THE LONDON CIGARETTE ~~CARD COMPANY'S~~

TRADE C

Return items to **any** Swind
time on or before the date
and Audio Books can be renewed - phone your

2014 edition

Compiled by

IAN A. LAKER

and

Y. BERKTAY

39th Revised Edition 2014

ISBN 978-1-906397-15-9

THE LONDON CIGARETTE CARD CO. LTD
Sutton Road, Somerton, Somerset, England TA11 6QP

Telephone: Somerton 01458-273452
Fax: 01458-273515
E-Mail: cards@londoncigcard.co.uk
International Calls: Telephone: ++44 1458-273452
Fax: ++44 1458-273515

www.londoncigcard.co.uk

Cards illustrated on front cover are from the series:
Brooke Bond Tea. History of the Motor Car 1968
Sporting Profiles. Carry On Up The Card Set 2005
Diamond Collection. Rock N Roll 1998
Brooke Bond Tea. Olympic Challenge 1992

Back cover
Cryptozoic. The Big Bang Theory Seasons 3 & 4 2012
Cryptozoic. The Vampire Diaries Season 1 2011

CARD COLLECTING

Wills
Garden Flowers
(1939)

When you mention cigarette cards, most people think of cricketers, footballers and film stars of the 1930s. This was the hey-day of cigarette card issues when virtually every packet contained a little picture and the major companies like Wills and Players had their own studios and artists devoted entirely to the production of cigar-ette cards. It was big business, and mas-sive print-runs often ran into hundreds of millions for each series. That's why there are still lots of them around today — sets can still be bought for around £20 upwards in very good condition, which is a major reason for their popularity for those of us wishing to indulge in nostalgia for Hollywood legends, sporting heroes, military hardware, famous trains and graceful ocean liners from a golden age.

Players
Uniforms of the
Territorial Army
(1939)

In The Beginning

In fact the hobby goes back to the 1890s, to a time when cigarettes were wrapped in paper packets. Manufacturers began inserting pieces of card to protect the contents, quickly realising that these would be useful for advertising their products. Soon these were followed by pictorial sequences, which would build up into sets. The object was to encourage repeat purchases and establish brand loyalty, and the subjects chosen were those most likely to appeal to the predominantly male customer base. Beautiful young women, sportsmen and soldiers dom-inated the earliest series, followed by ever more diverse topics in the early 20th century as companies competed for trade by offering something new.

Wills. Ships (1902)

Remember this was before the days of cinema, radio or TV, let alone the modern technological wonders we now take for granted. Newspapers carried few illustrations, and living standards were much lower. For most smokers, therefore, the cards they collected from their packets were their window on the world, serving to educate, excite or amuse — they were colourful, informative and free!

Many of these early cards were from firms whose names would mean nothing to a non-collector, little companies which went out of business or were swallowed up by the big boys before World War I. And it is these cards, few of which have survived, which are often the most valuable.

The 1920s and 1930s

The 1920s and 1930s are generally regarded as the golden age of cards. Competition was fierce and rival firms were constantly looking for something different to stand out from the crowd. Players and Wills went in for adhesive-backed cards and offered special albums to stick them in. So many were produced that there are still loads around today, and they fetch only a few pounds.

Wills. Railway Engines (1936)

Another idea was cards that made up into a sectional picture of a work of art, a map or an historic event like the 1937 Coronation Procession. Some makers developed cards with push-out sections which could be made into models, whilst others came out with sequences of silk embroidered flowers, cards in miniature frames, bronze plaques, metal charms to hang on a bracelet — even little gramophone records which could actually be played!

A New Dawn

Paper shortages halted card production in 1940. Cigarette cards would never be issued on the same scale as before the war, but even so there have been quite a few over the years, starting with the blue and white pictures of film stars and footballers printed in the sliding trays in Turf Cigarettes, and progressing to many series of popular cards in packets of Tom Thumb, Doncella and Grandee Cigars. Recent anti-smoking legislation has ended any hope of new cards with tobacco products, but we will continue to welcome new trade card issues.

Brooke Bond Tea. Famous People (1969)

Trade cards, or 'trading cards' as they are often called, are picture cards issued with non-tobacco products and they have a distinguished history which pre-dates even the earliest cigarette cards. On the continent of Europe, one of the first to recognise the sales potential of cards was the Liebig Meat Extract Company, which over a period of 120 years from 1872 onwards issued no fewer than 1,800 different series. In the 1920s and '30s firms like chocolate makers Frys and Cadburys, tea companies such as Typhoo, periodical publishers etc. mimicked their tobacco counterparts by producing a regular flow of picture cards. But it was in the post-war environment that trade cards really came into their own, filling the gap left by the demise of cigarette cards.

From the 1950s onwards came a flood of 'trade' cards issued with tea, confectionery, biscuits, cereals, ice cream and so on. Among them were companies such as A & BC Gum, Bassetts and Brooke Bond, who regularly released one set after another year after year. I expect many of you will remember collecting them — and really there has been a notable trend for this age group to begin collecting them again, which can be satisfyingly inexpensive with some Brooke Bond cards from the 1960s and '70s priced at around £4 or £5 for a mint set.

Cards at War

During World War I many patriotic collections were issued — 'Recruiting Posters', 'Infantry Training', 'Modern War Weapons', 'Military Motors', 'Allied Army Leaders', 'Britain's Part in The War' and so on. All were subject to Government scrutiny to ensure no secrets reached the enemy, and 'passed for publication by the Press Bureau' is printed on many of these

Wills. Military Motors (1916)

cards. In the run-up to World War II, out came cards demonstrating the nation's apparent military strength and preparedness for action — 'Britain's Defences', the 'R.A.F. at Work' and 'Life in the Royal Navy' to name a few. 'Aircraft of the R.A.F.' cards showed our latest fighters, the Spitfire and Hurricane ('the performance of this machine is an official secret' we are warned). It is rumoured that German agents were buying up Player's 1939 'British Naval Craft' in London to send back to U-Boat crews. Meanwhile the authorities sponsored a series of 'Air Raid Precautions', 'cigarette cards of national importance', endorsed by Home Secretary Samuel Hoare, with useful hints on how to put on a gas-mask or extinguish an incendiary bomb. How effective or otherwise these proved in the blitz we shall never know, but they raised public awareness.

The Cards That Never Were

Wills. Waterloo (c1916)

The Wagner cards were not the only ones never to see the light of day. Britain's biggest maker, W. D. & H. O. Wills of Bristol prepared a series of 50 cards to celebrate Wellington's victory over Napoleon at the Battle of Waterloo, but when the date for issue came up in 1915 their release was cancelled so as not to offend the French who were our allies fighting the Germans. And in a series of 'Musical Celebrities' all the German subjects were withdrawn and substituted by lesser-known individuals from other nationalities. Another Wills casualty was a series of 50 cards prepared to mark the coronation of King Edward VIII. Edward's abdication in 1936 put paid to this and the cards were destroyed — all except, that is, for a handful of sets presented to the firm's directors and top management.

A World Record

Early in 2007, a world record price was paid in America for a single card — $2,350,000, roughly equivalent to £1,200,000. This card was sold later on in the year for another world record price, $2,800,000 (approximately £1,500,000). The card in question featured Honus Wagner, one of the great names in U.S. baseball at the turn of the 20th century. Wagner was a dedicated non-smoker and objected when America's biggest tobacco corporation planned to picture him on a cigarette card without his permission. Threats of legal action prevented its release, but a few slipped out, and it was one of these that stunned the collecting world when it was auctioned.

Today's Hobby

Remember *The Saint*, *The Avengers*, *The Prisoner*, *Thunderbirds*, *Captain Scarlet* and *Doctor Who*? They all have huge followings and collectors are snapping up new sets as they come onto the market. The same goes for *Star Trek*, Buffy, Disney, Harry

Potter and *The Lord of the Rings*. Cult TV series and blockbuster movies are sure to be pictured on cards. That goes for football too. There are hundreds of different sets to chose from, some going back to the days of Matthews, Finney and Lofthouse, others bringing us right up to date with the latest Premiership players and stars like Lampard and Rooney.

The thing is, card collecting is a living

Strictly Ink
Doctor Who 3rd Series (2002)

Topps UK
Star Wars (1978)

hobby with many new series being produced each year attracting a new generation of collectors. Whatever your age or interests, you're going to be pleasantly surprised by what cards can offer. Collecting cards has come a long way since its pre-war image and people from all walks of life are now keen collectors.

The London Cigarette Card Company

In 2014 the London Cigarette Card Company will be celebrating its 87th anniversary. The firm's remarkable history as the world's first company devoted solely to the needs of card collectors began in 1927 when Colonel C.L. Bagnall D.S.O, M.C., set up business at 47 Lionel Road, Brentford with a capital of just £500. The enterprise proved popular with collectors, and card stocks quickly grew to the point where an extension had to be built to house them, and the first catalogue was published in 1929. Four years later came another momentous event — the launch of the monthly magazine *Cigarette Card News* now renamed **Card Collectors News** and still being published today. By 1933, the business had expanded to such a degree that larger premises were essential and, in October of that year, the L.C.C.C. moved to Wellesley Road, Chiswick, their address until 1977 when they moved again, this time to Somerset. Today, the company's headquarters in Sutton Road, Somerton houses one of the world's largest stocks of cigarette cards and trade cards — **MORE THAN 50 MILLION** — and serves collectors around the world. In September 1999 they set up their website (**www.londoncigcard.co.uk**) which now offers over 6,000 different series, all with sample colour illustrations.

They publish the hobby's essential reference catalogues with prices for over 13,000 different series on every subject imaginable. The 2014 editions — The **Cigarette Card Catalogue** at £7.50 and the **Trade Card Catalogue** at £7.00, are widely regarded as the definitive guides to collecting. They also publish a monthly magazine, **Card Collectors News** (available by post, at £2.20 each or £26 for a year's subscription) which keeps everyone up to date with news about the latest card issues, stories and features. Cards can be ordered by post, telephone, fax or e-mail and through this website.

For further information contact The London Cigarette Card Company Ltd, Sutton Road, Somerton, Somerset TA11 6QP, telephone 01458-273452, e-mail cards@londoncigcard.co.uk.

PUBLISHER'S ANNOUNCEMENTS

PRICES AND CONDITIONS

The prices quoted in this volume are the London Cigarette Card Company's selling prices for the supply of odd cards in finest possible condition — to complete a collector's set — or for complete sets in finest possible condition.

Collectors are reminded that rapidly diminishing stock and greatly increasing demands for cards mean that all prices in this Catalogue are subject to alteration without notice.

The lack of any figures in the price column does not mean the item is unobtainable. It indicates that, at the time of going to press, insufficient stocks are available to fix a definite price, and collectors wishing to acquire any specific items in this category should ask for a current quotation.

TERMS

Remittances should be sent with all orders and should take the form of crossed cheques or money orders. Notes and coins should be sent by registered post. We accept Mastercard, Visa, American Express, Visa Delta, Electron, JCB and Maestro credit/debit cards.

POSTAGE AND HANDLING FEE

Orders are sent post free to UK addresses, but **please note** orders under £20.00 will incur a handling fee of £2.00. Overseas postage is charged at cost and there is no handling fee.

VAT

Value Added Tax where applicable is included in all prices shown, at the current rate of 20%.

HOW TO ORDER

Full and *clearly* written name and address should be shown on all pages of all communications.

The order should be written very clearly giving the maker's name, the set title and, where odds are required, every number needed should be written, i.e. do not take a short cut by saying 1-5 are needed but write '1, 2, 3, 4, 5'.

Cheques, money orders or postal orders should be drawn in favour of THE LONDON CIGARETTE CARD COMPANY LIMITED, and crossed. Overseas payments can only be accepted by Sterling cheque drawn on a British bank or by credit/debit card. We accept Mastercard, Visa, American Express, Visa Delta, Electron, JCB and Maestro credit/debit cards. Quote your card number, expiry date and the card security code, which is the last three numbers on the signature strip (and, for Maestro cards, the issue number, if one is shown, or start date). Cash should always be registered. Send your order to:

The London Cigarette Card Co. Ltd, Sutton Road, Somerton, Somerset TA11 6QP, England

Please note:
Orders sent to addresses outside the European Community will have 15% (UK tax) deducted off card and album prices.

24 hour Telephone Order Line (01458-273452)

For the convenience of customers, an answering machine is in operation to receive orders when the office is closed. Just leave your order, name and address with credit or debit card number, expiry date and the card security code, which is the last three numbers on the signature strip (and, for Maestro cards, the issue number, if one is shown, or start date). Your order will be dealt with as soon as possible. Please note that we can only deal with general enquiries in office hours. Tel. No. **01458-273452** (international ++44 1458-273452).

Fax Machine (01458-273515)

Our fax machine is on 24 hours a day to receive orders. Just place your order stating your name, address, credit or debit card number, expiry date and the card security code, which is the last three numbers on the signature strip (and, for Maestro cards, the issue number, if one is shown, or start date). The Fax number is **01458-273515** (international ++44 1458 -273515).

E-mail (cards@londoncigcard.co.uk) & Website (www.londoncigcard.co.uk)

Our e-mail address is **cards@londoncigcard.co.uk**   Orders can also be placed using our secure website through the cards page (**www.londoncigcard.co.uk**).

OPENING TIMES AT SUTTON ROAD

Collectors are welcome to call at our offices in Sutton Road, Somerton, where you will be able to purchase your requirements direct from the massive stocks held at the premises – sets, albums, books and accessories plus odd cards. We do not have items on display, but we are more than happy to get things out for you to view.

Our offices are open to customers Monday to Friday
9.30am-12.30pm and 2.30pm-4.30pm

SIZE CODE

Where a letter appears with the quantity number it indicates that the series concerned is other than standard size. The abbreviations used are:

EL = Extra Large   L = Large   LT = Large Trade (size 89 × 64mm)
M = Medium   K = Miniature Size   P = Photographic.

The exceptions are on the Brooke Bond pages where the letterings are that Company's code to show the chronological sequence of issue.

DATE OF ISSUE

The Year of Issue is shown alongside each entry. Where the precise year is not known, an approximate date is given preceded by 'c'.

SALE OF COLLECTIONS

Our buying department welcomes offers of collections (whether large or small) and high prices will be paid for early and rare cards in good condition. Stamped addressed envelope should be enclosed with all queries.

New Issues

We usually have between 5 and 20 new issues (mostly trade card issues) added to stock each month, and if you wish to keep up-to-date why not subscribe to *Card Collectors News* **magazine** (see page ix), in which Frank Doggett, the magazine editior, gives a description of all new additions and includes sample illustrations of most of them. A sample of the back and front of each new issues can also be found on our website each month (www.londoncigcard.co.uk).

☆ BARGAIN 25 OFFER ☆

25 sets for £30, that's our terrific special bargain offer

We have selected twenty-five sets of cards issued between the 1950s and the 1990s, chosen for their wide range of interesting subjects and all in top condition. Each of the sets is individually catalogued at £2.50 or more, so this collection represents a huge saving on normal prices.

Ask for 'Bargain 25' when ordering

☆ SAMPLER COLLECTIONS ☆

We have taken one card from each of 450 post-war card series and assembled them into nine different groups of fifty. These are particularly useful for the collector who wishes to see sample cards before buying complete sets, and are also a great foundation for a 'type' collection. Each group of 50 costs only £6.

Order one collection from groups A, B, C, D, E, F, G, H or I for £6
or all nine groups for £45

2014 AUCTIONS

We have been auctioning for over 75 years cards to suit every collector

Monthly 400-lot postal auctions of cigarette and trade cards and associated items with estimated values from as little as £1 up to many hundreds.
Lots to interest every collector and suit their pocket.

Postal Auctions for 2014 are as follows:

Thursday,	2nd January	Saturday,	28th June
Saturday,	25th January	Saturday,	26th July
Saturday,	22nd February	Saturday,	30th August
Saturday,	29th March	Saturday,	27th September
Saturday,	26th April	Saturday,	25th October
Saturday,	31st May	Saturday,	29th November

Each postal auction finishes at midnight on the above dates.

A guide to how we assess condition and how to bid can be found on our bidding sheet which comes with the free auction catalogue, so it couldn't be easier if you are an 'auction beginner'.

There are no additional charges to bidders for buyer's premium, so bidding is straightforward, with no 'hidden extras'.

Each lot is described with an estimate of its value reflecting the condition of the cards, ranging from poor right through to mint condition, and for over 75 years collectors have bid with complete confidence, knowing that every effort is made to describe the lots accurately.

Each auction contains a selection of rare sets, rare and scarce individual cards, pre-1918 issues, 1920-40 series, old and modern trade issues including Brooke Bond, errors and varieties, silks, albums, books, Liebigs, cigarette packets etc – in fact plenty to interest everyone.

Auction catalogues are available **FREE OF CHARGE**, 4 weeks before the date of sale from
The London Cigarette Card Company Limited
Sutton Road, Somerton, Somerset TA11 6QP
Telephone: 01458-273452   Fax: 01458-273515
E-mail: auctions@londoncigcard.co.uk

The Auction Catalogue can also be found on our website, which contains a preview of each auction as well as facilities for on-line bidding – visit www.londoncigcard.co.uk for further details.

Also a copy of the auction catalogue is automatically sent each month to subscribers to our magazine *Card Collectors News*
(subscription details on page ix of this catalogue)

The FIRST EVER card collecting magazine!
First published in 1933

You get so much with a 12 month subscription

— 12 Copies of the Card Collectors News Magazine
— FREE sample card with every issue
— FREE monthly auction List which has at least 400 lots
— Special offers (only for subscribers) which could save you up to 25% on over 150 sets every month
— Discount on a Set of the month (only to Subscribers)
— Details of any new issues that arrive into stock every month
— Informative articles from readers and collectors all around the world
— Competitions and prizes! (You could get a 12 month subscription for free)

**Collect back issues of the magazine starting from £1
(see our website for issues available)**

Subscription is £26 for the UK
£50 for European countries and
£60 for countries outside of Europe

**Why not try our new E-magazine Subscription for only £26
(See website for details)**

**Keep your magazines safe in a purpose designed luxury binder
to hold 12 copies — £9.00 each**

CARTOPHILIC REFERENCE BOOKS

BOOKS FOR THE COLLECTOR

Cigarette Card Catalogue, 2014 Edition with **colour illustrations**. This is the original price guide, now in its 85th year, updated for the year 2014 with every item dated and priced. Covers cigarette cards and silks issued by hundreds of manufacturers in Britain and around the world from the 19th century to the present day. 232 pages giving selling prices for odd cards and sets in first class condition from our extensive stocks, with details of over 7,000 series. Contains eight-page section with new full colour illustrations. **£7.50**

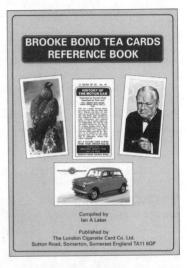

Liebig Card Catalogue, 2009 edition. This price guide (not illustrated) lists over 1,500 of these fascinating sets issued in different European languages (all except the earliest) by this manufacturer. It includes a brief history of the company, an English translation of each set title, together with Fada reference, the number in each set and date of issue from 1891 to 1973. The prices in the 2009 catalogue will remain valid until further notice. **£4.50**

Brooke Bond Tea Cards Reference Book. The definitive reference book with 319 colour illustrations of cards and albums including overseas issues and the story of the company's first hundred years from one shop to market leader. Published 2007. **£12.50**

Brooke Bond Picture Cards 'The First Forty Years'. This invaluable 72-page reference book detailing all the issues of Brooke Bond Tea from 1954 to 1994. It includes British issues as well as overseas issues with illustrations. **£7.00**

Classic Brooke Bond Picture Card Collections. Mark Knowler's 320-page hardback book should appeal to all collectors, not just those specialising in Brooke Bond, because it is a wonderful advert for the hobby. Impeccably presented and with superb colour illustrations throughout, it is the kind of book you can dip into for a few minutes or browse through for hours.

As described by the publisher, 'this beautifully produced nostalgic book comprises the best 12 original albums, presented slightly larger than they were 40 to 50 years ago, to bring out the best in the wonderfully detailed illustrations. Every card is printed in its correct position, making every page an enormously colourful feast for the eyes.'

The albums that have been included are Out Into Space, British Wild Life, Wild Flowers Series 2, Freshwater Fish, African Wild Life, Asian Wild Life, British Butterflies, Wild Birds in Britain, Transport Through The Ages, Trees in Britain, Flags and Emblems of the World and History of The Motor Car, although other UK issues from Frances Pitt British Birds through to the 1999 Thank You Card are covered in the introduction. **£25.00**

BOOKS FOR THE COLLECTOR

Collecting Cigarette & Trade Cards by Gordon Howsden. Traces the history and development of cards from their beginning to the present day and includes the background of the issuing firms, thematic collecting, printing and production, grading, pricing and so on. Authoritatively written in an easy-to-read style and beautifully illustrated in colour, the book approaches the subject from a fresh angle which will appeal to seasoned collectors and newcomers alike. Cigarette & Trade Cards is not only an indispensable reference work but also a joy to read or just browse through. 152 large-format pages with 220 colour illustrations featuring 750 cards and related ephemera.
. . . . **£17.50**

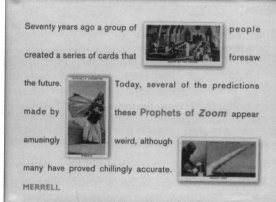

'**Prophets of Zoom**'. An unusual but fascinating book, 'Prophets of Zoom', with 112 pages, reproduces the front and back of each card in Mitchell's 1936 series of 50 The World of Tomorrow, opposite which is pictured a modern equivalent – and it's surprising how many of the predictions have become true!

From author Alfredo Marcantonio's introduction, we learn that the card set was inspired by a book called The World of Tomorrow and drew upon images from contemporary films, in particular Alexanda Korda's Things to Come, as well as inventions then at the cutting edge of technology. The individual predictions range from the amazing to the amusing, and together they paint a unique picture of the world we live in now, as pre-war Britain imagined it would be.

To take just one example. The very first card informs us that 'coal-mines and oil-wells will not last forever. We shall have to gain the energy we need, not from fuel, but from the inexhaustible forces of nature', and the set forecasts wind turbines, atomic energy and solar motors as being the power sources of the future.

From space travel and giant television screens, robots and bullet trains, to London's skyscraper skyline, this is highly entertaining stuff, and excellent value. **£7.95**

Orders are sent post free to UK addresses, but PLEASE NOTE orders under £20.00 will incur a handling fee of £2.00. Overseas postage is charged at cost and there is no handling fee.

REGIMENTAL BOOKS

The following series of books featuring the different Regiments and Corps of the British Army illustrated on Cigarette and Trade cards, contain History, Uniforms, Badges, Regimental Colours, Victoria Cross Winners and Personalities. Approximately 200 illustrations in each book, 56 pages with 16 in full colour, all produced by David J. Hunter.

The Coldstream Guards £8.50

The Gordon Highlanders. £8.50

Queen's Own Highlanders (Seaforth & Camerons) £8.50

The Queen's Royal Lancers £8.50

The Regiments of Wales (The Welsh Guards, The Royal Welsh Fusiliers & The Royal Regiment of Wales). £8.50

The Royal Army Medical Corps £8.50

The Royal Marines £8.50

The Royal Regiment of Fusiliers — Part 1 (The Royal Northumberland Fusiliers & The Royal Warwickshire Regiment). . £8.50

The Royal Regiment of Fusiliers — Part 2 (The Royal Fusiliers (City of London Regiment) & The Lancashire Fusiliers) . £8.50

The Scotts Guards. £8.50

The Worcestershire & Sherwood Foresters Regiment £8.50

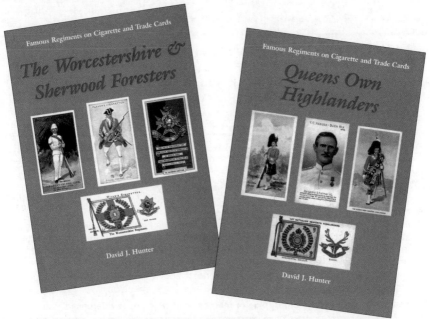

Orders are sent post free to UK addresses, but PLEASE NOTE orders under £20.00 will incur a handling fee of £2.00. Overseas postage is charged at cost and there is no handling fee.

LUXURY ALBUMS

LUXURY BINDER WITH 30 LEAVES £13.00
MATCHING SLIP-CASE £6.00 (only supplied with binder)
EXTRA LEAVES 17p EACH
☆ **GREY CARD INTERLEAVES — 30 FOR £4.00** ☆

Orders are sent post free to UK addresses, but PLEASE NOTE **orders under £20.00 will incur a handling fee of £2.00. Overseas postage is charged at cost and there is no handling fee.**

Full display, front and back, is given to your cards in top quality transparent leaves held in a luxurious binder. The leaves are made from a tough, clear optical film. Binders are available in a choice of blue or maroon covers (with matching slip-cases as an optional extra) and each is supplied complete with 30 leaves, of which various sizes are available as listed below.

Page Ref.	Suitable for	Pockets Per Page	Pocket size (mm) wide × deep
A	Standard size cards	10	43 × 83
M	Medium size cards	8	55 × 83
D	Doncella/Grandee/Typhoo size cards	6	111 × 55
L	Large size cards	6	73 × 83
X	Extra large cards	4	111 × 83
P	Postcards	2	111 × 170
C	Cabinet size cards, booklets etc	1	224 × 170
K	Miniature size cards	15	43 × 55

Remember to state which colour (blue or maroon) and which page reference/s you require.

Order by telephone (01458-273452), fax (01458-273515), or e-mail (cards@londoncigcard.co.uk), or through our website (www.londoncigcard.co.uk) 24 hours a day, 7 days a week using your credit or debit card or you can order by post..

ALBUMS FOR LARGE TRADE CARDS

☆ An album designed specifically for modern trade cards like Skybox, Comic Images, Rittenhouse, Inkworks, Topps etc

☆ The ideal way to display your large modern trade cards to their best advantage

☆ 3-ring luxury padded binders in a choice of maroon or blue

☆ There are two types of leaves:

9 pockets per sheet size 91 × 68mm, reference LT
6 pockets per sheet size 138 × 66mm, reference WV

Orders are sent post free to UK addresses, but PLEASE NOTE orders under £20.00 will incur a handling fee of £2.00. Overseas postage is charged at cost and there is no handling fee.

COMPLETE ALBUM WITH 30 LEAVES IN A CHOICE OF
'LT' OR 'WV' LEAVES £16.50 · EXTRA LEAVES 22p EACH

☆ COLLECTORS' ACCESSORIES ☆

A neat and tidy way for you to deal with incomplete sets is to use our
numbered, printed 'wants' lists

30 adhesive lists numbered 1 to 50 . . . . **75p**

The professional way to wrap sets is with our translucent
glascine wrapping strips

200 strips size 123 × 68mm for standard size cards **£5.00**
200 strips size 175 × 83mm for large cards **£5.50**
200 strips size 228 × 83mm for extra-large cards **£6.00**

THEMATIC LISTINGS

If you are interested in a particular subject the thematic listings on our website may be of help. Alternatively, lists can be sent on request.

SUBJECTS COVERED

American Football, Baseball etc.
Animals and Wildlife
Aviation, Space Travel and
    Astronomy
Birds, Butterflies and Moths
Boxing
Brooke Bond Tea Cards
Cricket
Dinosaurs
Dogs and Pets
Fantasy Art
Film and Stage Stars (1920-40
    issues)
Fish, Fishing and the Ocean
Flags, Arms and Maps
Flowers and the Garden
Football
Golf
Horses and the Turf
Liebig Card Issues
Military
Motoring

Native North American Indians and
    Cowboys
Pop Stars and Singers
Railways
Reprints
Royalty
Rugby League and Union
Ships, Shipping and Naval
Speedway
Sports (general)
Star Trek
Star Wars
Tennis
TV, Films and Sci-Fi
Wrestling
Miscellaneous Cigarette Card
    Issues
Miscellaneous Trade Card Issues
Selection of Cigarette Card Sets £20
    and under
Selection of Trade Card Sets under
    £5

Website
www.londoncigcard.co.uk

INDEX OF BRANDS

ADVENTURE — see D.C. Thomson
AMBROSIA — see J. Pascall
BELL BOY — see Anglo-American Gum
CHAMPION — see Amalgamated Press
DISCWORLD — see Cunning Articifer
DOCTOR TEA — see Harden Brothers
EAT MORE FISH — see Fish Marketing
  Board
FUTERA — see Trade Cards (Europe) Ltd
HORNET — see D.C. Thomson
HOTSPUR — see D.C. Thomson
HUSTLER — see J. Knight
JAG — see Fleetway Publications
JIBCO — see J.I. Batten
JOLLY SAILOR — see Cunning Articifer
JUBBLY — see Freshmaid Ltd
K THE B — see Local Authorities Caterers'
  Association
LAUGHING COW — see Bell UK
LION — see Fleetway Publications
LORD NIELSON — see Mister Softee Ltd
MICKEY MOUSE WEEKLY — see Caley

NEW HOTSPUR — see D.C. Thomson
ROVER — see D.C. Thomson
ROXY — see Fleetway Publications
SCOREBOARD — see Merlin
SIFTA SAM — see Palmer Mann & Co
  (reprint section)
SKIPPER — see D.C. Thomson
STIMOROL GUM — see Scanlen
SUBBUTEO — see P.A. Adolf
SUNLIGHT SOAP — see Lever Brothers
TIGER — see Fleetway Publications
TOP FLIGHT — see T.P.K. Hannah
TREBOR BASSETT — see Bassett
TREBOR/TOPPS — see Topps (UK)
TRIUMPH — see Amalgamated Press
VAL FOOTER GUM — see Klene
VANGUARD — see D.C. Thomson
VICTOR — see D.C. Thomson
VICTORY BUBBLE GUM — see Trebor
  Ltd
WIZARD — see D.C. Thomson
ZIP BUBBLE GUM — see Trebor Ltd

TOP TRUMPS

We have available the following Top Trumps sets that were issued between 1978 and 1980. These sets of colour photos can also be used as a card game.

TOP TRUMPS (UK) (CARD GAMES)

L33	Dragsters (Series 7)	1978	£4.00
L33	Flowers (Quartets)	1978	£4.00
L35	Prehistoric Monsters	1979	£4.00
L33	Rockets	1980	£4.00

MINI TRUMPS SERIES 1

K25	Dragsters	1978	£3.00

MINI TRUMPS SERIES 2

* K25	Grand Prix Cars	1978	£3.00
* K25	Hot Rods	1978	£3.00
* K25	Jumbos and Jets	1978	£3.00
K25	Rally Cars	1978	£3.00
K25	Super Trains	1978	£3.00

SUPER MINI TRUMPS SERIES 1

* M25	Dragster Bikes	1978	£3.00
* M25	Formula Cars	1978	£3.00
M25	Helicopters	1978	£3.00
* M25	Stock Cars	1978	£3.00

SUPER MINI TRUMPS SERIES 2

M25	Dragsters	1978	£3.00
* M25	HP Giants (Lorries etc)	1978	£3.00
* M25	Super Cars	1978	£3.00
* M25	Super Dragsters	1978	£3.00

SPECIAL OFFER:
The 9 sets marked with an asterisk * for £19.00 (saving £8.00)

Qty		Date	Odds	Sets
	A-1 DAIRIES LTD			
25	Birds and Their Eggs	1964	£1.60	£40.00
25	Butterflies and Moths	1965	20p	£5.00
25	The Story of Milk...	1967	£1.00	—
	A-1 DOLLISDALE TEA			
25	Do You Know about Shipping and Trees?	1962	20p	£2.50
	AAA SPORTS (USA)			
LT100	Decision 92 (United States Presidential Election)...	1992	—	£8.00
	ABC (Cinema)			
10	An Adventure in Space (Set 3)	1950	£3.00	—
10	Animals (Set 5)	1952	£2.00	—
10	Birds (Set 19)	1958	£1.20	—
10	Birds and Bird Watching (Set 7)	1953	£3.00	—
10	British Athletes (Set 11)	1955	£1.80	£18.00
20	British Soldiers (brown back)	1950	60p	£12.00
20	British Soldiers (black back)	1950	£1.00	—
10	Colorstars 1st Series	1961	70p	£7.00
10	Colorstars 2nd Series	1962	£3.75	—
10	Colorstars 3rd Series	1962	£2.50	—
10	Dogs (Set 17)	1957	£2.50	£25.00
10	Film Stars (Set 1)	1950	£3.00	—
10	Horses (Set 21)	1959	£2.00	—
10	Interesting Buildings (Set 10)	1955	80p	£8.00
10	Journey by Land (Set 8)	1954	£2.75	—
10	Journey by Water (Set 9)	1954	£2.75	—
10	Journey to the Moon (Set 12)	1956	£2.75	—
10	Parliament Buildings (Set 18)	1958	£1.00	£10.00
10	Railway Engines (Set 4)	1951	£4.50	—
10	Scenes from the Films (Set 6)	1953	£4.50	—
10	Sea Exploration (Set 16)	1958	£1.00	£10.00
10	Sea Scenes (Set 20)	1958	80p	£8.00
10	Sports on Land (Set 15)	1956	80p	£8.00
10	Travel of the Future (Set 14)...	1957	£1.00	£10.00
10	Water Sports (Set 13)	1957	£1.00	£10.00
	ABC (Monogram)			
L16	Film Stars	1935	£5.00	—
12	Star Series (Film Stars)	1936	£5.00	—

A & BC
(AMERICAN & BRITISH CHEWING GUM LTD)
(44-page Illustrated Reference Book, revised 2004 edition — £4.50)

Qty		Date	Odds	Sets
M120	All Sports	1954	£4.50	—
EL17	Banknotes	1971	£3.50	—
L55	Batman (pink back):			
	A With 'Batman Fan Club'	1966	£2.50	—
	B Without 'Batman Fan Club'	1966	£1.80	£100.00
L55	Batman (number on front)	1966	£2.60	—
L44	Batman (Nd 1A to 44A)	1966	£3.30	—
L44	Batman (Nd 1B to 44B)	1966	£5.00	—

Qty			Date	Odds	Sets

Qty			Date	Odds	Sets
L38	Batman (black back):				
	A	English text	1966	£4.00	—
	B	Dutch text	1966	£6.00	—
M1	Batman Secret Decoder (For Series of 38)				
	(3 lines of code)		1966	—	£15.00
	Battle:				
L73	A	Complete set................................	1966	—	£130.00
L69/73	B	(Minus Nos 32, 39, 42, 44)	1966	£1.50	£105.00
LT66	Battle of Britain		1970	£1.50	—
LT60	Bazooka Joe and His Gang		1968	£4.00	—
L60	Beatles (black and white)		1964	£4.50	—
L45	Beatles (black and white) 2nd Series		1965	£7.00	—
L40	Beatles (coloured)		1965	£11.00	—
K114	Car Stamps		1971	£2.50	—
L45	The Champions (TV Series)		1969	£3.70	—
M1	The Champions Secret Decoder (4 lines of code)		1969	—	£20.00
M56	Christian Name Stickers		1967	£3.00	—
EL15	Civil War Banknotes		1965	£3.50	—
L88	Civil War News		1965	£3.50	—
EL43	Comic Book Foldees		1968	£2.50	—
EL24	Crazy Disguises		1970	£9.00	—
L66	Creature Feature................................		1974	£1.50	£100.00
L48	Cricketers		1959	£2.50	—
L48	Cricketers 1961 Test Series:				
	A	Size 90 × 64mm................................	1961	£3.00	—
	B	Size 94 × 68mm................................	1961	£3.00	—
L66	Elvis Presley Series................................		1959	£15.00	—
L36	Exploits of William Tell		1960	£2.50	—
M22	Famous Indian Chiefs		1968	£5.00	—
EL54	Fantastic Twisters		1972	£6.00	—
M48	Film and TV Stars 1st Series		1953	£3.50	—
M48	Film and TV Stars 2nd Series		1953	£3.50	—
M48	Film and TV Stars 3rd Series		1954	£3.50	—
L48	Film Stars:				
	A	Set of 48 (grey back)	1955	£2.50	—
	B	Set of 48 (white back)...............	1955	£2.70	—
	C	Set of 24 (white back with stand)	1955	£2.70	—
40	Flag Stickers		1966	£5.00	—
L73	Flags................................		1971	£1.00	—
L80	Flags of the World:				
	A	Size 95 × 67mm................................	1959	£1.25	£100.00
	B	Size 82 × 57mm................................	1963	£1.25	£100.00
L46	Footballers 1st Series:				
	A	Front without 'Planet Ltd'...............	1958	£3.00	—
	B	Front inscribed 'Planet Ltd'	1958	£2.75	—
L46	Footballers 2nd Series:				
	A	Front without 'Planet Ltd'...............	1958	£8.00	—
	B	Front with 'Planet Ltd'	1958	£6.00	—
L49	Footballers (in Action) 1st Series (red)		1959	£4.00	—
L49	Footballers (in Action) 2nd Series (red)		1959	£6.50	—
LT42	Football 1st Series (black)		1960	£3.50	—
LT42	Football 2nd Series (black)		1960	£6.50	—
LT64	Footballers		1961	£5.50	—
LT44	Footballers — Scottish................................		1961	£12.00	—
L82	Footballers (Bazooka)		1962	£7.00	—

Qty		Date	Odds	Sets
	A & BC (continued)			
L55	Footballers 1st Series (blue)	1963	£4.50	—
L55	Footballers 2nd Series (blue)	1963	£4.50	—
L81	Footballers — Scottish (green)	1963	£12.00	—
L58	Footballers 1st Series (red)	1964	£4.00	—
L45	Footballers 2nd Series (red)	1964	£10.00	—
L46	Footballers 3rd Series (red)	1964	£12.00	—
L81	Footballers — Scottish (green)	1964	£12.00	—
M110	Footballers (black and white, issued in pairs) 1st Series	1966	£4.50	—
M110	Footballers (black and white, issued in pairs) 2nd Series	1966	£7.00	—
M54	Footballers — Scottish (coloured, Nos 1 to 42, issued in pairs)	1966	£10.00	—
L55	Football Star Players	1967	£3.50	£190.00
EL12	Footballers (Posters)	1967	£8.00	—
L54	Footballers 1st Series (yellow)	1968	£4.50	—
L47	Footballers 2nd Series (yellow)	1968	£3.50	—
L45	Footballers — Scottish (yellow)	1968	£8.50	—
EL26	Football Team Pennants — English	1968	£7.00	—
M20	Football Team Emblems	1968	£6.50	—
L65	Footballers 1st Series (green)	1969	£2.25	—
L54	Footballers 2nd Series (green)	1969	£2.25	£125.00
L55	Footballers 3rd Series (green)	1969	£2.25	£125.00
MP36	Footballers	1969	£2.50	—
L42	Footballers — Scottish 1st Series (blue)	1969	£7.00	—
L35	Footballers — Scottish 2nd Series (blue)	1969	£8.00	—
MP15	Football Photos — Scottish	1969	£5.50	—
LT84	Footballers 1st Series (orange)	1970	£1.20	£100.00
LT85	Footballers 2nd Series (orange)	1970	£1.00	£85.00
LT86	Footballers 3rd Series (orange)	1970	£4.00	—
EL14	Footballers Pin Ups	1970	£6.50	—
M72	Football Colour Transparencies	1970	£7.00	—
LT85	Footballers — Scottish 1st Series (green)	1970	£4.00	—
LT86	Footballers — Scottish 2nd Series (green)	1970	£4.00	—
EL28	Footballers Pin Ups — Scottish	1970	£8.00	—
L109	Footballers 1st Series (purple)	1971	£2.50	—
L110	Footballers 2nd Series (purple)	1971	£2.50	—
L71	Footballers 3rd Series (purple)	1971	£5.00	—
M23	Football Club Crests	1971	£2.50	—
M23	Football Superstars	1971	£7.00	—
L73	Footballers — Scottish 1st Series (purple)	1971	70p	£50.00
L71	Footballers — Scottish 2nd Series (purple)	1971	£6.50	—
M16	Football Club Crests — Scottish	1971	£3.00	£50.00
L109	Footballers 1st Series (orange/red)	1972	£3.00	£330.00
L110	Footballers 2nd Series (orange/red)	1972	£3.50	£385.00
M22	Football Card Game	1972	£1.25	—
L89	Footballers — Scottish 1st Series (blue)	1972	£4.50	£400.00
L88	Footballers — Scottish 2nd Series (orange/red) (No. 164 not issued)	1972	£6.00	—
L131	Footballers 1st Series (blue)	1973	£4.50	—
L130	Footballers 2nd Series (blue) (Nos 235 and 262 not issued)	1973	£4.50	—
M32	Football Photos	1973	£3.00	—
EL16	Football Giant Team Posters	1973	£10.00	—
L90	Footballers — Scottish 1st Series (red)	1973	£5.00	—

3

Qty		Date	Odds	Sets
	A & BC (continued)			
L88	Footballers — Scottish 2nd Series (red)	1973	£5.00	—
L132	Footballers (red)	1974	£1.70	£225.00
L132	Footballers — Scottish (green)	1974	£4.00	—
L40	Fotostars	1961	£3.50	—
LT66	Funny Greetings	1961	£1.20	—
LT66	Funny Valentines...	1961	£3.50	—
L25	Girl from Uncle	1967	£3.00	—
	Golden Boys:			
L36	A Size 96 × 67mm...	1960	£5.00	—
LT40	B Size 89 × 64mm...	1960	£6.00	—
M27	Grand Prix (sectional)	1970	40p	£10.00
L36	The High Chaparral	1969	£2.50	£90.00
L55	Huck Finn:			
	A Inscribed 'Hanna-Barbera Production Inc.' ...	1968	£2.75	£150.00
	B Inscribed ILAMI 1968'	1968	£2.75	—
L60	Kung Fu...	1974	£2.00	—
L55	Land of the Giants	1969	£4.50	—
L54	The Legend of Custer	1968	£2.50	—
L55	Lotsa Laffs	1970	£2.20	—
L84	Love Initials	1970	£1.75	—
L36	Magic	1967	£3.50	£125.00
L55	Man from UNCLE	1965	£1.20	£70.00
	Man on the Moon:			
LT55	Space Ship Back	1970	£3.00	—
LT19	Text Back	1970	£3.00	—
L52	Mickey Takers...	1970	£3.50	—
M24	Military Emblem Stickers	1966	£4.00	—
L55	Monkees (black and white)	1967	£1.40	£75.00
L55	Monkees (coloured)	1967	£2.60	—
L30	Monkees Hit Songs	1967	£3.50	—
EL16	Monster Tattoos	1970	£5.00	—
EL16	Olympic Posters	1972	£3.50	—
L36	Olympics	1972	£4.00	—
L55	Partridge Family	1972	£2.00	—
L120	Planes:			
	A Size 94 × 67mm...	1958	£2.20	—
	B Size 88 × 64mm...	1958	£2.20	—
L44	Planet of the Apes	1968	£4.50	—
L33	Put-on Stickers	1969	£3.00	—
LT48	Railway Quiz	1958	£1.00	£50.00
L72	Railway Quiz	1959	£2.25	—
L40	The Rolling Stones	1965	£10.00	—
M24	Royal Portraits	1953	£2.50	£60.00
L25	Sir Francis Drake	1961	£4.00	—
LT88	Space Cards	1958	£5.00	—
L44	Stacks of Stickers	1971	£4.00	—
L55	Star Trek	1969	£9.00	—
L66	Superman in the Jungle	1968	£2.20	—
L16	Superman in the Jungle (jig-saw)	1968	£3.50	—
L50	Top Stars	1964	£3.50	—
L40	Top Stars	1964	£5.00	—
EL15	TV Cartoon Tattoos	1972	£8.00	—
L44	Ugly Stickers	1967	£3.00	—
EL88	Wacky Plaks	1965	£2.50	—
EL15	Walt Disney Characters Tattoos...	1973	£10.00	—

Qty		Date	Odds	Sets
	A & BC (continued)			
EL16	Wanted Posters	1968	£5.00	—
L56	Western Series	1959	£2.75	—
LT70	Who-Z-At Star?	1961	£2.70	—
L55	Winston Churchill	1965	75p	£40.00
L37	World Cup Footballers	1970	£6.00	—
EL16	World Cup Posters	1970	£6.00	—
L48	You'll Die Laughing	1967	£1.50	—

AMA GROUP (USA)

Qty		Date	Odds	Sets
LT60	Desert Storm Operation Yellow Ribbon	1991	—	£9.50

A & P PUBLICATIONS

Qty		Date	Odds	Sets
24	Post-war British Classic Cars	1992	20p	£4.00

A.W. SPORTS (USA)

Qty		Date	Odds	Sets
LT100	All World Racing (Motor Racing)	1991	—	£9.50
LT100	All World Racing (Motor Racing)	1992	—	£9.50

ABBEY GRANGE HOTEL

Qty		Date	Odds	Sets
15	Fighting Vessels	1986	—	£5.00

ACTION STARS

Qty		Date	Odds	Sets
20	Action Stars (1950s Footballers) 1st Series...	2010	—	£7.50
20	Action Stars (1950s Footballers) 2nd Series	2010	—	£7.50
20	Action Stars (1950s Footballers) 3rd Series	2011	—	£7.50

P.A. ADOLPH (Subbuteo Table Soccer)

Qty		Date	Odds	Sets
24	Famous Footballers 1st Series of 24	1954	£1.00	£25.00
24	Famous Footballers 2nd Series of 24...	1954	£1.00	£25.00
50	Famous Footballers 'A Series of 50'	1954	£16.00	—

AHC (Ace High Confectionery)

Qty		Date	Odds	Sets
25	Wonders of the Universe	1955	70p	£17.50

ALICE'S ATTIC

Qty		Date	Odds	Sets
EL16	Fry's Chocolate Advertising Postcards from the Early 1900s	2012	—	£10.00

ALL SPORTS INC. (USA)

Qty		Date	Odds	Sets
LT100	Exotic Dreams — Cars	1992	—	£9.50

A.W. ALLEN LTD (Australia)

Qty		Date	Odds	Sets
32	Bradman's Records	1931	£40.00	—
72	Butterflies and Moths	c1920	£2.00	—
36	Cricketers (brown fronts)	1932	£15.00	—
36	Cricketers (dark brown fronts)	1933	£15.00	—
36	Cricketers (flesh tinted, frameline back)	1934	£12.00	—
36	Cricketers (flesh tinted, no frameline back)	1936	£12.00	—
36	Cricketers (coloured)	1938	£12.00	—
144	Footballers (striped background)	1933	£7.00	—
72	Footballers (Club flag)	1934	£7.00	—
48	Footballers (players in action)	1939	£10.00	—
49	Kings and Queens of England	1937/53	£1.60	—

A.W. ALLEN LTD (Australia) (continued)

Qty		Date	Odds	Sets
36	Medals	1938	£3.00	—
36	Soldiers of The Empire...	1938	£3.00	—
36	Sports and Flags of Nations	1936	£3.00	—

J. ALLEN SPORTS

25	Sportsmen	1997	—	£9.50

ALMA CONFECTIONERY

48	James Bond 007 Moonraker	1980	£4.50	—

JAMES ALMOND

25	Sports and Pastimes	c1925	£9.00	—

AMABILINO PHOTOGRAPHIC

M30	Display Fireworks	1988	—	£7.00

AMALGAMATED PRESS LTD

24	Aeroplanes (plain back)	c1930	£3.50	—
M12	Catchy Tricks and Teasers	1933	£4.50	—
M22	English League (Div. 1) Footer Captains...	1926	£4.00	—
M16	Exploits of the Great War	1929	£2.75	—
16	Famous Aircraft	1927	£3.50	—
M24	Famous Footer Internationals	1926	£5.00	—
M22	Famous Shipping Lines	1926	£6.00	—
M32	Famous Test Match Cricketers	1926	£6.00	—
24	Famous Trains & Engines	c1930	£3.50	—
M16	Great War Deeds	1927	£3.25	—
M32	Great War Deeds	1928	£3.25	—
M24	The Great War — 1914-1918	1928	£3.25	—
M16	The Great War — 1914-1918 — New Series	1929	£3.25	—
M16	Heroic Deeds of the Great War	1927	£3.25	—
32	Makes of Motor Cars and Index Marks	1923	£2.50	—
24	Motors (plain black)	c1930	£4.00	—
M16	RAF at War (plain black)	1940	£5.25	—
24	Ships of the World	1924	£2.50	—
33	Ships of the World	c1935	£3.25	—
M12	Sports 'Queeriosities'	1933	£4.00	—
MP66	Sportsmen	1922	£1.60	—
32	Sportsmen of the World	c1935	£3.00	—
M32	Thrilling Scenes from the Great War	1927	£3.25	—
M16	Thrills of the Dirt Track	1929	£9.00	—
M16	Tip-Top Tricks and Teasers	1927	£3.50	—
M14	VCs and Their Glorious Deeds of Valour (plain back)	c1930	£4.00	—
	AUSTRALIAN ISSUES			
M32	Australian and English Cricket Stars	1932	£12.50	—
M16	England Test Match Cricketers	1928	£11.00	—
M16	Famous Australian Cricketers	1928	£12.50	—
16	Famous Film Stars	1927	£6.00	—
32	Makes of Motor Cars and Index Marks (with date)	1924	£4.00	—
16	Modern Motor Cars	1926	£6.00	—
M24	Wonderful London	1926	£6.00	—

Qty		Date	Odds	Sets

AMANDA'S FLOWERS

Qty		Date	Odds	Sets
L12	Flower Children	1990	35p	£4.00

AMARAN TEA

Qty		Date	Odds	Sets
25	The Circus	1968	36p	£9.00
25	Coins of the World	1965	50p	£12.50
25	Dogs' Heads	1965	50p	£12.50
25	Do You Know	1969	60p	£15.00
25	Flags and Emblems...	1964	40p	£10.00
25	Naval Battles	1971	80p	—
25	Old England	1969	20p	£2.50
25	Science in the 20th Century	1966	20p	£2.50
25	Veteran Racing Cars	1966	80p	£20.00

AMBER TIPS TEA (New Zealand)

Qty		Date	Odds	Sets
M20	The Living Seashore	1975	20p	£3.00

THE ANGLERS MAIL

Qty		Date	Odds	Sets
EL3	Terminal Tackle Tips	1976	—	£6.00

ANGLING TIMES

Qty		Date	Odds	Sets
M15	Series 1 Floats	1980	30p	£4.50
M15	Series 2 Species...	1980	30p	£4.50
M15	Series 3 Baits	1980	30p	£4.50
M15	Series 4 Sea Fish	1980	30p	£4.50
M24	Fish	1987	25p	£6.00
M24	Fishing Floats...	1986	20p	£4.50

ANGLO-AMERICAN CHEWING GUM LTD

Qty		Date	Odds	Sets
LT66	The Horse	1966	40p	£25.00
L36	Kidnapped	c1955	£5.00	—
M12	M.G.M. Film Stars	1935	£10.00	—
40	Underwater Adventure	1966	20p	£4.00
50	Zoo Stamps of the World	1966	80p	£40.00
	Waxed Paper Issues:			
M72	Animal World (2 pictures per card)...	c1965	£2.50	—
M72	Coaching Secrets	1964	£2.00	—
M32	Famous International Teams (inscribed 'Series of 72')	1960	£2.50	—
M128	Famous Soccer Clubs	1960	£2.50	—
M36	Flags of The Nations	c1965	£2.00	—
M36	Men of Courage	1958	£3.00	—
M48	Men of Progress	1958	£3.00	—
M72	Noted Football Clubs	1961	£2.00	—
M48	Race Around The World	1959	£3.00	—
M72	Soccer Hints	1961	£2.00	—
M48	Sports Gallery...	c1960	£4.00	—
M48	Sports Parade	1957	£4.00	—
M48	Strange But True...	1957	£3.00	—
M72	Strange World...	1964	£2.00	—
M72	Swimming Know-How	1962	£2.00	—
M36	Transport Through the Ages	c1960	£3.00	—
M48	World of Wonders	1957	£3.00	—
M36	World Airlines	1960	£4.00	—
	Albums or Folders with cards printed therein:			
72	Strange World...	1965	—	£10.00

Qty		Date	Odds	Sets

ANGLO CONFECTIONERY LTD

Qty		Date	Odds	Sets
LT66	The Beatles — Yellow Submarine	1968	£12.00	—
LT66	Captain Scarlet and the Mysterons	1968	£2.50	—
L12	Football Hints (Booklet Folders)	1970	£1.50	—
L84	Football Quiz	1969	£1.50	—
LT66	The Horse	1966	£2.00	—
LT66	Joe 90	1968	£4.00	—
L56	The New James Bond 007	1970	£12.00	—
L84	Railway Trains and Crests	1974	£1.00	—
LT66	Space	1967	£1.35	£90.00
LT66	Tarzan	1967	£1.35	£90.00
L64	UFO	1970	£3.00	£190.00
L78	Walt Disney Characters	1971	£5.00	—
L66	Wild West	1970	£2.00	—
L48	World Cup 1970 (Football)	1970	£2.50	—

APLIN & BARRETT

Qty		Date	Odds	Sets
L25	Whipsnade (Zoo)	1937	£1.50	£37.50

ARDMONA (Australia)

Qty		Date	Odds	Sets
L50	International Cricket Series III	1980	—	£12.50

ARMITAGE BROS. LTD

Qty		Date	Odds	Sets
25	Animals of the Countryside	1965	20p	£2.50
25	Country Life	1968	20p	£2.50

ARMY RECRUITING OFFICE

Qty		Date	Odds	Sets
M24	British Regiments 1st Series (without text)	1992	30p	£7.50
M24	British Regiments 2nd Series (with text)	1992	30p	£7.50

THE ARROW CONFECTIONERY CO.

Qty		Date	Odds	Sets
13	Conundrums	c1905	£32.00	—
12	Shadowgraphs	c1905	£32.00	—

ARTBOX (USA)

Qty		Date	Odds	Sets
LT90	Charlie and The Chocolate Factory — The Film ...	2005	—	£9.50
LT72	Dexter's Laboratory	2001	—	£8.00
LT72	Finding Nemo — Film Cardz (Disney Film)	2003	—	£12.00
LT54	Harry Potter and the Deathly Hallows Part 2	2011	—	£9.50
LT90	Harry Potter & The Goblet of Fire 1st Series	2005	—	£12.00
LT90	Harry Potter & The Goblet of Fire 2nd Series	2006	—	£9.50
LT90	Harry Potter & The Half-Blood Prince 1st Series ...	2009	—	£11.00
LT90	Harry Potter & The Order of The Phoenix 1st Series	2008	—	—
LT90	Harry Potter & The Order of The Phoenix 2nd Series	2008	—	£9.50
LT90	Harry Potter & The Prisoner of Azkaban 1st Series	2004	—	£15.00
LT90	Harry Potter & The Prisoner of Azkaban 2nd Series	2004	—	£9.50
LT72	Harry Potter & The Prisoner of Azkaban Film Cardz	2004	—	£12.00
LT90	Harry Potter & The Sorcerer's Stone	2005	—	£11.00
LT72	Harry Potter Memorable Moments 1st Series	2006	—	£12.00
LT72	Harry Potter Memorable Moments 2nd Series	2009	—	£9.50
M18	Pokemon Chrome Series	1999	—	£6.00
M80	Pokemon 3-D Action Cards	1999	25p	£16.00
M40	Pokemon Premier Edition (3-D Action Cards)	1999	—	£12.00
LT72	The Powerpuff Girls 1st Series	2000	—	£8.50
LT12	The Powerpuff Girls 1st Series Foil Series	2000	—	£3.50

Qty		Date	Odds	Sets
	ARTBOX (USA) (continued)			
M40	Sailor Moon — 3D	2000	—	£10.00
LT45	The Simpsons	2000	—	£16.00
LT72	Terminator 2 Judgment Day — Film Cardz	2003	20p	£9.50
LT24	Terminator 2 Judgment Day — Film Cardz			
	Cyberetch Series...	2003	40p	£9.50
LT40	World Wrestling Federation Lenticular Series 2 ...	2001	—	£10.00
	ASKEYS			
25	People and Places	1968	20p	£3.00
25	Then and Now	1968	20p	£4.00
	THE ASSEMBLY ROOMS (Briggate)			
50	War Portraits	1916	£90.00	—
	ASTON & ERDINGTON POLICE			
L24	Cop Card-Toons (including album)...	1989	—	£6.00
	ASTON CARDS			
LT24	Speedway Programme Covers 1st Series Inaugural			
	Season 1928	2002	—	£16.00
LT24	Speedway Programme Covers ,2nd Series The Early			
	Years 1920/30s	2003	—	£16.00
LT24	Speedway Programme Covers 3rd Series More Early			
	Years 1920/30s	2003	—	£16.00
LT24	Speedway Programme Covers 4th Series			
	The Fabulous '40s	2004	—	£16.00
LT24	Speedway Programme Covers 5th Series			
	More Early Years 1930s	2005	—	£16.00
LT24	Speedway Programme Covers 6th Series			
	More Early Years 1920/40s	2006	—	£16.00
LT24	Speedway Programme Covers 7th Series			
	More Fabulous '40s...	2008	—	£16.00
	ATLANTIC SERVICE STATIONS (Australia)			
M32	Australia in the 20th Century 1st Series	1959	£1.25	—
M32	Australia in the 20th Century 2nd Series...	1960	80p	£25.00
M32	English Historical Series	c1961	£1.25	—
M32	Queensland's Centenary	1959	£1.25	—
	AUSTIN MOTOR CO. LTD			
L13	Famous Austin Cars	1953	£12.00	—
	AUSTRALIAN BUTTER			
L54	Cricketers	1982	—	£15.00
L50	Cricketers	1983	25p	£12.50
	AUSTRALIAN DAIRY CORPORATION			
L63	Kanga Cards (Cricket)	1985	—	£15.00
	AUTOBRITE (Car Polish)			
25	Vintage Cars	1965	60p	£15.00
	AUTOGRAPH ADICTS			
L16	England Rugby World Cup Winners	2003	—	£10.00

Qty		Date	Odds	Sets

AUTOMATIC MACHINE CO. LTD

Qty		Date	Odds	Sets
25	Modern Aircraft	1958	30p	£7.50

AUTOMATIC MERCHANDISING CO. LTD

L25	Adventure Twins and the Treasure Ship	1959	£1.20	£30.00

AVON & SOMERSET POLICE

L37	British Stamps	1985	£1.20	—

AVON RUBBER CO. LTD

30	Leading Riders of 1963 (Motor Cyclists)	1963	£2.00	£60.00
	Folder		—	£4.00

B.B.B. PIPES

25	Pipe History	c1925	£12.00	—

B.J.B. CARDS (Canada)

L25	Famous Golfers of the 40s and 50s	1992	—	£15.00

B.N.A. (Canada)

LT49	Canadian Winter Olympic Winners	1992	—	£8.00

B.P. PETROL

25	Team England (Football World Cup)	1998	30p	£7.50
	Album		—	£3.00

B.T. LTD

25	Aircraft	1964	£1.00	—
25	British Locomotives	1961	£1.00	—
25	Do You Know?	1967	40p	£10.00
25	Holiday Resorts	1963	20p	£3.50
25	Modern Motor Cars	1962	£1.60	—
25	Occupations	1962	36p	£9.00
25	Pirates and Buccaneers	1961	£1.40	—
25	The West	1966	30p	£7.50

BAD AXE STUDIOS (USA)

LT52	Dungeon Dolls — Adult Fantasy Art	2011	—	£9.50

BADSHAH TEA CO.

25	British Cavalry Uniforms of the 19th Century	1963	60p	£15.00
25	Butterflies and Moths	1967	20p	£2.50
25	Fish and Bait	1965	24p	£6.00
25	Fruit of Trees and Shrubs...	1965	36p	£9.00
25	Garden Flowers	1963	50p	£12.50
24	The Island of Ceylon	1962	£4.00	—
25	Naval Battles	1968	60p	£15.00
25	People and Places	1968	20p	£2.50
25	Regimental Uniforms of the Past	1971	20p	£2.50
25	Romance of the Heavens...	1968	£1.40	—
25	Wonders of the World	1967	36p	£9.00

Qty		Date	Odds	Sets

J. BAINES & SON

Qty		Date	Odds	Sets
L?	Cricket and Football Cards, etc. (Shapes)	c1905	£40.00	—

BAKE-A-CAKE LTD

56	Motor Cars	1952	£5.00	—

BAKER, WARDELL & CO. LTD

25	Animals in the Service of Man	c1964	£2.60	—
36	Capital Tea Circus Act	c1960	£4.00	—
25	Do You Know 1st Series	c1962	£3.40	—
25	Do You Know 2nd Series	c1962	£3.40	—
25	History of Flight 1st Series	c1966	£9.00	—
25	History of Flight 2nd Series	c1966	£9.00	—
25	Irish Patriots	c1960	£9.00	—
25	They Gave Their Names	c1963	£3.00	—
25	Transport — Present and Future	c1956	£5.00	—
25	World Butterflies	c1960	£6.00	—

BARBERS TEA LTD

1	Advertisement Card — Cinema & TV Stars	1955	—	£5.00
1	Advertisement Card — Dogs	1960	—	£1.50
1	Advertisement Card — Railway Equipment	1958	—	£4.00
25	Aeroplanes	1954	80p	—
24	Cinema and Television Stars	1955	£3.00	—
24	Dogs	1960	20p	£4.00
25	Locomotives	1953	£1.40	£35.00
24	Railway Equipment	1958	50p	£12.00

JOHN O. BARKER (Ireland) LTD (Gum)

EL24	Circus Scenes	1960	£2.00	£50.00
EL24	Famous People	1960	£1.60	£40.00
25	The Wild West	1960	£4.00	—

BARRATT & CO. LTD
(AFTER 1973 SEE GEO. BASSETT)

M30	Aircraft	1941	£6.00	—
M30	Aircraft	1943	£6.00	—
25	Animals in the Service of Man	1964	20p	£3.50
16	Australian Cricketers Action Series	1926	£15.00	—
15	Australian Test Players	1930	£30.00	—
45	Beauties Picture Hats	c1910	£20.00	—
25	Birds	1960	70p	£17.50
50	Botany Quest	1966	£1.80	—
25	British Butterflies	1965	£2.60	—
25	Butterflies and Moths	1960	20p	£5.00
25	Cage and Aviary Birds	1960	50p	£12.50
50	Captain Scarlet and The Mysterons	1967	£3.50	—
50	Cars of the World	1965	£1.80	£90.00
	Characters From Fairy Stories and Fiction (plain back):			
M50	Characters From Fairy Stories	c1940	£10.00	—
M12	Gulliver's Travels	c1940	£10.00	—
M12	Pinocchio	c1940	£10.00	—
M36	Snow White and the Seven Dwarfs	c1940	£10.00	—
M12	The Wizard of Oz	1939	£10.00	—

11

BARRATT & CO. LTD (continued)

Cricketers, Footballers and Football Teams:

Qty		Date	Odds	Sets
80	Cricketers	c1925	£30.00	—
186	Footballers	c1925	£15.00	—
3	Football Teams	c1925	—	—
M20	Cricket Team Folders	1933	£22.00	—
M60	Disneyland 'True Life'	1956	£1.65	—
M50	FA Cup Winners 1883-1935	1935	£25.00	—
25	Fairy Stories	c1925	£3.20	—
11	Famous British Constructions, Aircraft Series	c1930	£18.00	—
M25	Famous Cricketers — 1930	1930	£12.00	—
M50	Famous Cricketers — 1932	1932	£12.00	—
M9	Famous Cricketers — 1932	1932	£22.00	—
M34	Famous Cricketers — 1934	1934	£16.00	—
M7	Famous Cricketers — 1936	1936	£16.00	—
M60	Famous Cricketers — 1937, unnumbered	1937	£12.00	—
M40	Famous Cricketers — 1938, numbered	1938	£12.00	—
35	Famous Film Stars	1960	£3.00	—
M100	Famous Footballers — 1935-36, unnumbered (black back)	1935	£12.00	—
M98	Famous Footballers — 1936-37, unnumbered (sepia back)	1936	£12.00	—
M100	Famous Footballers — 1937-38, numbered	1937	£12.00	—
M20	Famous Footballers — 1938-39, numbered	1938	£12.00	—
M110	Famous Footballers — 1939-40, numbered	1939	£12.00	—
M50	Famous Footballers — 1947-48	1947	£11.00	—
M50	Famous Footballers — 1948-49	1948	£11.00	—
M50	Famous Footballers — 1949-50	1949	£11.00	—
M50	Famous Footballers New Series — 1950-51	1950	£7.50	—
M50	Famous Footballers New Series — 1951-52	1951	£7.50	—
M50	Famous Footballers New Series — 1952-53	1952	£7.50	—
M50	Famous Footballers, Series A.1	1953	£6.00	—
M50	Famous Footballers, Series A.2	1954	£6.00	—
M50	Famous Footballers, Series A.3	1955	£6.00	—
60	Famous Footballers, Series A.4	1956	£6.00	—
60	Famous Footballers, Series A.5	1957	£6.00	—
60	Famous Footballers, Series A.6	1958	£6.00	—
60	Famous Footballers, Series A.7	1959	£6.00	—
50	Famous Footballers, Series A.8	1960	£6.00	—
50	Famous Footballers, Series A.9:			
	A Back Series A.8 Error printing	1961	£6.50	—
	B Back Series A.9	1961	£6.00	—
50	Famous Footballers, Series A.10	1962	£2.00	—
50	Famous Footballers, Series A.11	1963	£5.00	—
50	Famous Footballers, Series A.12	1964	£5.00	—
50	Famous Footballers, Series A.13	1965	£5.00	—
50	Famous Footballers, Series A.14	1966	£5.00	—
50	Famous Footballers, Series A.15	1967	£1.00	£50.00
50	Famous Sportsmen	1971	£2.00	—
M45	Fastest on Earth	1953	£2.00	—
32	Felix Pictures	c1930	£25.00	—
50	Film Stars (without name of film company)	c1940	£7.50	—
48	Film Stars (with name of film company)	c1940	£7.50	—
25	Fish and Bait	1962	80p	£20.00
12	Footballers Action Caricatures	c1930	£25.00	—
100	Football 'Stars'	c1930	£25.00	—

Qty		Date	Odds	Sets
	BARRATT & CO. LTD (continued)			
50	Football 'Stars' … … … … … … … … … … …	1973	£6.00	—
M66	Football Teams — 1st Division … … … … … … …	c1930	£15.00	—
M22	Football Team Folders, English League Division I	1932	£25.00	—
M22	Football Team Folders, English League Division I	1933	£25.00	—
M22	Football Team Folders, English League Division I	1934	£25.00	—
M22	Football Team Folders, English League Division II	1932	£25.00	—
M22	Football Team Folders, English League Division II	1933	£25.00	—
M22	Football Team Folders, English League Division II	1934	£25.00	—
M1	Football Team Folder, English League Division III	c1933	£25.00	—
M20	Football Team Folders, Scottish League Divison I	1934	£25.00	—
M3	Football Team Folders, Irish League … … … … …	c1933	£40.00	—
M1	Football Team Folder, Rugby Union … … … … …	1934	£40.00	—
48	Giants in Sport … … … … … … … … … … … …	1959	£6.00	—
EL12	Gold Rush (Package Issue) … … … … … … … …	c1960	£8.00	—
25	Head-Dresses of the World … … … … … … … …	1962	30p	£7.50
25	Historical Buildings … … … … … … … … … …	1960	30p	£7.50
25	History of the Air … … … … … … … … … … … …	1960	36p	£9.00
32	History of the Air … … … … … … … … … … … …	1959	£4.50	—
48	History of the Air:			
	A Cream card … … … … … … … … … … …	1959	£1.20	—
	B White card … … … … … … … … … … …	1959	£1.20	—
25	Interpol — back with chain frameline … … … … …	1964	£3.00	—
25	Interpol — back without chain frameline			
	(different subjects) … … … … … … … … … …	1964	£8.00	—
48	Leaders of Sport … … … … … … … … … … … …	c1930	£15.00	—
35	Magic Roundabout … … … … … … … … … … …	1968	£1.60	—
25	Merchant Ships of the World:			
	A Black back … … … … … … … … … … …	1962	70p	£17.50
	B Blue back … … … … … … … … … … … …	1962	50p	£12.50
M40	Modern Aircraft … … … … … … … … … … …	1955	£2.50	—
M45	Modern British Aircraft … … … … … … … … … …	1949	£3.50	—
12	National Flags … … … … … … … … … … … …	c1915	£20.00	—
64	Natural History Series … … … … … … … … … …	c1935	£6.00	—
M24	Naval Ships … … … … … … … … … … … … …	c1940	£8.00	—
M6	Our King and Queen … … … … … … … … … …	c1940	£9.00	—
25	People and Places … … … … … … … … … … …	1965	20p	£3.00
25	Pirates and Buccaneers … … … … … … … … …	1960	£1.00	£25.00
12	Prominent London Buildings … … … … … … … …	c1910	£20.00	—
M5	Regimental Uniforms … … … … … … … … … …	c1930	£12.00	—
36	Robin Hood … … … … … … … … … … … … …	1957	£2.00	—
30	Robin Hood … … … … … … … … … … … … …	1961	£2.50	£75.00
36	Sailing Into Space … … … … … … … … … … …	1959	£2.50	—
35	Sea Hunt … … … … … … … … … … … … … …	1961	£2.50	—
50	The Secret Service … … … … … … … … … … …	1970	£2.20	—
50	Soccer Stars … … … … … … … … … … … … …	1972	£3.50	—
50	Soldiers of the World … … … … … … … … … …	1966	50p	£25.00
16	South African Cricketers Series … … … … … … …	c1930	£20.00	—
25	Space Mysteries … … … … … … … … … … … …	1966	40p	£10.00
L20	Speed Series … … … … … … … … … … … … …	c1930	£8.00	—
50	Tarzan … … … … … … … … … … … … … … …	1967	35p	£17.50
35	Test Cricketers by E.W. Swanton, Series A … … … …	1956	£6.00	—
48	Test Cricketers, Series B … … … … … … … … …	1957	£7.50	—
50	Thunderbirds 1st Series … … … … … … … … …	1966	£3.60	—
50	Thunderbirds 2nd Series … … … … … … … … …	1967	£1.00	£50.00
50	Tom and Jerry… … … … … … … … … … … … …	1971	50p	£25.00

Qty		Date	Odds	Sets
	BARRATT & CO. LTD (continued)			
50	Trains	1970	30p	£15.00
50	Trains of the World	1964	30p	£15.00
35	TV's Huckleberry Hound and Friends	1961	£1.60	£55.00
35	TV's Yogi Bear	1963	£4.40	—
35	TV's Yogi Bear and Friends	1964	80p	—
70	UFO	1971	£1.20	—
M35	Walt Disney Characters	1955	£5.00	—
50	Walt Disney Characters 2nd Series	1957	£5.50	—
35	Walt Disney's True Life	1962	£1.40	—
25	Warriors Through the Ages	1962	80p	£20.00
25	What Do You Know?	1964	20p	£3.00
L72	Wild Animals	1970	80p	—
M50	Wild Animals by George Cansdale:			
	A With 'printed in England'	1954	£1.60	—
	B Without 'printed in England'	1954	£1.60	—
36	Wild West Series No.1	1959	£2.00	—
24	The Wild West	1961	50p	£12.50
25	The Wild West	1963	36p	£9.00
50	The Wild Wild West	1968	£1.60	—
25	Willum	1961	£6.50	—
50	Wisecracks 1st Series	1969	20p	£4.00
50	Wisecracks 2nd Series	1970	40p	£20.00
50	Wisecracks 3rd Series	1971	40p	£20.00
50	Wonders of the World	1962	20p	£6.00
25	World Locomotives	1963	80p	—
50	Wunders der Welt	1968	20p	£7.50
25	The Young Adventurer	1964	£2.40	£60.00
50	Zoo Pets	1964	£1.20	£60.00
	GEO. BASSETT & CO. LTD			
30	Adventures With Ben and Barkley	2001	20p	£6.00
50	Age of the Dinosaurs:			
	A Complete set	1979	£1.20	—
	B 35 Different	1979	—	£25.00
40	Ali-Cat Magicards	1978	£2.00	—
50	Asterix in Europe	1977	50p	£25.00
M20	The A Team	1986	75p	—
50	Athletes of the World	1980	40p	—
48	Bananaman	1985	20p	£4.00
	Album		—	£3.50
M20	Battle (Package Issue)	1985	£2.50	—
50	The Conquest of Space — 1980-81	1980	50p	£25.00
50	Cricket	1978	£9.00	—
50	Cricket 2nd Series	1979	£3.50	—
48	Dandy Beano Collection (black back)	1989	20p	£10.00
48	Dandy/Beano 2nd Series (blue back)	1990	20p	£8.00
48	Dinosaurs and Prehistoric Creatures	1994	£2.00	—
8	Dinosaurs and Prehistoric Creatures	1997	—	—
50	Disney/Health and Safety	1977	25p	£12.50
EL6	Europe's Best (Footballers)	1992	—	—
EL6	Europe's Best — Captains (Footballers)	1992	—	£6.00
EL6	Europe's Best — Goalkeepers (Footballers)	1992	—	£6.00
EL6	Europe's Best — Midfielders (Footballers)	1992	—	£6.00
EL6	Europe's Best — Strikers Series 1 (Footballers) ...	1992	—	£6.00
EL6	Europe's Best — Strikers Series 2 (Footballers) ...	1992	—	£6.00

GEO. BASSETT & CO. LTD (continued)

Qty		Date	Odds	Sets
50	Football Action	1976	£4.50	—
50	Football Action	1977	£4.50	—
EL6	Football Action	1991	—	—
50	Football — 1978-79:			
	A Complete set...	1978	—	£125.00
	B 42 Different (Minus Nos 26, 31, 33, 43, 44,			
	45, 49, 50)	1978	£1.00	£45.00
50	Football — 1979-80...	1979	50p	£25.00
50	Football — 1980-81...	1980	50p	£25.00
50	Football — 1981-82...	1981	£3.00	—
50	Football — 1982-83...	1982	£2.50	—
50	Football — 1983-84...	1983	20p	£8.00
	Album		—	£4.00
50	Football — 1984-85...	1984	£1.20	—
48	Football — 1985-86...	1985	20p	£10.00
48	Football — 1986-87...	1986	30p	£15.00
	Album		—	£4.00
48	Football — 1987-88...	1987	£1.00	—
48	Football — 1988-89...	1988	20p	£10.00
48	Football 1989-90:			
	A Red back	1989	20p	£10.00
	B Purple-red back	1989	20p	£9.00
48	Football 1990-91...	1990	35p	£17.50
48	Football 1991-92...	1991	60p	£30.00
48	Football 1992-93...	1992	30p	£15.00
48	Football 1995-96...	1995	60p	£30.00
50	Football Stars	1974	£2.00	—
50	Football Stars — 1975-76...	1975	£3.50	—
EL6	Great Defenders (Footballers)	1992	—	£6.00
EL6	Great Goalkeepers (Footballers)	1991	—	—
EL6	Great Grounds (Football)	1991	—	—
EL6	Great Managers 1st Series (Football)...	1991	—	—
EL6	Great Managers 2nd Series (Football)	1992	—	£6.00
M50	Guinness Book of Records	1990	—	£15.00
48	Hanna Barbera's Cartoon Capers	1983	£1.50	—
	Album		—	£4.00
24	Hologrems:			
	A Red back	1986	25p	£6.00
	B Plain back...	1986	50p	£12.00
	Album, Poster and Badge		—	£4.00
50	House of Horror	1982	£1.50	—
20	Jurassic Park (package issue)	1993	—	£10.00
40	Knight Rider	1987	40p	£16.00
	Album		—	£4.00
50	Living Creatures of Our World	1979	20p	£10.00
45	Looney Tunes (blue border & blue back)	1995	20p	£9.00
30	Looney Tunes Cartoons (yellow border)	1997	25p	£7.50
25	Looney Tunes Cartoons (blue border, purple back)	1999	40p	£10.00
32	Lord of The Rings	2003	80p	£25.00
12	The Magic Sword Quest for Camelot	1998	20p	£2.50
EL6	Midfield Dynamos (Footballers)	1992	—	£6.00
25	Motor Cars — Vintage and Modern	1968	80p	£20.00
25	Nursery Rhymes	1967	80p	£20.00
50	Play Cricket	1980	32p	£16.00
	Album		—	£10.00

Qty		Date	Odds	Sets
	GEO. BASSETT & CO. LTD (continued)			
25	Pop Stars	1974	40p	£10.00
EL25	Pop Stars	1984	£1.00	—
25	Popular Dogs	1966	50p	£12.50
48	Premier Players (Footballers)	1994	20p	£10.00
EL6	Premier Players — Goalkeepers (Footballers)......	1994	—	£6.00
EL6	Premier Players — Midfielders (Footballers)	1994	—	—
35	Secret Island 1st Series	1976	£1.40	—
40	Secret Island 2nd Series	1976	20p	£3.00
20	Sky Fighters (Package Issue)	1986	£2.00	—
48	Sonic the Hedgehog	1994	20p	£6.00
50	Space 1999:			
	A Complete set...............................	1976	—	£80.00
	B 49 different (minus No. 42)	1976	60p	£30.00
50	Super Heroes.......................................	1984	£1.00	—
	Album		—	£10.00
50	Survival on Star Colony 9......................	1979	40p	£20.00
40	Swim and Survive	1982	40p	£16.00
50	Tom and Jerry......................................	1974	£2.25	—
EL6	Top Strikers 1st Series (Footballers)	1991	—	—
EL6	Top Strikers 2nd Series (Footballers)	1992	—	—
70	UFO	1974	25p	£17.50
25	Victoria Cross Heroes in Action:			
	A Title black print on white	1970	60p	£15.00
	B Title white print on black	1970	£3.00	—
EL6	Winners in 1992 (Football Teams)	1992	—	£6.00
48	World Beaters (Footballers)	1993	30p	£15.00
EL6	World Beaters (Footballers)	1993	—	£6.00
50	World Cup Stars/World Cup '74.................	1974	20p	£8.00
40	World Heroes (Footballers):			
	A 'Bassett's & Beyond' at top	1999	£1.00	£40.00
	B 'Barratt' at top	1999	£1.25	—
40	World of The Vorgans	1978	£2.25	—
50	World Record Breakers	1983	£1.20	—
48	World Stars (Football)	1997	£1.00	—
EL6	World's Greatest Teams (Football)	1991	—	—
50	Yogi's Gang	1976	£1.70	—
	BATGER & CO.			
20	Batgers Sweet Advertisement Series	c1905	£45.00	—
	J.I. BATTEN & CO. LTD ('Jibco' Tea)			
28	Dominoes	c1955	£3.50	—
K25	Screen Stars 1st Series	1955	£4.00	—
K25	Screen Stars 2nd Series	1956	80p	£20.00
	S.P. BATTEN			
50	War Portraits	1916	£90.00	—
	BATTLE PICTURE WEEKLY			
16	Weapons of World War II — Germany	c1975	£1.25	—
16	Weapons of World War II — Great Britain	c1975	£1.25	—
16	Weapons of World War II — Japan	c1975	£1.25	—
16	Weapons of World War II — USA	c1975	£1.25	—
16	Weapons of World War II — USSR	c1975	£1.25	—

Qty		Date	Odds	Sets
	BATTLEAXE TOFFEE			
24	British and Empire Uniforms	1915	£28.00	—
	J.C. BATTOCK			
?M78	Cricket and Football Cards	c1920	£60.00	—
	BAYTCH BROS LTD			
64	Fighting Favourites	1951	£12.00	—
	BEANO LTD			
50	Conquest of Space	1956	20p	£7.50
25	Fascinating Hobbies	1950	£4.00	—
50	Modern Aircraft	1953	£1.20	—
50	Ships of the Royal Navy	1955	40p	£20.00
50	This Age of Speed — No.1 Aeroplanes	1954	50p	£25.00
50	This Age of Speed — No. 2 Buses and Trams... ...	1954	£2.00	—
50	Wonders of Modern Transport	c1955	80p	£40.00
	BEANSTALK CARDS			
15	Saturday Afternoon Heroes (Footballers)	2003	—	£5.50
15	Vintage Football Stars	2003	—	£5.50
	BEATALLS			
?19	Beauties	c1920	£30.00	—
	J.J. BEAULAH LTD			
1	Boston Stump Advertisement Card			
	A 'Boston Stump' in black	1953	—	60p
	B 'Boston Stump' in blue	1954	—	60p
25	Coronation Series	1953	£1.60	£40.00
24	Marvels of the World	1954	20p	£3.00
24	Modern British Aircraft	1953	20p	£5.00
	BEAUTIFUL GAME LTD			
LT50	Football Greats	1999	—	£20.00
LT4	Football Greats Sir Tom Finney	1999	—	£4.00
	BEAVERBROOK NEWSPAPERS (Daily Express)			
L59	Car Cards '71	1971	20p	£6.00
L53	Star Cards (pop stars)	1972	£1.00	—
	T.W. BECKETT & CO. LTD (South Africa)			
M50	Animals of South Africa, Series 3	1966	20p	£9.00
M50	Birds of South Africa 1st Series	1965	20p	£9.00
M50	Birds of South Africa 2nd Series	1966	20p	£9.00
	THE BEEHIVE			
25	British Uniforms of the 19th Century	1959	80p	£20.00
	BEL UK (Laughing Cow)			
M12	Animal Antics	1997	£1.25	—
L8	Chicken Run	2000	£1.25	—
	BELL TEA (New Zealand)			
EL20	Historic New Zealand	1991	—	£12.00

Qty		Date	Odds	Sets

BELL'S WHISKY

Qty		Date	Odds	Sets
42	Other Famous Bells (shaped)	1975	60p	£25.00

J. BELLAMY & SONS LTD

25	Vintage and Modern Trains of the World 1st Series	1968	30p	£7.50

BENSEL WORKFORCE LTD

20	Occupations	1991	—	£5.00

BETTER PUBS LTD

EL20	East Devon Inn Signs + 2 varieties	1976	75p	£15.00

J. BIBBY & SONS LTD (Trex)

L25	Don't You Believe It	1956	£1.00	—
L25	Good Dogs...	1956	£2.60	—
L25	How, What and Why?	1956	£1.00	—
L25	Isn't It Strange?	1956	£1.00	—
L25	They Gave it a Name	1956	£2.20	—
L25	This Wonderful World	1956	£1.00	—

BIRCHGREY LTD

L25	Panasonic European Open (Golf)	1989	—	£15.00

ALFRED BIRD & SONS

K49	Happy Families	1938	£1.50	—

BIRD'S EYE

EL12	Recipe Cards	c1965	33p	£4.00
30	Wonders of the Seven Seas	c1975	£1.25	—

BIRKUM

25	Motor Cars...	1956	£1.20	—

BISHOPS STORTFORD DAIRY FARMERS LTD (Tea)

25	Dogs' Heads	1965	£1.00	£25.00
25	Freshwater Fish	1964	£1.40	—
25	Historical Buildings	1964	50p	£12.50
25	History of Aviation	1964	60p	£15.00
25	Passenger Liners	1965	20p	£3.00
25	Pond Life	1966	20p	£3.00
25	Science in the 20th Century	1966	20p	£3.00
25	The Story of Milk...	1966	30p	£7.50

BLACK ROOK PRESS

10	Classic Football Stars (1960s) Series 1	1998	—	£4.50

BLACKCAT CARDS

15	Sunderland F.C. Cup Kings of '73	2003	—	£5.50

BLACKPOOL PROGRAMME & MEMORABILIA COLLECTORS CLUB (BPMCC)

13	Blackpool FC Legends...	2004	—	£10.00

BLAKEY'S BOOT PROTECTORS LTD

72	War Pictures	c1916	£6.50	—

Qty					Date	Odds	Sets

BLUE BAND

Qty				Date	Odds	Sets
24	History of London's Transport:					
	A	Black printing		1954	£1.00	—
	B	Blue printing		1954	£1.00	—
	C	Red printing		1954	£1.00	—
24	History of London's Transport 2nd Series			1955	£2.50	—
16	See Britain by Coach:					
	A	Black back		1954	30p	£5.00
	B	Blue back		1954	£1.00	—

THE BLUE BIRD

Qty		Date	Odds	Sets
M10	Famous Beauties of the Day	1922	£9.00	—

BLUE BIRD STOCKINGS

Qty		Date	Odds	Sets
EL12	Exciting Film Stars 3rd Series	1954	—	£30.00

BLUE CAP LTD

Qty				Date	Odds	Sets
	Flixies Coloured Film Transparencies:					
K12	i	Ancient Monuments		1959	£1.00	—
K12	ii	Aviation Series		1959	£1.00	—
K12	iii	British Bird Series		1959	£1.00	£12.00
K12	iv	Butterflies		1959	£1.00	—
K12	v	Dog Series		1959	£1.00	£12.00
K12	vi	Flowers		1959	£1.00	£12.00
K12	vii	Football Teams		1959	£1.00	—
K12	viii	Military Uniforms		1959	£1.00	—
K12	ix	Robin Hood		1959	£1.00	£12.00
K12	x	Ships		1959	£1.00	—
K12	xi	Sport Series		1959	£1.00	—
K12	xii	Tropical Fish		1959	£1.00	—
	Album for Series ii, iii, v, xi				—	£6.00
	Album for Series i, viii, ix, xii				—	£6.00
	Album for Series iv, vi, vii, x				—	£6.00

BON AIR (USA)

Qty		Date	Odds	Sets
LT50	Birds and Flowers of the States	1991	—	£8.00
LT20	Civil War The Heritage Collection 1st Series	1991	—	£10.00
LT12	Civil War The Heritage Collection 2nd Series	1992	—	£6.00
LT100	18 Wheelers 1st Series (Lorries)	1994	—	£9.50
LT100	18 Wheelers 2nd Series (Lorries)	1995	—	£9.50
LT62	Federal Duck Stamps (ducks featured on stamps)	1992	—	£8.50
LT100	Fire Engines 1st Series	1993	—	£12.00
LT100	Fire Engines 2nd Series	1993	—	£15.00
LT100	Fire Engines 3rd Series	1994	—	£15.00
LT100	Fire Engines 4th Series	1994	—	£15.00
LT100	Fire Engines 5th Series	1998	—	£12.00
LT90	Native Americans	1995	—	£9.50
LT63	On Guard The Heritage Collection	1992	—	£9.50
LT50	Wildlife America	1991	—	£8.00

E.H. BOOTH & CO. LTD (Tea)

Qty		Date	Odds	Sets
25	Badges and Uniforms of Famous British Regiments and Corps	1964	20p	£4.00
24	The Island of Ceylon	c1955	£5.00	—
25	Ships and Their Workings	1963	£1.20	—

Qty		Date	Odds	Sets
	BOW BELLS			
MP6	Handsome Men of the British Screen...	1922	£8.00	—
	BOWATER-SCOTT			
EL9	Scotties Famous Football Teams	1969	£3.00	—
EL3	Scotties Grand Prix Series I	1968	£3.00	—
EL4	Scotties Grand Prix Series II...	1969	£3.00	—
	BOWMAN GUM INC. (USA)			
M108	Jets-Rockets-Spacemen	1951	—	—
	BOYS' CINEMA			
M24	Boys' Cinema Famous Heroes	1922	£4.50	—
MP6	Cinema Stars (plain back)	c1925	£4.50	—
MP6	Famous Film Heroes	1922	£4.50	—
EL8	Favourite Film Stars	c1930	£4.50	—
7	Film Stars	c1930	£3.50	—
MP8	Film Stars, brown glossy photos	1930	£4.50	—
MP8	Film Stars, black glossy photos...	1931	£4.50	—
	BOYS' COMIC LIBRARY			
4	Characters from Boys' Fiction	c1910	£16.00	—
4	Heroes of the Wild West	c1910	£16.00	—
6	One and All Flowers	c1910	£16.00	—
	BOYS' FRIEND			
3	Famous Boxers Series...	1911	£15.00	—
3	Famous Flags Series	1911	£10.00	—
3	Famous Footballers Series	1911	£20.00	—
3	Famous Regiments Series	1911	£10.00	—
MP4	Footballers, half length studies	1923	£6.00	—
MP5	Footballers, two players on each card	1922	£6.00	—
MP15	Rising Boxing Stars...	1922	£4.00	—
	BOYS' MAGAZINE			
M8	Coloured Studies of Famous Internationals...	1922	£6.00	—
P10	Famous Cricketers Series	1928	£6.00	—
P12	Famous Footballers Series	c1930	£6.00	—
MP10	Football Series	c1930	£4.50	—
EL9	Football Teams	c1925	£13.00	—
	Sportsmen:			
M8	Boxers	c1926	£9.00	—
M10	Cricketers	c1926	£10.00	—
M30	Footballers (picture 49 × 39mm)	c1926	£6.00	—
M64	Footballers and Miscellaneous			
	(picture 56 × 35mm)	c1926	£6.00	—
12	'Zat' Cards, Cricketers	c1930	£9.00	—
M11	'Zat' Cards, Cricketers	1932	£9.00	—
	BOYS' REALM			
MP15	Famous Cricketers	1922	£3.50	—
MP9	Famous Footballers...	1922	£5.00	—
	BREWER'S			
24	Nursery Rhymes	c1920	£10.00	—

Qty		Date	Odds	Sets

BREYGENT (USA)

Qty		Date	Odds	Sets
LT72	Dexter Seasons 1 and 2	2009	—	£8.00
LT72	Dexter Season 3	2011	—	£8.00
LT72	Ghost Whisperer Seasons 1 and 2	2009	—	£8.00
LT72	Ghost Whisperer Seasons 3 and 4	2010	—	£8.00
LT72	The Tudors Seasons I, II & III	2011	—	£9.50
LT72	Vampirella — Adult Fantasy Art	2011	—	£8.00
LT72	The Wizard of Oz	2006	—	£8.50

C. & T. BRIDGEWATER LTD

Qty		Date	Odds	Sets
KP48	Coronation Series	1937	20p	£7.50
KP96	Film Stars (CE over No.) (No. 54 without CE)	1932	50p	£50.00
KP96	Film Stars (E below No.)	1933	£1.00	£100.00
KP96	Film Stars (number only)	1934	£1.00	£100.00
KP48	Film Stars 4th Series	1935	40p	£20.00
KP48	Film Stars 5th Series	1937	£1.75	£85.00
KP48	Film Stars 6th Series (F before No.)	1938	£2.00	—
P48	Film Stars 7th Series	1939	£1.75	£85.00
KP48	Film Stars 8th Series	1940	60p	£30.00
KP48	Radio Stars 1st Series	1935	£1.50	£75.00
KP48	Radio Stars 2nd Series	1936	40p	£20.00

BRIMSTONE PRODUCTIONS

Qty		Date	Odds	Sets
10	Hollywood Beauties (of the 40s & 50s)	2009	—	£5.00

J.M. BRINDLEY

Qty		Date	Odds	Sets
30	Australian Cricketers	1986	—	£12.00
30	Bentley Cars	1993	—	£12.00
M20	Birds of Britain 1st Series Nos 1-20	1991	—	—
M20	Birds of Britain 2nd Series Nos 21-40...	1992	—	—
M20	Birds of Britain 3rd Series Nos 41-60	1993	—	—
M20	Birds of Britain 4th Series Nos 61-80	1993	—	—
M20	Birds of Britain 5th Series Nos 81-100	1993	—	—
M12	British Birds of Prey	1995	—	£8.00
20	Car Badges and Emblems	1987	—	£6.00
30	Cricketers 1st Series	1984	—	£15.00
30	Cricketers 2nd Series	1985	—	£20.00
L16	Cricketers 3rd Series	1985	—	£12.00
30	Cricketers 4th Series	1985	33p	£10.00
L20	Cricket (cartoons) 5th Series...	1985	—	£10.00
12	Cricket Caricatures 1st Series Nos 1-12	1992	50p	£6.00
18	Cricket Caricatures 2nd Series Nos 13-30	1993	—	£9.00
30	Cricket — The Old School	1987	—	£10.00
20	Cricket Old Timers	1993	—	£7.50
30	Cricket — Surrey v Yorkshire	1988	—	£9.00
20	Cricketers of the 1880s	1992	30p	£6.00
25	Cricketing Greats	1987	24p	£6.00
EL1	Cricketing Greats — W.G. Grace	1987	—	50p
18	Famous Operatic Roles	1992	—	£7.00
18	Fish	1989	—	£6.00
EL35	Full Dress Uniforms of the British Army c1914 1st Series	1990	—	£12.00
EL35	Full Dress Uniforms of the British Army c1914 2nd Series	1990	—	£12.00

21

Qty		Date	Odds	Sets
	J.M. BRINDLEY (continued)			
EL35	Full Dress Uniforms of the British Army c1914 3rd Series	1990	—	£12.00
EL35	Full Dress Uniforms of the British Army c1914 4th Series	1990	—	£12.00
EL35	Full Dress Uniforms of the British Army c1914 5th Series	1990	—	£12.00
20	Golf	1987	—	£10.00
38	Hampshire County Cricket Club	1991	30p	£12.00
24	Hampshire Cricket Sunday League Era	1987	—	£6.00
20	Horse Racing	1987	—	£6.00
20	Loco's	1987	40p	—
30	London, Brighton and South Coast Railway	1986	—	£8.00
20	Military	1987	—	£6.00
25	Old Golfing Greats	1987	50p	£12.50
EL1	Old Golfing Greats — H. Vardon	1987	—	50p
12	Old Motor Cycles	1993	—	—
30	Opera Stars	1988	—	£12.00
16	Players of the Past — 1930s Football	1992	—	£10.00
EL6	Regimental Drum Majors	1992	—	£3.00
EL7	The Royal Hussars Bandsmen 1979-1989	1989	—	—
20	S.E.C.R. Locos	1995	40p	£8.00
16	Sea Fish	1992	—	£8.00
20	South African Test Cricket 1888-1988...	1989	40p	£8.00
20	Trains — London & S.W. Railways	1992	—	£6.00
30	Victorian and Edwardian Soldiers in Full Dress ...	1988	—	£10.00
M6	World Boxers 1st Series Nos 1-6	1992	—	£4.50
M6	World Boxers 2nd Series Nos 7-12	1993	—	£4.50

BRISTOL–MYERS CO. LTD

Qty		Date	Odds	Sets
25	Speed 1st Series...	1966	£5.00	—
25	Speed 2nd Series	1966	£5.00	—

THE BRITISH AUTOMATIC CO. LTD (Weight Cards)

Qty		Date	Odds	Sets
K24	British Aircraft	1950	£1.80	£45.00
K24	British Birds	1950	£2.25	—
K24	British Locomotives	1948	£1.00	£25.00
K36	British Motor Cars	1950	£3.50	—
K44	Coronation Information...	1953	£1.20	—
K32	Dogs 1st Series	1953	75p	£24.00
K32	Dogs 2nd Series	1953	£1.10	£35.00
K24	Famous Trains of the World 1st Series	1952	£1.50	—
K24	Famous Trains of the World 2nd Series	1952	£1.25	£30.00
K30	Fortunes, Horoscopes, Quotations...	1953	£1.00	—
K32	Fortunes, Horoscopes, Quotations...	1953	£1.00	—
K32	Fortunes 2nd Series	1953	70p	—
K24	Fresh Water Fish	1950	£1.75	—
K24	History of Transport	1948	50p	£12.00
K44	Jokes	1951	60p	—
K24	Olympic Games	1952	£5.00	—
K24	Racing and Sports Cars	1957	£3.00	—
K24	Space Travel	1955	£2.00	—
K24	Speed	1949	50p	£12.00
K24	Sportsman	1955	£3.00	—
K20	Twenty Questions	1952	£2.50	—
K24	Warships of the World	1950	£1.00	£24.00

Qty		Date	Odds	Sets

BRITISH EDUCATIONAL SERIES

Qty		Date	Odds	Sets
50	Modern Aircraft	1953	20p	£10.00

BRITISH TOURIST AUTHORITY

25	Industrial Heritage Year	1993	—	£15.00

C. BRITTON

L24	Golf Courses of the British Isles	1993	30p	£7.50

BROOK MOTORS LTD (Motor Engineers)

EL12	Motor Cars 1910-1931	1961	£2.50	£30.00
EL12	Railway Engines (size 120 × 83mm)	1962	£3.00	£36.00
EL12	Railway Engines (size 125 × 105mm)...	c1970	£1.00	£12.00
EL12	Traction Engines	1968	£2.00	£24.00

BROOKE BOND & CO. LTD

(104-page illustrated reference book 'Brooke Bond Tea Cards', published 2007 — £12.50)

Qty			Date	Odds	Sets
50	Adventurers and Explorers		1973	20p	£4.00
	Album			—	£4.00
50	African Wild Life:				
	A	Blue back	1961	25p	£12.50
	B	Black back	1973	20p	£4.00
50	Asian Wild Life		1962	20p	£10.00
	Album			—	£35.00
50	Bird Portraits:				
	A	With address	1957	£1.20	£60.00
	B	Without address	1957	£2.50	—
50	British Butterflies:				
	A	Blue back	1963	70p	£35.00
	B	Black back	1973	20p	£5.00
50	British Costume:				
	A	Blue back	1967	20p	£5.00
	B	Black back	1973	20p	£4.00
	Album (reprint, glossy cover with price)		—	£4.00
	C	Error and Corrected Cards of Nos 3, 4, 23, 24		—	£30.00
50	British Wild Life:				
	A	Brooke Bond (Great Britain) Ltd	1958	£1.80	—
	B	Brooke Bond Tea Ltd	1958	80p	£40.00
	C	Brooke Bond & Co. Ltd	1958	£1.80	—
50	Butterflies of the World...		1964	20p	£7.50
	Album			—	£30.00
	Creatures of Legend:				
M24	A	Standard set	1994	30p	£7.50
EL12	B	Two pictures per card	1994	80p	£10.00
	Album			—	£6.00
	Wallchart		1994	—	£5.00
	The Dinosaur Trail:				
20	A	Standard set:			
		i Postcode BB1 1PG	1993	80p	£16.00
		ii Postcode BB11 1PG	1993	20p	£3.00
L10	B	Two pictures per card:			
		i Postcode BB1 1PG	1993	£1.80	—
		ii Postcode BB11 1PG	1993	60p	£6.00
	Album			—	£4.00

BROOKE BOND & CO. LTD (continued)

Qty		Date	Odds	Sets
	Discovering Our Coast:			
50	A Standard set Blue back	1989	20p	£4.00
50	B Standard set Black back	1992	20p	£5.00
L25	C Two pictures per card	1989	40p	£10.00
	Album		—	£4.00
	Wallchart	1989	—	£4.00
50	Famous People:			
	A Blue back	1969	20p	£4.00
	Album (original with printer's credit and price) ..		—	£15.00
	B Black back	1973	20p	£4.00
	Album (reprint, cover without price and printer's credit)		—	£4.00
	Features of the World:			
50	A Standard set	1984	20p	£5.00
L25	B Two pictures per card	1984	80p	£20.00
	Album		—	£4.00
50	Flags and Emblems of the World:			
	A Blue back	1967	20p	£5.00
	Album (original, matt cover with printer's credit)		—	£7.00
	B Black back	1973	40p	£10.00
	Album (reprint, glossy cover without printer's credit)		—	£4.00
48	40 Years of Cards:			
	A Dark Blue back	1994	20p	£7.00
	B Light Blue back	1994	20p	£6.00
	C Black back	1994	20p	£6.00
LT40	40 Years of the Chimps Television Advertising	1995	25p	£10.00
	Album		—	£4.00
20	Frances Pitt — British Birds:			
	A Cream Card	1954	£4.00	£80.00
	B White Card	1954	£3.00	£60.00
50	Freshwater Fish:			
	A Blue back	1960	£1.00	£50.00
	B Black back	1973	50p	£25.00
	Going Wild — Wildlife Survival:			
M40	A Standard set	1994	20p	£6.00
EL20	B Two pictures per card	1994	50p	£10.00
	Album		—	£4.00
50	History of Aviation	1972	20p	£5.00
	Album		—	£4.00
50	History of the Motor Car:			
	A Blue back	1968	25p	£12.50
	Album (original, cover with price)		—	£7.00
	B Black back	1974	25p	£12.50
	Incredible Creatures:			
40	A Standard set:			
	i 'Sheen Lane' address	1985	30p	£12.00
	ii 'Walton' address with Dept. IC	1986	20p	£4.00
	iii 'Walton' address without Dept. IC ...	1986	50p	£20.00
L20	B Two pictures per card:			
	i 'Sheen Lane' address	1985	£2.50	—
	ii 'Walton' address with Dept. IC	1986	£1.50	£30.00
	iii 'Walton' address without Dept. IC ...	1986	£3.00	—
	Set of 4 Wallcharts		—	£6.00

Qty		Date	Odds	Sets
	BROOKE BOND & CO. LTD (continued)			
LT20	International Soccer Stars	1998	50p	£10.00
	Album		–	£4.00
50	Inventors and Inventions	1975	20p	£4.00
	A Journey Downstream:			
25	A Standard set	1990	20p	£3.50
L25	B Two pictures per card	1990	50p	£12.50
	Album		–	£4.00
12	The Language of Tea (flags)	1988	20p	£2.50
LT45	The Magical, Mystical World of Pyramids:			
	A Red & black back	1996	40p	£18.00
	B Black back	1998	30p	£14.00
	Album		–	£4.00
	The Magical World of Disney:			
25	A Standard set	1989	20p	£5.00
L13	B Two pictures per card	1989	60p	£8.00
	Album		–	£4.00
	Natural Neighbours:			
40	A Standard set	1992	25p	£10.00
L20	B Two pictures per card	1992	50p	£10.00
	Album		–	£4.00
	Olympic Challenge 1992:			
40	A Standard set	1992	25p	£10.00
L20	B Two pictures per card	1992	60p	£12.00
	Album		–	£4.00
40	Olympic Greats:			
	A Green back	1979	30p	£12.00
	B Black back	1988	£1.00	–
	Album		–	£4.00
50	Out Into Space:			
	A 'Issued with Brooke Bond ...'	1956	£9.00	–
	B 'Issued in packets ...'	1958	£1.00	£50.00
40	Play Better Soccer	1976	20p	£4.00
	Album		–	£4.00
40	Police File	1977	20p	£4.00
	Album		–	£4.00
EL10	Polyfilla Modelling Cards	1974	£9.00	–
50	Prehistoric Animals	1972	20p	£7.00
	Album		–	£20.00
	Queen Elizabeth I — Queen Elizabeth II:			
50	A Blue back	1983	20p	£5.00
50	B Black back	1988	20p	£6.00
L25	C Two pictures per card	1983	£1.40	£35.00
	Album		–	£4.00
50	The Race Into Space:			
	A Blue back	1971	20p	£6.00
	Album (original with printer's credit, 45mm)		–	£25.00
	B Black back	1974	20p	£5.00
50	Saga of Ships:			
	A Blue back	1970	20p	£4.00
	Album (original, cover light blue sky)		–	£20.00
	B Black back	1973	20p	£5.00
	Album (reprint, cover dark blue sky)		–	£4.00
50	The Sea — Our Other World...	1974	20p	£4.00
	Album (original, with printer's credit)		–	£10.00
	Album (reprint, without printer's credit)		–	£4.00

BROOKE BOND & CO. LTD (continued)

Qty		Date	Odds	Sets
LT50	The Secret Diary of Kevin Tipps	1995	20p	£10.00
	Album		—	£4.00
40	Small Wonders:			
	A Blue back	1981	20p	£5.00
	B Black back	1988	20p	£4.00
	Album		—	£4.00
LT19	Tea Leaf Oracle	1999	£4.00	—
	Teenage Mutant Hero Turtles:			
12	A Standard set	1991	20p	£2.50
L6	B Two pictures per card	1991	80p	£5.00
	Album		—	£4.00
12	30 Years of The Chimps:			
	A Thin Card plain back	1986	£6.00	—
	B Thick Card plain back	1986	85p	£10.00
	C Thin Card Tak Tik back	1986	£5.00	—
50	Transport Through the Ages:			
	A Blue back	1966	20p	£5.00
	B Black back	1973	£1.00	—
50	Trees in Britain:			
	A Blue back	1966	20p	£4.00
	Album (original, cover with price and printer's			
	credit)		—	£7.00
	B Black back	1973	20p	£4.00
	Album (reprint, cover with price without printer's			
	credit)		—	£4.00
50	Tropical Birds:			
	A Blue back	1961	30p	£15.00
	B Black back	1974	20p	£4.00
	Album (reprint, without price and printer's credit)		—	£4.00
	Unexplained Mysteries of the World:			
40	A Standard set	1987	20p	£4.00
L20	B Two pictures per card	1987	50p	£10.00
	Album		—	£4.00
40	Vanishing Wildlife:			
	A Brown back	1978	20p	£4.00
	B Black back	1988	20p	£5.00
	Album		—	£5.00
50	Wild Birds in Britain:			
	A Blue back	1965	20p	£4.00
	B Black back	1973	20p	£6.00
50	Wild Flowers, Series 1:			
	A Thick Card	1955	£3.00	£150.00
	B Paper Thin Card	1955	£9.00	—
50	Wild Flowers, Series 2:			
	A Blue back with 'issued by ...'	1959	25p	£12.50
	B Blue back without 'issued by ...'	1959	£2.50	—
	C Black back	1973	20p	£4.00
	Album (reprint, without price)		—	£4.00
50	Wild Flowers, Series 3	1964	20p	£6.00
50	Wild Life in Danger:			
	A Blue back	1963	20p	£4.00
	Album (original, with price, WWF 44mm)		—	£12.00
	B Black back	1973	20p	£4.00
LT30	The Wonderful World of Kevin Tipps	1997	40p	£12.00
	Album		—	£4.00

Qty		Date	Odds	Sets

BROOKE BOND & CO. LTD (continued)

Qty		Date	Odds	Sets
50	Wonders of Wildlife … … … … … … … … … … …	1976	20p	£4.00
	Error and corrected card of No. 37… … … … … …		—	£18.00
	Album … … … … … … … … … … … … … …		—	£4.00
40	Woodland Wildlife:			
	A Green back … … … … … … … … … … …	1980	20p	£6.00
	B Black back … … … … … … … … … … …	1988	20p	£7.00
	Album … … … … … … … … … … … … … …		—	£4.00
L50	Zena Skinner International Cookery Cards … … …	1974	£20.00	—

BROOKE BOND OVERSEAS ISSUES

IRELAND

Qty		Date	Odds	Sets
40	Incredible Creatures … … … … … … … … … …	1986	£2.00	£80.00

CANADA

Qty		Date	Odds	Sets
CU1 48	Songbirds of North America:			
	A Back 'Red Rose Tea & Coffee' Album			
	clause reading:			
	a 'Mount Your Collection, Send 25c'…	1959	£6.00	—
	b 'Album available at your grocer's or			
	from us 25c' … … … … … … …	1959	£3.50	—
	B Back 'Red Rose and Blue Ribbon Tea and			
	Coffee' … … … … … … … … … … …	1959	£1.80	£90.00
CU2 48	Animals of North America:			
	A 'Rolland' back … … … … … … … … … …	1960	£2.75	—
	B 'Roland' back:			
	a Text between lines 47mm … … … …	1960	£2.50	£125.00
	b Text between lines 49mm … … … …	1960	£13.00	—
CU3 48	Wild Flowers of North America … … … … … …	1961	90p	£45.00
CU4 48	Birds of North America… … … … … … … … …	1962	£1.00	£50.00
CU5 48	Dinosaurs … … … … … … … … … … … … …	1963	£3.00	£150.00
CU6 48	Tropical Birds:			
	A Top line in red … … … … … … … … …	1964	£8.00	—
	B Top line in black … … … … … … … … …	1964	90p	£45.00
CU7 48	African Animals … … … … … … … … … … …	1964	20p	£6.00
	Album … … … … … … … … … … … … …		—	£20.00
CU8 48	Butterflies of North America … … … … … … …	1965	80p	£40.00
CU9 48	Canadian/American Songbirds … … … … … …	1966	£2.50	£125.00
CU10 48	Transportation Through the Ages:			
	A Top line in red … … … … … … … … …	1967	£8.00	—
	B Top line in black … … … … … … … … …	1967	35p	£17.50
CU11 48	Trees of North America … … … … … … … …	1968	40p	£20.00
CU12 48	The Space Age … … … … … … … … … … …	1969	30p	£15.00
	Album … … … … … … … … … … … … …		—	£15.00
CU13 48	North American Wildlife in Danger … … … … … …	1970	20p	£7.50
	Album … … … … … … … … … … … … …		—	£15.00
CU14 48	Exploring the Ocean … … … … … … … … …	1971	20p	£5.00
	Album … … … … … … … … … … … … …		—	£5.00
CU15 48	Animals and Their Young:			
	A Text ends 'Products' … … … … … … …	1972	40p	£20.00
	B Text ends 'Tea/Coffee'… … … … … … …	1972	£9.00	—
CU16 48	The Arctic … … … … … … … … … … … … …	1973	20p	£10.00
	Album … … … … … … … … … … … … …		—	£4.00
CU17 48	Indians of Canada … … … … … … … … … …	1974	£1.00	£50.00
	Album … … … … … … … … … … … … …		—	£4.00

BROOKE BOND & CO. LTD (continued)

USA

Qty		Date	Odds	Sets
CU2 48	Animals of North America:			
	A Blue text on back	1960	£9.00	—
	B Black text on back	1960	£12.00	—
CU3 48	Wild Flowers of North America:			
	A Dark Blue back	1961	£5.00	—
	B Light Blue back	1961	£20.00	—
CU4 48	Birds of North America...	1962	£7.00	—
CU5 48	Dinosaurs	1963	£9.00	—
CU6 48	Tropical Birds	1964	£5.00	—
CU8 48	Butterflies of North America	1965	£5.00	—
CU9 48	Canadian/American Songbirds	1966	£3.00	—

SOUTHERN RHODESIA AND EAST AFRICA

Qty		Date	Odds	Sets
SR2 50	African Wild Life	1961	£6.00	—
SR3 50	Tropical Birds	1962	£5.00	—
SR4 50	Asian Wild Life	1963	£6.00	—
SR5 50	Wild Life in Danger	1964	£6.00	—
SR6 50	African Birds	1965	£5.00	—
SR7 50	Butterflies of the World...	1966	£5.00	£250.00

SOUTH AFRICA

Qty		Date	Odds	Sets
SA1 50	Wild van Africa (alternate cards English and Afrikaans)	1965	£12.00	—
SA2 50	Wild van Africa (bilingual)	1965	£5.00	£250.00
SA3 50	Out Into Space	1966	£5.00	£250.00
SA4 50	Our Pets:			
	A Printing A	1967	£5.00	£250.00
	B Printing B (revised numbering)	1967	£15.00	—

MUSGRAVE-BROOKE BOND (Eire)

Qty		Date	Odds	Sets
MBB1 20	British Birds	1964	£10.00	—
MBB2 50	British Wild Life	1964	£10.00	—
MBB3 50	Butterflies of the World...	1965	£10.00	—
MBB4 50	Transport Through the Ages	1966	£5.00	£250.00

BROOKE BOND-LIEBIG (Italy)

Qty		Date	Odds	Sets
EL6	F.1845 The Nativity	1971	—	£20.00
EL6	F.1850 Self-Portraits of Famous Artists	1972	—	£6.00
EL6	F.1851 Journey to the Moon (II)...	1972	—	£10.00
EL6	F.1852 Historical Fights	1972	—	£5.00
EL6	F.1853 The Resurrection	1972	—	£18.00
EL6	F.1854 History of the Typewriter	1972	—	£10.00
EL6	F.1855 How Animals See (I)	1973	—	£6.00
EL6	F.1856 Ludwig van Beethoven	1973	—	£7.00
EL6	F.1857 The Fight Against Microbes (I)	1973	—	£6.00
EL6	F.1858 How Animals See (II)...	1973	—	£5.00
EL6	F.1859 The Story of the Circus	1973	—	£11.00
EL6	F.1860 The Fight Against Microbes (II)	1973	—	£12.00
EL6	F.1861 The Circus	1974	—	£12.00
EL6	F.1862 War at Sea	1974	—	£35.00
EL6	F.1863 Animals	1974	—	£10.00
EL6	F.1867 Journey to the Moon (1)...	1975	—	£13.00
EL6	F.1868 Protected Birds...	1975	—	£11.00
EL6	F.1869 Old Military Dress (1)...	1975	—	£11.00
EL6	F.1871 Old Military Dress (II)...	1975	—	£35.00

BROOKE BOND & CO. LTD (continued)

BROOKE BOND NOVELTY INSERTS
ADVERTISEMENT CARD INSERTS (Great Britain)

Qty		Date	Odds	Sets
1	Why is Crown Cup 'Medium Roasted'?	1963	—	£5.00
1	3 Crown Cups and Saucers	1963	—	£12.00
2	Danish Designed Tableware	1964	£12.00	—
2	Radio London	1965	£12.00	—
2	Six-Piece Cutlery Set	1966	£12.00	—
1	Free Opal Glass Jar:			
	A Original card plain back	1967	—	£45.00
	B Reprint card printed back	2004	—	£1.50
	Place The Face Bingo:			
15	A Single Face with PG Tips	1972	£35.00	—
15	B Single Face without PG Tips	1972	£35.00	—
15	C Three Faces	1972	£35.00	—
K15	D Flap of Packet	1972	£40.00	—
1	Play Better Soccer set and album offer	1976	—	£4.00
1	Play Better Soccer 'Great New Series!'	1976	—	£12.00
1	Police File 'New picture Card Series'	1977	—	£45.00
LT1	P.G. Tips Tipps Family 1997 Calendar	1996	—	£10.00
LT3	Farewell to Picture Cards	1999	£1.50	£4.50
LT1	P.G. Tips Need Your Help	1999	—	£1.50
LT1	Thank You	1999	—	£1.50
LT1	PG Tips Bean Chimp:			
	A With Multi Coloured Circle	2001	—	£4.00
	B With Dark Brown Circle	2001	—	£7.00

ADVERTISEMENT CARDS (Eire)

Qty		Date	Odds	Sets
	Match-Maker Cards:			
	A Blue & black printing:			
39	a 'Musgrave Brooke Bond' on front	1967	£40.00	—
39	b 'PG Tips' on front	1967	£40.00	—
9	B Red & black printing	1967	£40.00	—

CARD GAMES

Qty		Date	Odds	Sets
L36	British Costume	1974	—	£25.00
L36	Flags and Emblems...	1974	—	£25.00
L36	Motor History	1974	—	£25.00
L55	P.G. Tips Card Game — Get Out	1995	—	£5.00
L54	P.G. Tips Card Game — Playing Cards	1995	—	£4.00
L36	P.G. Tips Card Game — Snap	1995	—	£4.00
L54	P.G. Tips Card Game — Trick Cards	1995	—	£4.00

BROOKFIELD SWEETS (Ireland)

Qty		Date	Odds	Sets
50	Animals of the World	c1956	£4.00	—
25	Aquarium Fish 1st Series	c1959	£4.00	—
25	Aquarium Fish 2nd Series	c1959	£4.00	—
25	Conquest of Space	c1956	£4.00	—
25	Motor Cars	c1954	£4.00	—

BROOKS DYE WORKS LTD

Qty		Date	Odds	Sets
EL4	Interesting Shots of Old Bristol	c1950	£1.50	£6.00

BROWN & POLSON

Qty		Date	Odds	Sets
L25	Brown & Polson Picture Cards (Recipe)	1925	£4.00	—

Qty		Date	Odds	Sets
	DAVID BROWN (Tractors)			
EL3	Is Your Slip Showing?	1954	£3.00	£9.00
	BROWNE BROS. LTD (Tea)			
25	Birds	1963	£1.40	—
25	British Cavalry Uniforms of the 19th Century	1964	80p	—
25	Garden Flowers	1965	£2.00	—
25	History of the Railway 1st Series	1964	40p	£10.00
25	History of the Railway 2nd Series	1964	36p	£9.00
24	The Island of Ceylon	1961	£5.00	—
25	Passenger Liners	1966	£2.00	—
25	People and Places	1967	20p	£2.50
25	Tropical Birds	1966	20p	£2.50
25	Wonders of the Deep	1965	20p	£2.50
25	Wonders of the World	1967	20p	£5.00
	BRYANT & MAY			
L12	The Thirties	1992	—	£12.00
	BUBBLES INC. (Chewing Gum)			
L55	Mars Attacks	1964	£25.00	—
L50	Outer Limits	1966	£5.00	—
	BUCHANAN'S (Jam)			
24	Birds and Their Eggs	1923	£9.00	—
	JOHNNY BUNNY			
25	Football Clubs and Badges	c1960	£3.00	—
	BUNSEN CONFECTIONERY CO.			
628	Famous Figures Series	c1925	£18.00	—
	BURDALL & BURDALL			
30	Wild Animals	c1920	£7.00	—
	BURLINGTON SLATE			
L20	Processing and Use of Slate...	1992	—	£15.00
	BURTONS (Wagon Wheels)			
25	Indian Chiefs	1972	70p	£17.50
EL8	NFL Heroes (American Football)	1987	—	£24.00
L7	Pictures of the Wild West	1983	£7.00	—
25	The West	1972	20p	£5.00
25	Wild West Action	1972	20p	£5.00
	BUTTAPAT DAIRIES			
?22	People of the World...	1915	£20.00	—
	BUTTERCUP BREAD (Australia)			
M24	Alan Border Tribute	1994	—	£18.00
M24	Border's Ashes Heroes	1993	—	£18.00
M24	1993-94 World Series All Stars	1993	—	£18.00

Qty		Date	Odds	Sets

BYRNES ENT. (USA)

Qty		Date	Odds	Sets
LT22	Firemen in Action	1981	—	£9.50
LT22	Firemen in Action	1982	—	£12.00

C.B.S. LTD

30	Glamorgan Cricketers	1984	—	£20.00

CCC LTD

L15	Arsenal FC Cup Winners 1992/1993	1993	—	£6.00
L20	Doctor Who (TV Series)	1993	—	£12.00
L6	Wild Cats by Joel Kirk	1994	—	£3.00

C & G CONFECTIONERY CO.

25	Box of Tricks 1st Series	1963	£4.40	—
25	Box of Tricks 2nd Series	1963	£4.40	—

C.H. PUBLICATIONS

L6	MG World 1st Series Nos 1-6 (Cars)	1999	—	£2.50
L6	MG World 2nd Series Nos 7-12 (Cars)	1999	—	£2.50
L6	Triumph World 1st Series Nos 1-6 (Cars)	1999	—	£2.50
L6	Triumph World 3rd Series Nos 13-18 (Cars)	2000	—	£2.50

CMA (UK)

LT82	Hammer Horror Series 2	1996	—	£15.00
LT74	Hammer Horror Entombed	2000	—	£20.00

C.N.G. (New Zealand)

M10	Trees of New Zealand	1992	—	£8.00

C.S. LTD (Cadet Sweets)

50	Footballers and Club Colours	1963	£1.40	—
25	Record Holders of the World 1st Series	1962	40p	£10.00
25	Ships Through the Ages 1st Series	1963	£1.20	—
25	Ships Through the Ages 2nd Series	1963	£1.20	—

CADBURY BROS. LTD

EL12	Antarctic Series	c1915	£30.00	—
EL6	Bay City Rollers	1975	£2.00	£12.00
L12	Birds in Springtime	1983	—	£3.50
6	Bourneville Series	c1905	£20.00	—
6	Bourneville Village Series	c1905	£20.00	—
EL25	British Birds (Reward Cards)	c1910	£9.00	—
12	British Birds and Eggs	c1910	£12.00	—
EL12	British Birds and Their Eggs (Reward Cards)	c1910	£11.00	—
EL32	British Butterflies and Moths (Reward Cards)	c1910	£6.00	—
6	British Colonies, Maps and Industries	c1910	£20.00	—
120	British Marvels Vol. I	1936	£1.75	—
120	British Marvels Vol. II	1936	£1.75	—
12	British Trees Series	1911	£7.00	—
80	Cadbury's Picture Making	c1935	£1.75	—
12	Cathedral Series	1913	£8.00	—
6	Colonial Premiers Series	c1910	£20.00	—
	Constellations Series:			
12	A Standard Size (size 65 × 37mm)	1912	£8.00	—
EL6	B Strip of two (size 152 × 36mm)	1912	£16.00	—

Qty		Date	Odds	Sets
	CADBURY BROS. LTD (continued)			
24	Copyright (Inventors) Series	c1915	£14.00	—
	Coronation:			
1	A Size 73 × 34mm...	1911	—	£30.00
EL1	B Size 149 × 38mm	1911	—	£40.00
48	Dangerous Animals	1970	40p	£20.00
6	Dogs Series	c1910	£35.00	—
EL12	English Industries	c1910	£32.00	—
25	Fairy Tales	1924	£3.60	—
27	Famous Steamships	1923	£3.50	—
12	Fish	c1910	£12.00	—
EL6	Fish and Bait Series	c1910	£36.00	—
	Flag Series (horizontal):			
12	A Standard Size (size 65 × 36mm)	1912	£3.75	—
EL6	B Strips of Two (size 150 × 36mm)	1912	£8.00	—
	Flag Series (vertical):			
EL12	A Size 107 × 35mm	1912	£25.00	—
EL12	B Size 146 × 50mm	1912	£25.00	—
EL12	Flight, The World's Most Spectacular Birds	1983	—	£6.00
1	Largest Steamers in the World	c1905	—	£50.00
6	Locomotive Series	c1910	£32.00	—
12	Match Puzzles	c1905	£35.00	—
6	Old Ballad Series	c1905	£22.00	—
EL6	Panama Series	c1910	£30.00	—
EL5	Pop Stars	1975	£1.50	—
EL8	Prehistoric Monsters	1975	£1.25	—
EL6	Rivers of the British Isles	c1910	£16.00	—
24	Shadow Series	c1915	£15.00	—
6	Shipping Series:			
	A Size 84 × 40mm...	c1910	£12.00	—
	B Size 134 × 58mm	c1910	£12.00	—
	C Size 153 × 39mm	c1910	£12.00	—
	D Size 164 × 81mm	c1910	£12.00	—
EL6	Sports Series	c1905	£45.00	—
24	Strange But True...	1969	20p	£2.50
25	Transport	1925	50p	£12.50

CADBURY-SCHWEPPES FOODS LTD

Qty		Date	Odds	Sets
12	The Age of the Dinosaur	1971	50p	£6.00

CADET (Sweets)

Qty		Date	Odds	Sets
48	Adventures of Rin Tin Tin:			
	A Size 60 × 32mm...	1960	£1.20	—
	B Size 65 × 37mm:			
	i 'Cadet Sweets' in two lines	1960	50p	£25.00
	ii 'Cadet Sweets' in one line	1960	£1.50	—
25	Arms and Armour	1960	20p	£2.50
50	Buccaneers:			
	A Size 58 × 30mm...	1959	£1.00	—
	B Size 63 × 33mm...	1959	35p	£17.50
50	Buccaneers (Different Series) Size 65 × 35mm ...	1959	50p	£25.00
50	Conquest of Space:			
	A Size 64 × 35mm...	1957	60p	—
	B Size 69 × 37mm...	1957	30p	£15.00
25	Daktari	1968	36p	£9.00
50	Doctor Who and The Daleks	1965	£3.00	£150.00

Qty		Date	Odds	Sets
	CADET (Sweets) (continued)			
25	Dogs 1st Series:			
	A Size 60 × 32mm...	1958	50p	£12.50
	B Size 65 × 35mm...	1958	£2.50	—
25	Dogs 2nd Series:			
	A Size 60 × 32mm...	1958	50p	£12.50
	B Size 65 × 35mm...	1958	£2.50	—
25	Evolution of the Royal Navy	1960	20p	£3.50
22	Famous Explorers (Package Issue)	c1960	£8.00	—
50	Footballers...	1957	60p	£30.00
50	Footballers:			
	A Title 19 mm	1958	35p	£17.50
	B Title 28 mm	1958	35p	£17.50
25	How?...	1968	36p	£9.00
25	Prehistoric Animals	1961	£1.00	—
50	Railways of the World	1955	20p	£7.50
50	Record Holders of the World...	1956	20p	£10.00
50	Stingray	1965	70p	£35.00
25	Treasure Hunt...	1964	20p	£2.50
50	UNCLE (TV Series):			
	A Photos	1966	£1.30	£65.00
	B Drawings	1966	£2.50	—
25	What Do You Know?	1965	50p	£12.50

A.J. CALEY & SON

K24	Film Stars	c1930	£9.00	—
48	Mickey Mouse Wisequacks	1939	£10.00	—
L50	Tricks & Puzzles	c1930	£6.00	—

CALFUN INC (Canada)

LT100	Fantazy Cards (Pin Up Girls)	1992	—	£15.00

CALICO GRAPHICS (USA)

LT54	League of Nations 2nd Series	1990	—	£9.50
EL1	League of Nations 2nd Series advert card	1990	—	£1.00

CALRAB (USA)

LT24	The California Raisins World Tour	1988	—	£5.00

CALTEX OIL (Australia)

EL6	Stargazer (Haley's Comet)	1986	—	£3.00

F.C. CALVERT & CO. LTD (Tooth Powder)

K25	Dan Dare	1954	£4.00	£100.00

CANDY GUM

M50	Auto Sprint 1st Series	1975	25p	—
M30	Auto Sprint 2nd Series	1975	20p	£6.00

CANDY NOVELTY CO.

25	Animals of the Countryside	1960	£5.00	—
50	Animals of the World	c1960	£4.00	—
M50	Dog Series A.1:			
	A Complete set...	c1955	£1.50	—
	B 25 different	c1955	20p	£3.50

Qty		Date	Odds	Sets

CANDY NOVELTY CO. (continued)

Qty		Date	Odds	Sets
32	Motor Car Series:			
	A Blue green	c1953	£6.00	—
	B Orange	c1953	£6.00	—
25	Ships through the Ages 2nd Series	c1960	£5.00	—
32	Western Series:			
	A Black on blue green	c1953	£6.00	—
	B Green on blue green	c1953	£6.00	—

CANNING'S

Qty		Date	Odds	Sets
25	Types of British Soldiers	c1914	£15.00	—

CANNON PRESS

Qty		Date	Odds	Sets
10	Screen Gems David Niven	2010	—	£5.00
20	Screen Gems Lana Turner	2009	—	£9.00
20	Screen Gems Natalie Wood	2009	—	£9.00
10	Screen Gems Rock Hudson	2010	—	£5.00
10	Screen Gems Will Hay...	2009	—	£5.00
10	Treasure Island	2009	—	£5.00

CAPERN (Bird Food)

Qty		Date	Odds	Sets
7	Cage Birds (blue backgrounds)	c1920	£12.00	—
7	Cage Birds (white backgrounds)	c1920	£12.00	—
	Cage Birds:			
EL51	A Plain back	c1925	£4.50	—
EL8	B Postcard back	c1925	£5.00	—
EL1	C Text back	c1925	£8.00	—
24	Capern Picture Aviary	1964	£1.00	—
1	Capern Picture Aviary Introductory Card	1964	—	25p

CAR AND DRIVER (USA)

Qty		Date	Odds	Sets
EL100	Cadillac Collection	1993	—	£15.00

CARAMAC

Qty		Date	Odds	Sets
M42	Railway Locomotives	1976	36p	£15.00

CARD CRAZY (New Zealand)

Qty		Date	Odds	Sets
LT90	High Velocity New Zealand Cricketers	1996	20p	£12.00
LT90	New Zealand Rugby League Superstars...	1995	20p	£12.00
LT110	New Zealand Rugby Union Superstars	1995	20p	£12.00
LT55	Shortland Street (TV Series)	1995	—	£6.00

CARD CREATIONS (USA)

Qty		Date	Odds	Sets
LT100	Popeye	1994	—	£12.00

CARD INSERT LTD

Qty		Date	Odds	Sets
1	Famous Footballers (only No.12 issued)	c1955	—	£8.00

CARDLYNX

Qty		Date	Odds	Sets
EL6	Bookmarks High Grade Series	2008	—	£4.50
L6	Butterflies	2007	—	£3.00
L6	Eagles	2007	—	£3.00
L6	Gangsters	2005	—	£3.00
L6	Golfers	2006	—	£3.00
L6	Horses	2007	—	£3.00

Qty		Date	Odds	Sets
	CARDLYNX (continued)			
L6	Jazz Greats	2005	–	£3.00
L6	Lighthouses	2008	–	£3.00
L6	Owls	2004	–	£3.00
L6	Parrots	2004	–	£3.00
L6	Poultry	2005	–	£3.00
L6	Poultry Breeds	2007	–	£3.00
L6	Sea Shells	2008	–	£3.00
L6	Space Firsts	2004	–	£3.00
EL6	UFOs & Aliens From Space	2010	–	£4.50
L6	Victorian Poultry	2007	–	£3.00
EL6	Wild West Outlaws	2013	–	£4.50
EL6	Wizards Past, Present & Future/ World's Most			
	Valuable Baseball Cards	2010	–	£4.50

CARDS INC
LT72	Beyblade	2000	–	£8.00
LT72	Captain Scarlet	2002	20p	£9.50
LT72	Harry Potter and The Prisoner of Azkaban	2004	20p	£9.50
LT17	Harry Potter and The Prisoner of Azkaban			
	Foil Series	2004	25p	£4.00
LT72	The Prisoner Volume 1 (1960/70s TV Series)	2002	–	£12.00
LT30	Scarface The Film	2003	–	£8.00
LT72	Shrek 2 The Film:			
	A Standard Series	2004	20p	£12.00
	B Foil Parallel Series	2004	40p	£30.00
LT72	Thunderbirds	2001	20p	£9.50
LT72	Thunderbirds The Movie	2004	–	£11.00
LT100	U.F.O. (TV Series)	2004	–	£12.00
LT100	The Very Best of The Saint	2003	–	£12.00

CARDTOON CREATIONS
24	Championship Champions 2005-2006			
	(Reading F.C.)	2006	–	£7.50

CARDTOONS (USA)
LT95	Baseball Parodies	1993	–	£8.00
LT9	Baseball Parodies Field of Greed Puzzle	1993	–	£3.00
LT11	Baseball Parodies Politics in Baseball	1993	–	£3.00

CARDZ (USA)
LT100	Hitchhiker's Guide to the Galaxy (Cartoon)	1994	–	£9.50
LT50	Lee MacLeod — Fantasy Art	1994	–	£6.00
LT10	Lee MacLeod Tekchrome Nos T1 to T10 — Fantasy			
	Art	1994	–	£8.00
LT100	The Mask — The Film	1994	–	£9.50
LT60	Maverick — The Movie	1994	–	£9.50
LT60	The Muppets	1993	–	£9.00
LT80	Muppets Take The Ice	1994	–	£8.00
LT60	Return of The Flintstones	1994	–	£9.00
LT110	San Diego Zoo	1993	–	£12.00
LT60	Tiny Toons Adventures	1994	–	£9.00
LT60	Tom & Jerry	1993	–	£9.00
LT100	WCW Main Event (Wrestling)	1995	–	£9.50
LT100	William Shatner's Tek World	1993	–	£9.50

Qty		Date	Odds	Sets
	CARDZ (USA) (continued)			
LT100	World War II	1994	—	£9.50
LT10	World War II Tekchrome Nos T1-T10	1994	—	£3.00
	CARNATION (Tinned Milk)			
EL12	Recipe Service	1971	33p	4.00
	CARR'S BISCUITS			
EL20	Cricketers	1968	£7.00	—
EL48	Sporting Champions	1966	£7.00	—
EL20	Sports — Soccer Card Series	c1967	£10.00	—
	CARSON'S CHOCOLATE			
72	Celebrities	1901	£16.00	—
	CARTER'S LITTLE LIVER PILLS			
28	Dominoes	c1910	£1.50	—
	F.C. CARTLEDGE			
L96	Epigrams (Rheuma Salts)...	1939	21p	£20.00
L48	Epigrams (Knock-out Razor Blades)	1939	20p	£10.00
L12	Epigrams (without maker's name)	1939	—	£10.00
L64	Epigrams (without product)	1939	20p	£12.00
50	Famous Prize Fighters:			
	A Complete set (matt)	1938	—	£125.00
	B 49/50 (—No. 23) (matt)	1938	£2.00	£100.00
	C 2 variety cards (matt) (Nos 13 & 19)	1938	—	£8.00
	D Complete set (glossy)...	1938	£3.00	—
	CASEY CARDS			
10	The Casey (Football Stars of the 1960s)	2010	—	£5.00
	CASH & CO.			
20	War Pictures	c1910	£15.00	—
	CASSELL'S			
M6	British Engines	c1925	£10.00	—
M12	Butterflies and Moths Series	c1925	£7.00	—
	CASTROL OIL			
L18	Famous Riders	1956	£5.00	—
L24	Racing Cars	1955	£4.00	—
	CAVE, AUSTIN & CO. LTD			
20	Inventors Series	1928	£11.00	—
	C.E.D.E. LTD			
25	Coins of the World	1956	20p	£4.00
	CENTRAL ELECTRICITY AUTHORITY			
M10	Careers in the Central Electricity Board	1957	25p	£2.50
	CEREBOS			
100	Sea Shells:			
	A Brown back	1925	£2.50	—
	B Grey back	1925	£4.50	—

Qty		Date	Odds	Sets
	CEYLON TEA CENTRE			
24	Island of Ceylon	1955	20p	£2.50
	CHAMPS (USA)			
LT100	American Vintage Cycles Series 1	1992	—	£9.50
LT100	American Vintage Cycles Series 2	1993	—	£9.50
	CHANNEL 4/CHEERLEADER			
L20	All Time Great Quarterbacks	1989	—	£25.00
	H. CHAPPEL & CO.			
?10	British Celebrities	1905	£32.00	—
? 4	Characters from Nursery Rhymes	1905	£40.00	—
	CHARTER TEA & COFFEE CO LTD			
25	Prehistoric Animals 1st Series	c1965	£1.20	—
25	Prehistoric Animals 2nd Series	c1965	£1.20	—
25	Strange but True 1st Series	1961	80p	£20.00
25	Strange but True 2nd Series	1961	60p	£15.00
25	Transport Through the Ages 1st Series	c1965	80p	£20.00
25	Transport Through the Ages 2nd Series	c1965	60p	£15.00
	CHEF & BREWER			
L20	Historic Pub Signs	1984	—	£15.00
	CHESDALE (New Zealand)			
M6	Action Sports	1983	50p	£3.00
	CHIVERS & SONS LTD			
M10	Firm Favourites 1st Series	c1930	£4.00	—
M10	Firm Favourites 2nd Series	c1930	£4.00	—
M10	Firm Favourites 3rd Series	c1930	£4.00	—
M95	Firm Favourites (Nos 31 to 125)	c1930	£2.50	—
EL6	Studies of English Fruits (Series 1)	c1930	£6.00	—
EL6	Studies of English Fruits (Series 2)	c1930	£6.00	—
24	Wild Wisdom	c1960	£3.00	—
48	Wild Wisdom in Africa	c1960	£3.00	—
48	Wild Wisdom, River and Marsh	c1960	£3.00	—
	Package Issues:			
L15	Children of Other Lands	c1955	£1.25	—
L15	Chivers British Birds	c1955	£1.50	—
L20	On Chivers Farms	c1955	£1.25	—
	CHIX CONFECTIONERY CO. LTD			
M12	Batman P.C. inset (Package issue)	1989	—	£6.00
M48	Facts & Feats (Waxed Paper issue)	c1960	£4.00	—
	Famous Footballers No.1 Series:			
L24	A Inscribed 'Set of 48' (Nos 1-24 only issued)	1955	£4.50	—
L24	B Inscribed 'Numbers 1 to 24'	1955	£4.50	—
L24	C Inscribed 'Numbers 25 to 48'	1955	£4.50	—
L48	D Inscribed 'Numbers 1 to 48'	1955	£4.50	—
L48	Famous Footballers 2nd Series	1957	£5.50	—
L48	Famous Footballers 3rd Series	1958	£6.50	—
L50	Famous Footballers	1961	£6.50	—
L50	Famous Last Words	1969	£1.50	—

Qty		Date	Odds	Sets

CHIX CONFECTIONERY CO. LTD (continued)

Qty		Date	Odds	Sets
L48	Footballers (double picture):			
	A 'Ask for Chix' back … … … … … … … …	1960	£2.00	—
	B Anonymous back … … … … … … … … …	1960	80p	£40.00
L50	Funny Old Folk … … … … … … … … … … … …	1970	40p	£20.00
L50	Happy Howlers … … … … … … … … … … … …	1969	£1.00	—
L6	Joker P.C. inset (Double Package issue) … … … …	1990	—	£9.00
L50	Krazy Kreatures from Outer Space … … … … … …	1968	£1.60	£80.00
L50	Military Uniforms … … … … … … … … … … … …	1969	60p	—
L50	Moon Shot … … … … … … … … … … … … … …	1966	£2.20	—
L50	Popeye … … … … … … … … … … … … … … …	1959	£3.50	—
L24	Scottish Footballers (SFBL 1 back) … … … … …	c1960	£8.00	—
L50	Ships of the Seven Seas … … … … … … … …	1964	£2.00	—
L50	Soldiers of the World … … … … … … … … … …	1960	£1.40	—
L50	Sports Through the Ages … … … … … … … … …	1963	£3.20	—
96	TV and Radio Stars … … … … … … … … … …	1955	£4.00	£400.00
L50	Wild Animals … … … … … … … … … … …	c1960	£1.70	—

CHOCOLAT DE VILLARS

Qty		Date	Odds	Sets
24	British Birds and Their Eggs … … … … … … … …	1926	£4.00	£100.00

CHUMS

Qty		Date	Odds	Sets
MP23	'Chums' Cricketers … … … … … … … … … … …	1923	£5.50	—
MP20	'Chums' Football Teams … … … … … … … … …	1922	£4.00	—
P8	'Chums' Football Teams, New Series … … … … … …	c1925	£4.00	—
LP10	'Chums' Real Colour Photos … … … … … … … …	c1925	£8.00	—

CHURCH & DWIGHT (USA)

Qty		Date	Odds	Sets
M60	Beautiful Flowers, New Series … … … … … …	c1888	£4.00	—
EL10	Birds of Prey … … … … … … … … … … … …	1975	—	£25.00
M30	Fish Series … … … … … … … … … … … … …	1900	£4.00	—
M30	New Series of Birds … … … … … … … … … …	1908	£3.50	—
M30	Useful Birds of America (no series number) … …	1915	£3.50	—
M30	Useful Birds of America 1st Series … … … … …	1915	£3.00	—
M30	Useful Birds of America 2nd Series … … … …	1918	£3.00	—
M30	Useful Birds of America 3rd Series … … … …	1922	£3.00	—
M30	Useful Birds of America 4th Series … … … … …	1924	£3.00	—
M15	Useful Birds of America 5th Series … … … … …	1928	£3.00	—
M15	Useful Birds of America 6th Series … … … … …	1931	£3.00	—
M15	Useful Birds of America 7th Series … … … … …	1933	£3.00	—
M15	Useful Birds of America 8th Series … … … … …	1936	£3.00	—
M15	Useful Birds of America 9th Series … … … … …	1938	£1.00	£15.00
M15	Useful Birds of America 10th Series … … … …	1938	£1.00	£15.00

THE CITY BAKERIES LTD

Qty		Date	Odds	Sets
8	The European War Series … … … … … … … …	1916	£40.00	—
4	Shadow Series … … … … … … … … … … …	1916	£35.00	—

CLARNICO

Qty		Date	Odds	Sets
30	Colonial Troops … … … … … … … … … … …	c1910	£30.00	—
25	Great War Leaders … … … … … … … … … …	c1915	£22.00	—
29	Wolf Cubs … … … … … … … … … … … …	c1910	£40.00	—

CLASSIC COLLECTIONS

Qty		Date	Odds	Sets
50	Newcastle United FC (Football) … … … … … …	1993	—	£20.00

Qty		Date	Odds	Sets
	CLASSIC GAMES INC. (USA)			
LT100	Deathwatch 2000	1993	—	£9.50
LT50	McDonalds History	1996	—	£8.00
LT150	WWF The History of Wrestle Mania Series 2	1990	—	£12.00
LT150	World Wrestling Federation Superstars	1991	—	£12.00

CLEVEDON CONFECTIONERY LTD

Qty		Date	Odds	Sets
K50	British Aircraft:			
	A Title in one line	1956	£3.00	—
	B Title in two lines	1956	£3.00	—
K25	British Orders of Chivalry and Valour:			
	A Black back	1960	£5.40	—
	B Blue back	1960	£5.40	—
K50	British Ships	1956	£3.50	—
M50	British Trains and Engines	1958	£8.00	—
K25	Dan Dare	1960	£8.00	—
K40	Did You Know?	1957	£5.50	—
K40	Famous Cricketers	c1960	£12.00	—
K25	Famous Cricketers	c1960	£12.00	—
K50	Famous Football Clubs	1961	£4.00	—
K50	Famous Footballers	1961	£6.50	—
K50	Famous International Aircraft	1963	£2.00	—
M50	Famous Screen Stars, Series A.1	1959	£4.50	—
K40	Film Stars	1958	£4.50	—
K50	Football Club Managers	1959	£15.00	—
K50	Hints on Association Football:			
	A Black back & front	1957	£4.00	—
	B Blue back, coloured front	1957	£4.00	—
	C Blue back & front	1957	£9.00	—
K50	Hints on Road Safety	1958	£3.00	—
K50	International Sporting Stars	1960	£4.50	—
M50	Regimental Badges	1956	£3.50	—
EL25	Sporting Memories	1960	£12.00	—
K50	The Story of the Olympics	1960	£3.00	—
K50	Trains of the World	1962	£2.50	—

CLEVELAND PETROL

Qty		Date	Odds	Sets
EL20	Golden Goals (numbered 1-41)	1972	£1.00	—
	Album		—	£15.00

CLIFFORD

Qty		Date	Odds	Sets
50	Footballers	c1950	£25.00	—

CLOVER DAIRIES LTD

Qty		Date	Odds	Sets
25	Animals and Reptiles	1965	20p	£3.00
25	British Rail	1973	20p	£2.50
25	People and Places	1970	20p	£3.00
25	Prehistoric Animals	1966	22p	£6.00
25	Science in the 20th Century	1965	20p	£3.50
25	Ships and Their Workings	1966	20p	£3.50
25	The Story of Milk	1964	24p	£6.00
25	Transport Through the Ages	1967	20p	£3.00

COACH HOUSE STUDIOS

Qty		Date	Odds	Sets
50	Railway Locomotives	1987	40p	—

Qty		Date	Odds	Sets
	COCA-COLA (UK)			
LT10	Football Match World Cup USA (scratch cards) ...	1994	—	£4.00
LT49	Football World Cup (yellow back)	2002	—	£15.00
	COCA-COLA (South Africa)			
M100	Our Flower Paradise	1964	50p	£50.00
	COCA-COLA (USA)			
	The World of Nature:			
EL12	Series I — Earth and Air and Sky	c1960	£1.00	—
EL12	Series II — Man's Closest Friends and Most			
	Inveterate Enemies	c1960	£1.00	—
EL12	Series III — Trees and Other Plants Useful to			
	Man	c1960	£1.00	—
EL12	Series IV — Some Common Wild Flowers	c1960	£1.00	—
EL12	Series V — Among Our Feathered Friends	c1960	£1.00	—
EL12	Series VI — Native Wild Animals	c1960	£1.00	—
EL12	Series VII — Life In and Around the Water	c1960	£1.00	—
EL12	Series VIII — Insects, Helpful and Harmful	c1960	£1.00	—
	COFTON COLLECTIONS			
L7	Alice in Wonderland...	2002	—	£3.00
15	Birmingham City F.C. Stars of The 1970s	2007	—	£5.50
25	Dogs 1st Series	1988	24p	£6.00
25	Dogs 2nd Series	1988	24p	£6.00
25	Dogs 3rd Series	1988	24p	£6.00
L25	Nursery Rhymes	1992	—	£7.50
15	West Brom. Heroes & Legends (Footballers)	2012	—	£5.50
L20	Worcestershire County Cricketers	1989	—	£7.50
	CECIL COLEMAN LTD			
24	Film Stars	c1935	£8.00	—
	COLGATE-PALMOLIVE			
EL4	Coronation Souvenir	1953	£2.50	£10.00
M24	Famous Sporting Trophies	1979	25p	£6.00
	Album		—	£6.00
	COLINVILLE LTD			
L28	Fantasy of Space 1st Series	1956	£9.00	—
L28	Fantasy of Space 2nd Series	1956	£9.00	—
L25	Prairie Pioneers	1960	£4.50	—
	COLLECT-A-CARD (USA)			
LT50	Adventures of Ronald McDonald — McDonald Land			
	500	1996	—	£6.00
LT100	American Bandstand (T.V. Music Show)	1993	—	£8.00
LT72	The Campbell's (Soup) Collection	1995	—	£8.00
LT120	Centennial Olympic Games	1996	—	£9.50
LT100	The Coca Cola Collection 2nd Series...	1994	—	£15.00
K8	The Coca Cola Collection 2nd Series Coke Caps	1994	—	£3.00
LT100	The Coca Cola Collection 3rd Series	1994	—	£12.50
LT100	The Coca Cola Collection 4th Series	1995	—	£12.50
LT50	The Coca Cola Polar Bears South Pole Vacation...	1996	—	£8.00
LT100	Country (Music) Classics	1992	—	£9.50

Qty		Date	Odds	Sets
	COLLECT-A-CARD (USA) (continued)			
LT72	Dinotopia — Fantasy Art Dinosaurs	1995	—	£9.50
LT100	Harley Davidson Series 2	1992	—	£9.50
LT100	Harley Davidson Series 3	1993	—	£9.50
LT100	King Pins (Ten Pin Bowling)	1990	—	£10.00
LT50	Norfin Trolls	1992	—	£5.00
LT72	Power Rangers 1st Series	1994	—	£9.50
LT72	Power Rangers 2nd Series	1994	—	£9.50
LT72	Power Rangers New Season	1994	—	£9.50
LT100	Stargate Plus Set LT12 Puzzle	1994	—	£9.50
LT100	Vette Set (Corvette Cars)	1991	—	£9.50
LT10	Vette Set (Corvette Cars) Bonus Series	1991	—	£4.00

COLLECTABLE PICTURES

L13	England Win The Ashes 2005 (Cricket)	2005	—	£8.50
L20	Liverpool F.C. European Champions 2005	2005	—	£12.00
L7	Views of Bath	2005	—	£5.00

COLLECTABLES OF SPALDING

25	British Cavalry Uniforms	1987	—	£7.50
25	Military Maids	1987	—	£7.50
25	Warriors Through the Ages	1987	30p	£7.50

THE COLLECTOR AND DEALER MAGAZINE

6	Animal Series	1953	£3.00	—

THE COLLECTOR & HOBBYIST

25	Fascinating Hobbies	1950	20p	£2.50

COLLECTORS' CORNER

L20	Halifax As It Was	1989	—	£4.50

COLLECTORS FARE

16	Reading Football Club Simod Cup Winners	1990	—	£6.00
EL16	Reading Football Club Simod Cup Winners	1990	—	£4.00

COLLECTORS SHOP

25	Bandsmen of the British Army	1960	60p	£15.00

COLONIAL BREAD (USA)

LT33	Star Trek The Motion Picture	1979	—	£9.50

COMET (Sweets)

25	Armand & Michaela Denis on Safari 1st Series ...	1961	30p	£7.50
25	Armand & Michaela Denis on Safari 2nd Series ...	1961	30p	£7.50
25	Modern Wonders:			
	A Black back	1961	20p	£3.00
	B Blue back	1961	80p	—
25	Olympic Achievements 1st Series	1959	60p	£15.00
25	Olympic Achievements 2nd Series	1959	60p	£15.00

COMIC ENTERPRISES

L15	Superman Action Comics	2005	—	£6.50

41

COMIC IMAGES (USA)

Qty		Date	Odds	Sets
LT70	The Art of Coca Cola	1999	—	£9.50
LT90	The Beast Within — Ken Barr Fantasy Art	1994	—	£9.50
LT72	The Beatles — Yellow Submarine	1999	—	£13.00
LT90	Beyond Bizarre — Jim Warren Surrealism			
	Fantasy Art	1993	—	£9.50
LT90	Bill Ward (Saucy Cartoons)	1994	—	£9.50
LT90	Blueprints of The Future — Vincent Di Fate			
	Fantasy Art	1994	—	£9.50
LT90	Bone	1994	—	£9.50
LT90	The Brothers Hildebrandt — Fantasy Art	1994	—	£8.00
LT72	The Cat In The Hat — The Film	2003	—	£8.00
LT72	Coca Cola — The Art of Haddon Sundblom	2001	—	£12.00
LT90	Colossal Conflicts (Marvel Heroes & Villains)			
	Series 2	1987	—	£9.50
LT72	Comic Greats 98	1998	—	£9.50
LT90	Conan The Marvel Years	1996	—	£12.00
LT72	Crimson Embrace — Adult Fantasy Art	1998	—	£9.50
LT72	Dark Horse Presents Ghost	1997	—	£9.50
LT72	Elvira Mistress of Omnichrome	1997	—	£9.50
LT72	Final Fantasy — The Spirits Within	2001	—	£8.50
LT90	Frazetta II The Legend Continues — Fantasy Art...	1993	—	£8.00
LT90	Greg Hildebrandt II — 30 Years of Magic	1993	—	£8.00
LT90	Harlem Globetrotters	1992	—	£9.50
LT90	Jack Kirby The Unpublished Archives — Fantasy			
	Art	1994	—	£8.00
LT72	Judgment Day (cartoon)	1997	—	£8.00
LT72	Julie Strain Queen of the 'B' Movies	1996	—	£9.50
LT72	Madagascar The Film	2005	—	£9.50
LT90	Magnificent Myths — Boris 4 Fantasy Art	1994	—	£9.50
LT90	Maxfield Parrish Portrait of America — Fantasy Art	1994	—	£8.00
LT61	Meanie Babies	1998	—	£8.00
LT90	Moebius — Fantasy Art	1993	—	£9.50
LT90	More Than Battlefield Earth — Ron Hubbard			
	Fantasy Art	1994	—	£9.50
LT72	The New American Pin Up (Pin Up Girls)	1997	—	£12.00
LT72	Olivia 98 (Adult Fantasy Art)	1998	—	£9.50
LT72	Olivia Obsessions in Omnichrome (Adult			
	Fantasy Art)	1997	—	£9.50
LT90	Other Worlds — Michael Whelan Fantasy Art	1995	—	£9.50
LT90	Other Worlds — Michael Whelan II Fantasy Art ...	1995	—	£9.50
LT72	The Painted Cow	1997	—	£9.50
LT90	The Phantom	1995	—	£9.50
LT90	Prince Valiant	1995	—	£8.00
LT90	Richard Corben Fantasy Art	1993	—	£9.50
LT72	The Rock's Greatest Matches — WWF	2000	—	£15.00
LT90	Ron Miller's Firebrands Heroines of Science			
	Fiction & Fantasy...	1994	—	£9.50
LT90	Sachs & Violens	1993	—	£8.00
LT90	The Savage Dragon	1992	—	£8.00
LT90	Shadow Hawk (Comic Book Art by Jim Valentino)	1992	—	£8.00
LT90	Shi Visions of The Golden Empire	1996	—	£9.50
LT72	Shrek 2 The Film...	2004	—	£9.50
LT70	South Park	1998	—	£9.50
LT90	Species — The Movie	1995	—	£9.50
LT90	Spiderman The McFarlane Era	1992	—	£9.50

Qty		Date	Odds	Sets
	COMIC IMAGES (USA) (continued)			
LT90	Spiderman II 30th Anniversary	1992	—	£9.50
LT90	Strangers in Paradise	1996	—	£8.00
LT90	Supreme — Adult Fantasy Art	1996	—	£9.50
LT72	Terminator 3 Rise of The Machines — The Movie	2003	—	£9.50
LT90	30th Salute G.I. Joe...	1994	—	£9.50
LT90	24 — TV Series	2003	—	£12.00
LT90	Ujena Swimwear Illustrated	1993	—	£9.50
LT90	Ujena Swimwear Illustrated	1994	—	£9.50
LT90	Unity Time Is Not Absolute	1992	—	£9.50
LT72	Van Helsing — The Film	2004	—	£9.50
LT90	William Stout 2 (Fantasy Art etc)	1994	—	£9.50
LT90	Wolverine From Then Till Now II	1992	—	£9.50
LT81	World Wrestling Federation No Mercy	2000	—	£12.00
LT90	Young Blood (Super Heroes)	1992	—	£8.00

COMIC LIFE

MP4	Sports Champions	1922	£6.00	—

COMMODEX (Gum)

M88	Operation Moon	1969	£2.00	—
L120	Super Cars...	1970	£2.00	—

COMMONWEALTH SHOE & LEATHER CO. (USA)

M12	Makes of Planes	c1930	£4.00	—

COMO CONFECTIONERY PRODUCTS LTD

K25	Adventures of Fireball XL5	c1970	£15.00	—
M25	History of the Wild West 1st Series	1960	£5.00	—
M25	History of the Wild West 2nd Series	1963	£1.00	£25.00
50	Lenny's Adventures	1960	£1.00	£50.00
50	Noddy and His Playmates	1962	£2.00	—
	Noddy's Adventures 1st Series:			
M25	A Size 63 × 63mm...	1961	£3.20	—
K25	B Size 46 × 46mm...	c1970	£6.00	—
M25	Noddy's Adventures 2nd Series...	1961	£3.20	—
25	Noddy's Budgie and Feathered Friends 1st Series	1959	£2.20	—
25	Noddy's Budgie and Feathered Friends 2nd Series	1959	£2.20	—
	Noddy's Friends Abroad:			
M25	A Size 62 × 62mm...	1959	£2.50	—
K25	B Size 46 × 46mm...	c1970	£6.00	—
	Noddy's Nursery Rhyme Friends:			
M25	A Size 63 × 60mm...	1959	£2.50	—
K25	B Size 46 × 46mm...	c1970	£6.00	—
M50	Sooty's Adventures	1961	£2.00	—
25	Sooty's Latest Adventures 3rd Series, No.1-25			
	A Black back	c1960	£2.00	—
	B Blue back	c1960	£2.00	—
	C Navy blue back	c1960	£2.00	—
	D Red back	c1960	£2.00	—
25	Sooty's Latest Adventures 3rd Series, No. 26-50			
	A Black back	c1960	£2.00	—
	B Blue back	c1960	£2.00	—
	C Navy blue back	c1960	£2.00	—
	D Red back	c1960	£2.00	—

Qty		Date	Odds	Sets
	COMO CONFECTIONERY PRODUCTS LTD (continued)			
M50	Sooty's New Adventures 2nd Series	1961	£2.00	—
25	Speed 1st Series...	1962	£1.60	£40.00
25	Speed 2nd Series	1962	60p	£15.00
	Album for 1st and 2nd Series combined	—		£15.00
25	Supercar 1st Series...	1962	£7.00	—
25	Supercar 2nd Series	1962	£5.00	—
25	Top Secret 1st Series	1965	£2.20	—
25	Top Secret 2nd Series	1965	£2.20	—
M26	XL5 1st Series	1965	£22.00	—
M26	XL5 2nd Series	1966	£22.00	—

COMPTONS

Qty		Date	Odds	Sets
22	Footballers Series A (coloured)	1925	£27.00	—
22	Footballers Series A (black and white)	1925	£27.00	—
22	Footballers Series B (coloured)	1925	£27.00	—
22	Footballers Series B (black and white)	1925	£27.00	—
22	Footballers Series C (coloured)	1925	£27.00	—
22	Footballers Series D (coloured)	1925	£27.00	—

CONNOISSEUR POLICIES

Qty		Date	Odds	Sets
M25	The Dorking Collection (Antiques)	2004	—	£7.00

CONTINENTAL CANDY CO. (U.K.)

Qty		Date	Odds	Sets
LT81	Snoots Nosy Bodies	1989	—	£9.00

COOPER & CO. STORES LTD

Qty		Date	Odds	Sets
50	Do You Know?	1962	20p	£5.00
25	Inventions and Discoveries 1st Series	1962	£1.60	—
25	Inventions and Discoveries 2nd Series	1962	£1.60	—
25	Island of Ceylon	1958	£4.00	—
25	Mysteries & Wonders of the World 1st Series	1960	60p	£15.00
25	Mysteries & Wonders of the World 2nd Series... ...	1960	40p	£10.00
25	Prehistoric Animals 1st Series	1962	£1.20	£30.00
25	Prehistoric Animals 2nd Series	1962	£1.20	£30.00
25	Strange but True 1st Series	1960	20p	£3.00
25	Strange but True 2nd Series	1960	20p	£3.50
25	Transport Through the Ages 1st Series	1961	30p	£7.50
25	Transport Through the Ages 2nd Series	1961	36p	£9.00
	Album for 1st and 2nd Series combined	—		£15.00

COORS BREWING CO. (USA)

Qty		Date	Odds	Sets
LT100	Coors	1995	—	£9.50

CORNERSTONE (USA)

Qty		Date	Odds	Sets
LT72	Austin Powers The Spy Who Shagged Me — The Movie...	1999	—	£9.50
LT81	The Avengers Return Series 3	1995	—	£15.00
LT110	Doctor Who 1st Series (TV Series)	1994	—	£25.00
LT110	Doctor Who 2nd Series (TV Series)	1995	—	£17.50
LT110	Doctor Who 3rd Series (TV Series)	1996	—	£15.00
LT90	Doctor Who 4th Series (TV Series)	1996	—	£15.00
LT90	Kiss Series 2, silver foil fronts (Pop Group)	1998	—	£12.00
LT81	Robot Carnival Masters of Japanese Animation ...	1994	—	£9.50

Qty		Date	Odds	Sets
	COUNTY PRINT SERVICES			
M25	Australian Test Cricketers	1993	–	£15.00
EL48	County Cricket Teams 1900-1914	1992	–	£10.00
50	County Cricketers 1990	1990	–	£25.00
20	Cricket Pavilions	1991	–	£15.00
EL24	Cricket Teams 1884-1900	1990	–	£7.00
M25	Cricket's Golden Age	1991	–	£10.00
EL12	Cricket's Pace Partners	1996	–	£8.00
EL12	Cricket's Spin Twins	1996	–	£8.00
50	Cricketers 1890	1989	–	£8.00
50	Cricketers 1896	1989	–	£8.00
50	Cricketers 1900	1990	–	£8.00
50	Cricketers 1906	1992	–	£10.00
EL5	Cricketing Knights	1994	–	£15.00
L25	Derbyshire Test Cricketers	1994	–	£12.50
14	England Cricket Team 1901-02	1991	–	£12.00
14	England Cricket Team 1903-04	1991	–	£4.00
15	England Cricket Team 1907-08	1992	–	£15.00
17	England Cricket Team 1932-33	1995	–	£6.00
16	England Cricket Team 1990-91	1990	–	£6.00
L25	Essex Test Cricketers	1993	–	£15.00
M27	Famous Cricket Crests...	1992	–	£12.50
M25	Famous Cricket Ties	1992	–	£12.00
EL12	First Knock Cricket's Opening Pairs	1994	–	£9.00
L25	Glamorgan Test Cricketers	1993	–	£12.50
L25	Gloucestershire Test Cricketers	1994	–	£12.50
L25	Hampshire Test Cricketers	1995	–	£12.50
L25	Kent Test Cricketers	1993	–	£12.50
L25	Lancashire Test Cricketers	1993	–	£12.50
L25	Leicestershire Test Cricketers	1995	–	£12.50
L25	Middlesex Test Cricketers...	1994	–	£12.50
50	1912 Triangular Tournament Cricket	1992	–	£9.00
M24	1920s Test Cricketers 1st Series	1994	–	£10.00
M24	1920s Test Cricketers 2nd Series	1996	–	£10.00
25	1950s England Cricket Characters...	1995	–	£20.00
50	1950s Test Cricketers	1992	–	£20.00
M50	1960s Test Cricketers	1992	–	£25.00
25	1995 England Cricket Characters	1996	–	£10.00
L25	Northamptonshire Test Cricketers	1993	–	£12.50
L25	Nottinghamshire Test Cricketers	1994	–	£12.50
50	Somerset County Championship Cricket			
	Series 1	1990	–	£10.00
50	Somerset County Championship Cricket			
	Series 2	1990	–	£10.00
L25	Somerset Test Cricketers	1994	–	£12.50
16	The South African Cricket Team 1894	1990	–	£8.00
M15	The South African Cricket Team 1965	1994	–	£6.00
L25	Surrey Test Cricketers	1994	–	£12.50
L25	Sussex Test Cricketers...	1994	–	£12.50
L25	Warwickshire Test Cricketers	1994	–	£12.50
L25	Worcestershire Test Cricketers	1995	–	£12.50
M30	World Stars of Cricket & Showbusiness	1992	–	£6.00
L25	Yorkshire Test Cricketers	1993	–	£20.00
	CECIL COURT			
L20	Christopher Columbus	1992	–	£6.50

Qty		Date	Odds	Sets
	CECIL COURT (continued)			
L12	Class of 66 (England World Cup Team)	2002	—	£7.50
L20	Famous Film Directors...	1992	—	£6.50
	COW & GATE			
L12	Advertisement Series 1st Series	1928	£2.50	£30.00
L12	Advertisement Series 2nd Series	1928	£2.00	£24.00
L48	Happy Families	1928	£1.25	—
	COWAN CO. LTD (Canada)			
EL24	Animal Cards	1923	£8.00	—
EL24	Birds Series	c1925	£8.00	—
EL24	Canadian Birds	1922	£8.00	—
EL24	Canadian Fish	c1924	£8.00	—
EL24	Chicken Cards	c1924	£8.00	—
M24	Dog Pictures	c1925	£8.00	—
M24	Learn To Swim	1929	£8.00	—
24	Noted Cats...	c1927	£8.00	—
EL12	Scenic Canada	c1925	£12.00	—
EL24	Wild Flowers of Canada	c1925	£8.00	—
	CRAIG & HALES (Australia)			
30	Footballers...	c1930	£25.00	—
	CRAWLEY CAKE & BISCUIT CO.			
24	World's Most Beautiful Birds	c1925	£9.00	—
	CREATURE FEATURES			
10	Spooky TV (The Addams Family)	2011	—	£5.00
	CRESCENT CONFECTIONERY CO. LTD			
48	Footballers...	c1925	£40.00	—
97	Sportsmen	c1925	£40.00	—
	CRICKET MEMORABILIA SOCIETY			
L50	Memorabilia Through the Ages (Cricket)	2000	—	£10.00
	CROMWELL STORES			
25	Do You Know?	1963	36p	£9.00
25	Racing Colours	1963	60p	—
	CROSBIE			
K54	Miniature Playing Cards	c1930	£1.00	—
	J. CROSFIELD			
36	Film Stars	1924	£9.00	—
	CROWN SPORTS CARDS (USA)			
LT10	Landforce Series 2 (Military)	1991	—	£5.00
LT9	Seaforce Series 3 (Naval)	1991	—	£5.00
	CROXLEY CARD CO.			
L20	British Lions Series 1 (Rugby Union)	1999	—	£10.00
LT20	Leicester Tigers Series 3 (Rugby Union)...	2001	—	£10.00
LT21	Leicester Tigers Series 5 (Rugby Union)...	2001	—	£10.00

Qty		Date	Odds	Sets

CROXLEY CARD CO. (continued)

Qty		Date	Odds	Sets
LT20	Saracens Series 2 (Rugby Union)	2000	—	£10.00
LT21	Saracens Series 4 (Rugby Union)	2001	—	£10.00

CRYPTOZOIC

LT68	The Big Bang Theory Seasons 3 & 4	2012	—	£9.50
LT72	Castle Seasons 1 & 2	2012	—	£9.50
LT72	Fringe — Imagine The Impossibilities Seasons 1 & 2	2012	—	£8.00
LT73	Fringe — Imagine The Impossibilities Seasons 3 & 4	2013	—	£8.50
LT63	The Vampire Diaries Season 1	2011	—	£9.50
LT69	The Vampire Diaries Season 2	2012	—	£9.50

CRYSELCO

EL25	Beautiful Waterways	1939	£1.20	£30.00
EL25	Buildings of Beauty	1938	£1.40	£35.00
EL12	Interesting Events of 60 Years Ago	1955	£2.25	£27.00

CRYSTAL CAT CARDS

LT6	Attitude Cats by Louis Wain Series LW5	2005	—	£3.00
LT6	Cats in Black by Louis Wain Series LW6	2005	—	£3.00
LT6	Cats Prize Winners by Louis Wain Series LW1 ...	2005	—	£3.00
LT6	Cats Sports & Leisure by Louis Wain Series LW2	2005	—	£3.00
LT6	Diabolo Cats by Louis Wain Series LW7	2005	—	£3.00
EL6	First World War Cats by Louis Wain Series LW12	2009	—	£3.00
LT6	Happy Days Cats by Louis Wain Series LW4	2005	—	£3.00
EL6	Mascots Cats by Louis Wain Series LW10	2009	—	£3.00
EL6	Mikado Cats by Louis Wain Series LW13	2010	—	£3.00
EL6	Out In All Weathers Cats by Louis Wain Series			
	LW8	2009	—	£3.00
EL6	Persians 1st Series Cats by Louis Wain Series			
	LW9	2009	—	£3.00
EL6	Persians 2nd Series Cats by Louis Wain Series			
	LW11	2009	—	£3.00
LT6	Purr-Fect Reaction Cats by Louis Wain Series LW3	2005	—	£3.00

D. CUMMINGS & SON

64	Famous Fighters (Boxers)	1948	£4.00	—

THE CUNNING ARTIFICER

6	Advertising Cards Discworld Emporium	2009	—	£2.50
20	Bernard Pearson's Clare Craft Pottery	2009	—	£5.00
	Album		—	£4.00
20	Discworld Advertisements and Labels	2009	—	£5.00
	Album		—	£4.00
25	Discworld Scout Insignia Collection (Terry			
	Pratchett's Scouting For Trolls)	2009	—	£7.50
	Album		—	£4.00
M25	The Discworld Stamp Collection (based on Terry			
	Pratchett's Discworld Books)	2009	—	£7.50
	Album		—	£4.00
M10	Discworld Toy Shop Collection (Props from The			
	Hogfather film)	2009	—	£4.00
	Album		—	£4,00
22	Famous Footballers of Ankh-Morpork (Terry			
	Pratchett's Discworld)	2010	—	£9.50
	Album		—	£6.00

47

Qty		Date	Odds	Sets
	D.S.I. (USA)			
LT50	Desert Storm	1991	—	£9.00
	DAILY HERALD			
32	Cricketers	1954	£4.25	—
32	Footballers	1954	£4.25	—
32	Turf Personalities	1955	£1.10	£35.00
	DAILY ICE CREAM CO.			
24	Modern British Locomotives	1954	£1.50	£36.00
	DAILY MIRROR			
M100	Star Soccer Sides	1971	70p	—
EL100	Star Soccer Sides 'My Club' Premium Issue	1971	£7.50	—
	DAILY SKETCH			
40	World Cup Souvenir	1970	£3.00	—
	DAILY TELEGRAPH			
26	England Rugby World Cup	1995	—	£6.00
26	Ireland Rugby World Cup	1995	—	£6.00
26	Scotland Rugby World Cup	1995	—	£6.00
26	Wales Rugby World Cup	1995	—	£6.00
	DAINTY NOVELS			
10	World's Famous Liners	1915	£12.00	—
	DANDY GUM			
M200	Animal Fables:			
	A Black back	1971	40p	—
	B Red back	1971	40p	—
M160	Cars and Bikes:			
	A Black back with 'Dandy'	1977	80p	—
	B Blue back, anonymous	1977	80p	—
M116	Flag Parade	1965	30p	£35.00
M160	Flag Parade	1978	30p	—
M210	Football Clubs and Colours of the World...	c1970	50p	—
M54	Football — European Cup (without firm's name) ...	1988	50p	—
M55	Football World Cup (with firm's name)	1986	50p	—
M80	Hippy Happy Tattoos (black and white)	c1965	80p	—
M72	Motor Cars	c1960	£1.25	—
M53	Our Modern Army	1956	£1.00	—
M53	Pin-up Girls (Original Set)...	1955	£1.70	£90.00
M53	Pin-up Girls (with 'Substitute' cards)	1955	£1.70	£90.00
M25	The Discworld Stamp Collection (based on Terry			
M54	Pin-up Girls	1977	60p	—
M80	Pirate Tattoos (coloured)	c1965	80p	—
M70	Pop Stars Series P	1977	£1.00	—
M56	Rock 'N' Bubble Pop Stars	1987	35p	£20.00
M100	Soldier Parade	1969	60p	—
M200	Struggle for the Universe (black back)	1970	30p	—
M72	Veteran and Vintage Cars:			
	A Numbers 1 to 48 British Issue	1966	£1.50	—
	B Numbers 49 to 72 Overseas Issue	1966	£1.50	—

Qty		Date	Odds	Sets

DANDY GUM (continued)

Qty			Date	Odds	Sets
M100	Wild Animals:				
	A	Danish/English text...	1969	25p	£25.00
	B	Arabic/English text	1978	30p	£30.00
M200	Wonderful World		c1975	30p	—

DART FLIPCARDS (USA)

Qty		Date	Odds	Sets
LT72	Battlestar Galactica	1996	—	£9.50
LT72	Betty Boop	2001	—	£20.00
LT100	Fern Gully The Last Rainforest	1992	—	£9.50
LT72	The Frighteners — The Film	1996	—	£12.00
LT72	I Love Lucy 50th Anniversary	2001	—	£9.50
LT72	The Lone Ranger	1997	—	£15.00
LT72	Mr Bean (Rowan Atkinson)	1998	—	£9.50
LT72	The Munsters All New Series	1998	—	£12.00
LT100	100 Years of Hersheys...	1995	—	£9.50
LT100	Pepsi Cola 1st Series	1994	—	£13.00
LT100	Pepsi Cola 2nd Series	1995	—	£9.50
LT72	Sabrina The Teenage Witch	1999	—	£9.50
LT72	Sailor Moon	1997	—	£9.50
LT72	Shrek The Film	2001	—	£8.00
LT72	Titanic (The Liner)	1998	—	£20.00
LT100	Vietnam Series 2...	1991	—	£9.50

DE BEUKELAER BISCUITS

Qty		Date	Odds	Sets
KP100	All Sports	1932	65p	£65.00
M125	Dumbo	c1940	£1.50	—
KP100	Film Stars 1st Series (Nd 1-100)	c1930	—	—
KP100	Film Stars 2nd Series (Nd 101-200)	c1930	£1.20	—
KP100	Film Stars 3rd Series (Nd 201-300)	c1930	£1.20	—
KP100	Film Stars 4th Series (Nd 301-400)	1932	£1.20	£120.00
KP100	Film Stars 5th Series (Nd 401-500)	c1935	£1.20	—
KP100	Film Stars 6th Series (Nd 501-600)	c1935	£1.20	—
KP100	Film Stars 7th Series (Nd 601-700)	c1935	£1.20	—
KP100	Film Stars 8th Series (Nd 701-800)	c1935	£1.20	—
KP100	Film Stars 9th Series (Nd 801-900)	c1935	£1.20	—
KP100	Film Stars 10th Series (Nd 901-1,000)	c1935	£1.20	—
KP100	Film Stars 11th Series (Nd 1,001-1,100)	1940	£1.20	—
KP100	Film Stars (A) (B1-B100) small figure	c1935	£1.20	—
KP100	Film Stars (B) (B1-B100) large figure	c1935	£1.20	—
K160	Film Stars (gold background)	1938	£1.60	—
132	Film Stars (gold background)	1939	£1.60	£210.00
M125	Gulliver's Travels	c1940	£1.25	—
M125	Pinocchio Series	c1940	£1.50	—
M60	Sixty Glorious Years	c1940	£2.00	—
M100	Snow White Series	c1940	£1.50	—

DERBY EVENING TELEGRAPH

Qty		Date	Odds	Sets
EL8	150 Years of British Railways (Derby)	1980	—	£5.00

DESIGN AT LONDON COLOUR LTD

Qty		Date	Odds	Sets
10	Bizarre	2013	—	£4.00
10	The Story of Barratt's Sweets Factory — The Early Years	2013	—	£5.50

Qty		Date	Odds	Sets

DESIGNS ON SPORT

Qty		Date	Odds	Sets
25	Test Cricketers	1992	–	£7.50

LIAM DEVLIN & SONS LTD

M36	Coaching Gaelic Football	c1960	£10.00	–
48	Corgi Toys	1971	£2.50	–
50	Do You Know?	1964	20p	£5.00
M50	Famous Footballers New Series	1952	£15.00	–
M50	Famous Footballers, Series A1	1953	£15.00	–
M50	Famous Footballers, Series A2	1954	£15.00	–
50	Famous Footballers, Series A3	1955	£15.00	–
M54	Famous Speedway Stars	c1960	£15.00	–
M45	Fastest on Earth	c1953	£5.00	–
36	Flags of All Nations	1958	£5.00	–
48	Gaelic Sportstars	c1960	£10.00	–
48	Irish Fishing	1962	70p	£35.00
50	Modern Transport	1966	20p	£10.00
48	Our Dogs	c1960	£9.00	–
48	Right or Wrong	c1960	£6.00	–
M35	Walt Disney Characters	c1955	£7.00	–
M50	Wild Animals by George Cansdale..............	1954	£5.50	–
48	Wild Wisdom	c1965	£3.00	–
50	Wonders of the World	1968	20p	£6.00
100	World Flag Series	c1965	£5.00	–

DIAMOND COLLECTION (UK)

L20	Rock 'n' Roll	1998	–	£7.50

DICKSON, ORDE & CO. LTD

50	Footballers	1960	40p	£20.00
25	Ships Through the Ages	1960	£3.40	–
25	Sports of the Countries	1962	£1.20	£30.00

DIGIT CARDS

LT40	Happy Puppy Your Best Friends (Game Cards) ...	c1995	–	£6.00

DIGITAL IMPACT

L20	Caricatures From The Movies	2002	–	£8.00
30	Victorian & Edwardian Soldiers in Full Dress	2001	–	£12.00

DINERS CLUB

EL8	Reminders	1976	40p	£3.00

DINKIE PRODUCTS LTD (Hair Grips)

M24	Stars and Starlets	1947	£3.00	–
M20	Stars and Starlets 2nd Series	1947	£3.00	–
M20	MGM Films 3rd Series	1948	£3.00	–
M24	Warner Bros. Artists 4th Series	1948	£5.00	–
M20	Gone With the Wind 5th Series	1948	£6.00	–
M24	Warner Bros. Films 6th Series	1949	£4.00	–
M24	MGM Stars 7th Series	1949	£4.00	–
M24	Paramount Pictures 8th Series	1950	£4.00	–
M24	M.G.M. Films 9th Series	1950	£6.50	–
M24	M.G.M. Films 10th Series	1951	£8.00	–
M24	United Artists Releases 11th Series	1951	£8.00	–

Qty		Date	Odds	Sets

DINOCARDZ (USA)

LT80	Dinosaurs Series 1	1992	—	£9.50

DIRECT ACCESS

L8	Atlanticard (British Sports Stars)	1992	£1.25	£10.00

DIRECT TEA SUPPLY CO.

25	British Uniforms of the 19th Century	c1960	£1.00	—

J. ARTHUR DIXON

Collectacard Series:

EL15	Vintage Steam (GWR), Set 6...	1978	—	£3.50
EL15	Vintage Steam (SR), Set 7	1978	—	£3.50
EL15	Vintage Steam (LMS), Set 8	1978	—	£3.50
EL15	Vintage Steam (LNER), Set 9	1978	—	£3.50
EL15	Vintage Steam (Scottish), Set 10	1978	—	£3.50

F. & M. DOBSON (SOUTHERN) LTD

L72	Flags of the World, Nos 1-72	1978	—	£10.00
L72	Flags of the World, Nos 73-144...	1978	—	£10.00
100	Newcastle and Sunderland's Greatest Footballers	1981	—	£20.00

A. & J. DONALDSON LTD

534	Sports Favourites	c1950	£9.00	—
64	Sports Favourites Golden Series (Footballers)... ...	c1950	£25.00	—

DONRUSS (USA)

LT56	Dallas	1981	—	£15.00
LT78	The Dark Crystal — The Film	1982	—	£10.00
LT66	Elvis	1978	—	£40.00
LT55	Knight Rider	1982	—	£20.00
LT66	Magnum P.I.	1983	—	£15.00
EL60	Major League All-Stars Baseball	1986	—	£12.00
LT66	Sgt Pepper's Lonely Hearts Club Band	1978	—	£15.00
LT66	Tron (including set 8 stickers)	1981	—	£15.00
LT92	Twister The Film	1996	—	£9.50

DORMY COLLECTION

25	Golf — The Modern Era	1994	60p	£15.00

DOUBLE Z ENTERPRISE (USA)

LT66	Zig & Zag	1994	—	£8.00

DRIFTER

M24	Pop Stars	1983	£1.00	—

DRYFOOD LTD

50	Animals of the World	1956	20p	£4.00
K50	Zoo Animals	1955	20p	£4.00

DUCHESS OF DEVONSHIRE DAIRY CO. LTD

L25	Devon Beauty Spots	1936	£4.40	£110.00

DUNHILLS

25	Ships and Their Workings...	1962	50p	£12.50

Qty		Date	Odds	Sets
	DUNKIN (Malta)			
L88	Martial Arts...	c1975	£1.00	—
M50	Motor Cycles of the World	1976	£2.20	—
	DUNN'S LONDON			
60	Animals	1924	£9.00	—
48	Birds	1924	£9.00	—
	J.A. DUNN & CO.			
26	Actresses 'FROGA A'	1902	£40.00	—
	DUO (USA)			
LT72	Abbott & Costello	1996	20p	£12.00
EL72	The Beatles — Yellow Submarine (152 × 102mm)	1999	—	£12.00
LT90	Gone with the Wind — The Film	1996	—	£9.50
LT72	Happy Days (1970s TV Series)	1998	—	£9.50
LT72	It's A Wonderful Life (The 1946 Film)	1996	—	£9.50
LT72	Lionel Greatest Trains	1998	—	£20.00
LT72	Lionel Legendary Trains	1997	—	£12.00
LT72	Lionel Legendary Trains 1900-2000 Centennial ...	2000	—	£20.00
LT81	The Outer Limits	1997	—	£9.50
LT72	The Wizard of Oz	1996	—	£15.00
LT72	WWF Smack Down (Wrestling)	1999	—	£12.00
LT72	Zorro — The Film	1998	—	£9.50
	MICKEY DURLING (Sunday Empire)			
48	Footballers of Today	c1950	£5.00	—
	DUTTON'S BEERS			
12	Team of Sporting Heroes	1980	20p	£2.50
	DYNAMIC (Australia)			
LT100	Disney's Aladdin	1995	20p	£9.50
LT60	Escape of the Dinosaurs	1997	—	£9.50
LT55	New Zealand All Blacks	1995	20p	£8.00
	DYNAMIC FORCES (USA)			
LT72	Lexx Premiere Series (TV, Sci-Fi Series)	2002	—	£9.50
	THE EAGLE			
16	Soccer Stars	1965	£4.00	—
	EAST KENT NATIONAL BUS CO.			
L8	British Airways Holidays	1984	—	£4.00
	EBRO			
EL69	Pop Singers	c1963	£4.00	—
	ECLIPSE ENTERPRISES (USA)			
LT110	The Beverly Hillbillies	1993	—	£9.50
LT110	National Lampoon Loaded Weapon I	1993	—	£9.50
	EDGE ENTERTAINMENT (USA)			
LT82	Judge Dredd — Movie & Comic	1995	—	£9.50

Qty		Date	Odds	Sets
	J. EDMONDSON & CO. LTD			
26	Actresses 'FROGA'	c1901	£60.00	—
4	Aeroplane Models	1939	£20.00	—
?72	Art Pictures	c1914	£14.00	—
15	Birds and Eggs	c1925	£12.00	—
?22	Boy Scout Proficiency Badges	c1925	£35.00	—
25	British Army Series	c1915	£25.00	—
20	British Ships	1925	£3.25	—
20	Dogs	c1930	£9.00	—
20	Famous Castles	1925	£7.00	—
30	Flags & Flags With Soldiers (Flags only)	c1905	£22.00	—
42	Flags of All Nations (3 printings)	c1930	£9.00	—
24	Pictures from the Fairy Stories	c1930	£6.00	—
24	Popular Sports	c1925	£12.00	—
25	Sports and Pastimes	c1910	£16.00	—
12	Throwing Shadows on the Wall	1937	£4.50	—
25	War Series	c1916	£15.00	—
12	Woodbine Village	c1930	£4.00	—
26	Zoo Alphabet	c1930	£7.50	—
	EDWARDS & SONS (Confectionery)			
27	Popular Dogs	1954	£4.00	—
12	Products of the World	1957	20p	£2.50
25	Transport — Present and Future:			
	A Descriptive back	1955	20p	£2.50
	B Album offer back	1955	20p	£5.00
25	Wonders of the Universe:			
	A With title	1956	20p	£2.50
	B Without title	1956	£1.00	£25.00
	THE 'ELITE' PICTURE HOUSE			
50	War Portraits	1916	£90.00	—
	ELKES BISCUITS LTD			
25	Do You Know? (Mechanical)	1964	20p	£3.00
	ELY BREWERY CO. LTD			
M24	Royal Portraits	1953	£2.25	£55.00
	EMERALD COLLECTABLES			
M72	Birds & their Eggs	1996	—	£15.00
	EMPIRE MARKETING BOARD			
12	Empire Shopping	c1925	£3.25	£40.00
	H.E. EMPSON & SON LTD			
25	Birds	1962	80p	—
25	British Cavalry Uniforms of the 19th Century	1963	60p	£15.00
25	Garden Flowers	1966	£1.00	£25.00
25	History of the Railways 1st Series	1966	£1.60	—
25	History of the Railways 2nd Series	1966	£1.60	—
24	The Island of Ceylon	1962	£4.00	—
25	Passenger Liners	1964	£1.60	—
25	Tropical Birds	1966	50p	£12.50
25	Wonders of the Deep	1965	20p	£3.00

Qty		Date	Odds	Sets
	ENESCO (USA)			
LT16	Precious Moments	1993	–	£8.00
	ENGLAND'S GLORY			
15	England '66 (Football World Cup)	2004	–	£5.50
	ENGLISH AND SCOTTISH CWS			
?23	British Sports Series	c1910	£35.00	–
25	Humorous Peeps into History (Nd 1-25)	1927	£3.20	£80.00
25	Humorous Peeps into History (Nd 26-50)	1928	£5.00	–
25	In Victoria's Days	1930	£3.20	£80.00
L12	The Rose of the Orient, Film Series	1925	50p	£6.00
L12	The Rose of the Orient 2nd Film Series	1925	50p	£6.00
L12	The Story of Tea (brown back)	1925	£1.00	£12.00
L12	The Story of Tea (blue back)...................	1925	£1.25	£15.00
	ENSIGN FISHING TACKLE			
L6	Advertising Blotters............................	2002	–	£3.00
L6	Advertising Cards	2002	–	£3.00
L6	The Art of Angling 1st Series	1997	–	£3.00
L6	The Art of Angling 2nd Series	1997	–	£3.00
L6	The Art of Angling 3rd Series	2002	–	£3.00
L6	Birds of Prey	1997	–	£3.00
L6	Fisherman's Lore	2002	–	£3.00
L6	Fishing Tackle Advertisements	1995	–	£3.00
L20	Freshwater Fish	1995	–	£7.50
L6	Game Birds (By Graham Payne)	1996	–	£3.00
L6	Garden Birds	1997	–	£3.00
L6	It's A Dog's Life	2002	–	£3.00
L6	Lifeboats	2002	–	£3.00
L6	Lighthouses	2002	–	£3.00
L6	Norman Neasom's Rural Studies Series 1	2002	–	£3.00
L6	Norman Neasom's Rural Studies Series 2	2002	–	£3.00
L6	Owls...	1997	–	£3.00
L25	Salmon Flies	1995	–	£7.50
L6	Sea Fish	2002	–	£3.00
L6	Sharks	2002	–	£3.00
L6	Water Loving Birds	2002	–	£3.00
	EPOL (South Africa)			
M30	Dogs...	1974	70p	£20.00
	JOHN E. ESSLEMONT LTD (Tea)			
25	Before Our Time................................	1966	30p	£7.50
25	Into Space.....................................	1966	80p	£20.00
24	The Island of Ceylon	c1960	£6.00	–
	ESSO			
EL20	Olympics (Nd 1-40)	1972	£2.00	–
M16	Squelchers Booklets (Football)	1970	£2.00	–
	ESSO (Australia)			
L18	Australia's Great Mineral Discoveries...........	1971	£1.00	£18.00

Qty		Date	Odds	Sets
	EUROSTAR			
LT125	Tour de France (Cycling)	1997	20p	—
	EVERSHED AND SON LTD			
25	Sports and Pastimes	c1910	£16.00	—
	EVERY GIRLS PAPER			
MP17	Film Stars	c1924	£5.00	—
	EWBANKS LTD			
25	Animals of the Farmyard	1960	30p	£7.50
25	British Uniforms	1957	20p	£4.00
25	Miniature Cars and Scooters...	1959	24p	£6.00
50	Ports and Resorts of the World	1958	20p	£9.00
25	Ships Around Britain	1961	20p	£2.50
25	Sports and Games	1958	36p	£9.00
25	Transport Through the Ages:			
	A Black back	1957	20p	£3.00
	B Blue back	1957	50p	£12.50
	EXPRESS WEEKLY			
	The Wild West:			
25	A No overprint	1958	30p	£7.50
25	B Red overprint...	1958	20p	£4.00
L25	C 2 Pictures per card...	1958	80p	—
	EXTRAS			
24	Prehistoric Monsters and the Present...	1979	£3.00	—
	F1 SPORTS CARD MARKETING INC. (Canada)			
LT200	Grid Formula 1 Racing...	1992	—	£20.00
	F.P.G. (USA)			
LT90	Barclay Shaw — Fantasy Art	1995	—	£9.50
LT90	Bernie Wrightson More Macabre Series 2 —			
	Fantasy Art	1994	—	£9.50
LT90	Bob Eggleton — Fantasy Art	1995	—	£9.50
LT90	Chris Foss — Fantasy Art...	1995	—	£9.50
LT90	Christos Achilleos — Fantasy Art	1992	—	£9.50
LT90	Darrell Sweet — Fantasy Art...	1994	—	£9.50
LT90	David Cherry — Fantasy Art	1995	—	£9.50
LT90	David Mattingly — Fantasy Art	1995	—	£9.50
LT90	Everway Vision Cards — Fantasy Art...	1995	—	£12.00
LT90	James Warhola — Fantasy Art	1995	—	£9.50
LT60	Janny Wurts — Fantasy Art	1996	—	£8.00
LT90	Jeffrey Jones Series 1 — Fantasy Art	1993	—	£9.50
LT90	Jeffrey Jones Series 2 — Fantasy Art	1995	—	£9.50
LT90	Joe Devito — Fantasy Art...	1995	—	£9.50
LT60	Joe Jusko's Edgar Rice-Burroughs Collection 1			
	(Tarzan)	1994	—	£12.00
LT60	Joe Jusko's Edgar Rice-Burroughs Collection 2 ...	1995	—	£15.00
LT90	John Berkey Series 2 — Fantasy Art	1996	—	£9.50
LT90	Michael Kaluta 1st Series — Fantasy Art	1994	—	£9.50
LT90	Michael Kaluta 2nd Series — Fantasy Art	1995	—	£9.50
LT90	Mike Ploog — Fantasy Art	1994	—	£9.50

		Date	Odds	Sets

F.P.G. (USA) (continued)

Qty		Date	Odds	Sets
LT90	Paul Chadwick — Fantasy Art	1995	—	£9.50
LT90	Robh Ruppel — Fantasy Art	1996	—	£9.50
LT90	Thomas Canty — Fantasy Art	1996	—	£9.50

FACCHINO

Cinema Stars:

K50	A Inscribed Series of 50	1936	£7.00	—
K100	B Inscribed Series of 100	1936	65p	£65.00
K50	How or Why	1937	60p	£30.00
K50	People of All Lands	c1935	£2.00	—
K50	Pioneers	c1935	£2.00	—

FACTORY ENTERTAINMENT

LT50	The Prisoner Volume 2	2010	—	£8.00

FAIRLEY'S RESTAURANT

20	The European War Series	1916	£25.00	—

FAITH PRESS

10	Boy Scouts...	1928	£7.00	—
10	Girl Guides...	1928	£7.00	—

FAMILY STAR

EL8	Good Luck Song Cards	c1930	£3.50	—
K52	Miniature Playing Cards	c1955	80p	—
M4	Film Stars	c1955	£5.00	—

FANTASY (USA)

LT50	Rocketship X-M	1979	—	£10.00

FANTASY TRADE CARD CO. (USA)

LT60	Alien Nation	1990	—	£18.00

FARM-TO-DOOR SUPPLIES

25	Castles of Great Britain	1965	£4.00	—
25	Cathedrals of Great Britain	1965	£4.00	—

FARROW'S

50	Animals in the Zoo	1925	£8.00	—

FAULDERS CHOCOLATE

10	Ancient v Modern Sports	1924	£10.00	—
10	Birds and Nests	1924	£7.00	—
10	Fruits...	1924	£7.00	—
10	Game	1924	£8.00	—
10	Zoology	1924	£8.00	—

FAX PAX

L40	The American West (19th Century)	1992	—	—
L40	Birds of the British Isles	1991	—	—
L40	Britain's Royal Heritage	1991	—	£4.00
LT50	Butterflies of the British Isles...	1996	—	£4.00
L40	Castles	1990	—	—
L40	Cathedrals and Minsters	1989	—	£4.00

Qty		Date	Odds	Sets
	FAX PAX (continued)			
L39	Dinosaurs	1993	—	£4.00
L36	Equestrianism...	1987	—	—
LT40	Famous Golfers	1993	—	£5.00
L42	First Ladies of the United States	1997	—	£4.00
L36	Football Greats	1989	—	—
L36	Football Stars	1989	—	£5.00
L40	Forty Great Britons	1992	—	—
L36	Golf	1987	—	£15.00
L40	Historic Houses	1990	—	£4.00
L40	Kings and Queens	1988	—	£4.00
L40	The Lake District...	1993	—	£4.00
L40	London	1992	—	£4.00
	Presidents of the United States 1993:			
L41	A Complete set	1993	—	—
L40	B Different (minus George Bush 1989-93) ...	1993	—	£5.00
L40	Scotland's Heritage	1990	—	£4.00
L38	Tennis	1987	—	£8.00
LT50	Wild Flowers of the British Isles...	1996	—	£4.00
L40	Wildlife of the British Isles...	1991	—	£4.00
LT40	World of Sport	1993	—	£6.00

FEATHERED WORLD

Qty		Date	Odds	Sets
EL?	Poultry, Pigeons, Cage Birds, etc. postcards...	c1910	£2.50	—

ALEX FERGUSON

Qty		Date	Odds	Sets
20	The European War Series	1917	£25.00	—
41	VC Heroes	1917	£20.00	—

FESTIVAL OF 1000 BIKES

Qty		Date	Odds	Sets
L24	The Vintage Motor Cycle Club	1993	—	£6.00

FIELD GALLERIES

Qty		Date	Odds	Sets
L7	Racehorses & Jockeys 1st Series	1997	—	£3.00
L7	Racehorses & Jockeys 2nd Series...	1997	—	£3.00

FIFE POLICE

Qty		Date	Odds	Sets
L36	British Stamps	1987	20p	£6.00
EL20	Intercity British Rail	1990	30p	£6.00

FILM PICTORIAL

Qty		Date	Odds	Sets
EL2	Film Stars (paper-backed silks)	c1930	£35.00	—

FILSHILL

Qty		Date	Odds	Sets
24	Birds and Their Eggs	c1920	£8.00	—
25	Footballers	1922	£20.00	—
25	Types of British Soldiers	c1920	£24.00	—

FINDUS (Frozen Foods)

Qty		Date	Odds	Sets
20	All About Pirates	1967	30p	£6.00

FINE FARE TEA

Qty		Date	Odds	Sets
25	Inventions and Discoveries 1st Series	1962	70p	£17.50
25	Inventions and Discoveries 2nd Series	1962	70p	£17.50
12	Your Fortune in a Teacup	1965	25p	£3.00

Qty		Date	Odds	Sets

FISH MARKETING BOARD

Qty		Date	Odds	Sets
18	Eat More Fish	c1930	£3.50	—

FIZZY FRUIT

25	Buses and Trams	c1960	£1.00	£25.00

FLEER

LT84	Believe It or Not	c1970	40p	—
LT192	Mad	1985	40p	—

FLEER (USA)

LT90	Aaahh! Real Monsters	1995	—	£8.00
LT10	Aaahh! Real Monsters Colouring Cards	1995	—	£3.00
LT120	Batman Forever:			
	A Fleer 1995 on front...	1995	—	£9.50
	B Fleer 95 Ultra on front...	1995	—	£9.50
LT100	Batman Forever Metal	1995	—	£12.00
LT119	Casper — The Movie (Nos 13 & 77 unissued,			
	2 different Nos 12 & 69)	1995	—	£9.50
LT42	Christmas Series...	1995	—	£10.00
LT66	Grossville High	1986	—	£8.00
LT72	Here's Bo Derek	1981	20p	£10.00
LT146	MTV Animation	1995	—	£12.00
LT42	Nursery Rhymes	1995	—	£8.50
LT150	Power Rangers The Movie	1995	—	£12.00
LT24	Power Rangers The Movie Power Pop Up	1995	—	£5.00
LT150	Reboot (TV Series)	1995	—	£12.00
LT100	Skeleton Warriors	1995	—	£8.00
LT50	Spiderman '97 with Fleer on front	1997	—	£9.50
LT50	Spiderman '97 without Fleer on front	1997	—	—
LT80	World Wrestling Federation Clash	2001	—	£10.00
LT100	WWF Wrestlemania...	2001	—	£10.00

FLEETWAY PUBLICATIONS LTD

L72	Adventures of Sexton Blake	1968	£4.00	—
EL1	The Bobby Moore Book of The F.A. Cup (booklet)	1968	—	£12.00
EL28	Football Teams 1958-59 (issued with 'Lion/Tiger')	1958	£4.00	—
EL28	Football Teams 1959-60 (issued with 'Lion/Tiger')	1959	£4.00	—
EL2	Pop Stars (Roxy)...	1961	£1.25	£2.50
50	Star Footballers of 1963 (issued with 'Tiger')	1963	£1.80	—

FLORENCE CARDS

24	Luton Corporation Tramways	1983	—	£3.00
M20	Tramway Scenes	1984	—	£3.00

FOOTBALL ASSOCIATION OF WALES

LT17	The Dragons Dream Team (Welsh International			
	Footballers)...	2000	—	£6.00

FOOTBALL CARD COLLECTOR

10	Association Footballers (of the 1960s) 1st Series...	2012	—	£5.00
10	Association Footballers (of the 1960s) 2nd Series	2012	—	£5.00
10	Association Footballers (of the 1950/60s) 3rd Series	2012	—	£5.00
10	Footballers 1960s 1st Series...	2011	—	£4.50

Qty		Date	Odds	Sets
	FOOTBALL CARD COLLECTOR (continued)			
10	Footballers 1960s 2nd Series	2011	—	£4.50
10	Footballers 1960s 3rd Series	2011	—	£4.50
10	Footballers 1960s 4th Series	2011	—	£4.50

FOOTBALL COLLECTOR CARDS

20	Football (1950s Footballers) blue fronts 1st Series	2011	—	£7.50
20	Football (1950s Footballers) yellow fronts 2nd Series	2011	—	£7.50
20	Football (1950s Footballers) green fronts 3rd Series	2011	—	£7.50

FOOTBALL FANFARE

20	Football Fanfare (1950s Footballers) 1st Series ...	2010	—	£7.50
20	Football Fanfare (1950s Footballers) 2nd Series ...	2010	—	£7.50
20	Football Fanfare (1950/60s Footballers) 3rd Series	2010	—	£7.50
20	Football Fanfare (1950/60s Footballers) 4th Series	2010	—	£7.50

FOOTBALL STAR COLLECTOR CARDS

20	Football Star	2010	—	£7.50

FOOTBALL TRADER

16	Legends of The Orient (Leyton Orient F.C.)...	2011	—	£5.00

FOOTBALLER MAGAZINE

24	Hall of Fame (Footballers)	1994	50p	£12.00
	Album		—	£10.00

FORD MOTOR CO. LTD

L50	Major Farming	c1955	£9.00	—

FOSTER CLARK (Malta)

50	The Sea Our Other World...	1974	40p	£20.00

FOTO BUBBLE GUM

25	Wonders of the Universe	1957	20p	£2.50

FRAME SET & MATCH

25	Wembley Magpies (Newcastle Utd Footballers) ...	1995	24p	£6.00

FRAMEABILITY

L17	British Steam Locomotives	2002	—	£6.00
L16	Fire Engines 1st Series	1996	—	£5.00
L16	Fire Engines 2nd Series	1998	—	£6.00
L10	Highwaymen	2003	—	£4.00
L17	Police — British Police Vehicles	2002	—	£6.00
L6	Traction Engines...	1999	—	£3.00
L10	World Cup Winners 1966 England	2002	—	£5.00

FRAMES OF MIND

L11	World Cup Winners 1966 (Football)	1997	—	£11.00

A.C.W. FRANCIS (West Indies)

25	British Uniforms of the 19th Century	c1965	£1.00	—
25	Castles of Britain...	c1965	£1.00	—

Qty		Date	Odds	Sets
	A.C.W. FRANCIS (West Indies) (continued)			
25	The Circus	1966	£1.00	—
25	Football Clubs and Badges	c1965	£1.00	—
25	Pond Life	1967	30p	£7.50
25	Sports of the Countries	1967	£1.00	—

	FREEDOM PRESS (USA)			
LT40	The JFK Assassination...	1991	—	£8.00
LT16	Official Currier and Ives Civil War	1994	—	£4.00

	LES FRERES			
25	Aircraft of World War II...	1966	£1.20	—

	FRESHMAID LTD (Jubbly)			
50	Adventurous Lives	1966	20p	£4.50

	J.S. FRY & SONS LTD (Chocolate)			
4	Advertisement Cards:			
	A G.H. Elliott size 63 × 38mm dark brown... ...	c1910	—	£30.00
	B G.H. Elliott size 66 × 38mm light brown	c1910	—	£30.00
	C Hello Daddy size 66 × 38mm	c1910	—	£30.00
	D Vinello size 80 × 62mm	c1920	—	£40.00
50	Ancient Sundials:			
	A With series title, text back	1924	£3.00	—
	B Without series title, plain back	1924	£7.00	—
50	Birds and Poultry...	1912	£3.00	£150.00
24	Birds and Their Eggs	1912	£4.50	£110.00
15	China and Porcelain	1907	£13.00	—
25	Days of Nelson	1906	£12.00	—
25	Days of Wellington	1906	£12.00	—
25	Empire Industries	1924	£8.00	—
	Exercises for Men and Women:			
13	A Exercises for Men	1926	£6.00	—
12	B Exercises for Men and Boys	1926	£6.00	—
13	C Exercises for Women	1926	£6.00	—
12	D Exercises for Women and Girls	1926	£6.00	—
K48	Film Stars	1934	£3.25	—
50	Fowls, Pigeons and Dogs...	1908	£4.50	£225.00
EL12	Fun Cards	1972	20p	£2.50
25	Match Tricks	c1921	£32.00	—
15	National Flags	1908	£7.00	—
50	Nursery Rhymes	1917	£4.00	£200.00
50	Phil May Sketches	1905	£4.00	—
25	Red Indians	1927	£8.00	—
25	Rule Britannia...	1915	£6.00	—
50	Scout Series	1912	£8.00	—
48	Screen Stars	1928	£3.50	—
120	This Wonderful World	1935	£2.00	—
50	Time and Money in Different Countries	1908	£3.50	£175.00
50	Tricks and Puzzles (blue back)	1918	£4.00	£200.00
50	Tricks and Puzzles (black back)	1924	£4.00	£200.00
6	War Leaders — Package Issue	1915	£30.00	—
25	With Captain Scott at the South Pole	1912	£12.00	£300.00

Qty		Date	Odds	Sets
	J.S. FRY & SONS LTD (Canada)			
50	Children's Pictures	c1915	£14.00	—
25	Hunting Series	c1915	£20.00	—
25	Radio Series	c1930	£12.00	—
50	Scout Series 2nd Series	c1930	£13.00	—
50	Treasure Island Map	c1915	£10.00	—
	FUTERA (Australia)			
LT60	Cricket Elite	1996	—	£15.00
LT110	Cricketers	1994	—	£16.00
	FUTERA			
	(SEE ALSO TRADE CARDS (EUROPE) LTD)			
LT18	Aston Villa F.C.	2000	—	£12.00
LT18	Derby County F.C.	2000	—	£12.00
LT18	Manchester City F.C.	2000	—	£15.00
LT18	Middlesbrough F.C.	2000	—	£12.00
LT64	Red Dwarf (TV Series)	2002	—	£15.00
LT18	West Ham United F.C.	2000	—	£15.00
LT50	World Stars Platinum Series (Footballers)	2001	—	£16.00
M24	World Stars 3D Footballers	2002	—	£7.50
	G.B. & T.W.			
L20	Golfing Greats	1989	—	£10.00
	G. D. S. CARDS			
L25	American Civil War Battles	2006	—	£12.50
L25	Birds by C.R. Bree	2007	—	£9.50
L25	Birds by Cassell 1860	2007	—	£9.50
L20	Birds of North America by John Cassin	2007	—	£8.50
L20	Birds of The United States	2007	—	£8.50
L20	British Birds of Prey Series 1	2006	—	£8.50
L20	British Birds of Prey Series 2	2008	—	£8.50
L20	British Butterflies (1841) Series 1	2008	—	£8.50
L20	British Butterflies (1841) Series 2	2008	—	£8.50
L20	British Fresh-Water Fish	2006	—	£8.50
EL4	Cattle Breeds	2007	—	£4.50
L20	Champion Hurdle — Winners 1976-1995	1997	—	£12.00
L20	Cheltenham Gold Cup — Winners 1976-1995	1997	—	£12.00
L20	Clippers and Yachts	2007	—	£8.50
L16	Derby Winners 1953-1968	1994	—	£10.00
L20	Dogs	2006	—	£8.50
L20	Earl of Derby Collection of Racehorse Paintings ...	2004	—	£13.00
L20	European Birds	2007	—	£9.50
L20	Famous Jockeys	2001	—	£9.50
L20	Famous Jockeys of Yesterday, Series 1	2003	—	£12.00
L20	Famous Titled Owners and Their Racing Colours,			
	Series 1	2003	—	£12.00
L20	Famous Trainers (Horse Racing)	2001	—	£9.50
L20	Finches by Butler and Frohawk (1899)	2010	—	£7.00
EL4	Fusiliers by Richard Simkin (1890-1905)	2008	—	£4.50
L20	Grand National — Winners 1976-1995	1997	—	£12.00
L20	Great Racehorses	2003	—	£12.00
L16	Great Racehorses of Our Time	1994	—	£14.00

Qty		Date	Odds	Sets

G. D. S. CARDS (continued)

L25	Hawks and Owls of The America	2007	–	£9.50
L20	Heads of Famous Winners (Racehorses)	2001	–	£9.50
L20	Horses	2008	–	£8.50
L20	Hummingbirds by M.E. Mulsant & J.B.E. Verreaux			
	(1876-77)	2010	–	£7.00
L25	Indian Chiefs of North America Series 1	2006	–	£9.50
L25	Indian Chiefs of North America Series 2	2007	–	£9.50
L20	Indian Tribes of North America	2007	–	£8.50
L16	Lester Piggott's Classic Winners	1994	–	£10.00
L25	Light Infantries and Regiments by Richard Simkin			
	(1890-1905)	2008	–	£9.50
EL4	Military (1890-1905) by Richard Simkin	2008	–	£4.50
L25	Monkeys by J.G. Keulemans	2007	–	£9.50
L25	1950's Racehorse Winners	2008	–	£10.50
L20	1960's Racehorse Winners	2007	–	£10.50
L25	1970's Racehorse Winners	2007	–	£10.50
L20	One Thousand Guineas Winners 1981-2000	2005	–	£10.50
L20	Orchids by Robert Warner & Thomas Moore (1882).	2010	–	£7.00
L20	Parakeets and Parrots (1903) by David Seth-Smith	2008	–	£8.50
L25	Parrots	2007	–	£9.50
L25	Pigeons	2006	–	£9.50
L20	Poultry	2006	–	£8.50
L25	Poultry by Harrison Weir 1904	2008	–	£9.50
L20	St Leger 1776-1815 Winning Owners Colours	2005	–	£10.50
EL6	Soldiers and Cavalry by Richard Simkin			
	(1890-1905)	2008	–	£7.00
L20	Tropical Birds	2007	–	£8.50
L20	Trotters (American Style Horse Racing)	2006	–	£8.50
L20	Two Thousand Guineas Winners 1981-2000	2005	–	£10.50
L25	World's Birds of Prey (1876) Series 1	2008	–	£9.50
L25	World's Birds of Prey (1876) Series 2	2008	–	£9.50

GALBRAITH'S STORES

25	Animals in the Service of Man	c1964	£5.00	–
50	Strange Creatures	c1963	£5.00	–

GALLERY OF LEGENDS

72	The British Open Golf Collection	1999	–	£12.00

GAMEPLAN LTD

L25	Open Champions (Golf)	1993	–	£8.00
L25	Vauxhall Motor Sport	1993	–	£10.00

GANONG BROS. LTD (Canada)

50	Big Chief	c1925	£8.00	–

GARDEN RAILWAYS MAGAZINE (USA)

20	Daventry Garden Railway	1991	–	£5.00
20	Garden Railway Structures Set E	1991	–	£5.00
20	Trains in the Garden: USA Set C	1991	–	£5.00
20	Trains in the Garden: Britain Set D	1991	–	£5.00

GAUMONT CHOCOLATE

K50	Film Stars	1936	£4.00	–

Qty		Date	Odds	Sets
	GAYCON PRODUCTS LTD (Confectionery)			
25	Adventures of Pinky and Perky 1st Series:			
	A Blue back	1961	£3.00	—
	B Black back	1961	£3.00	—
25	Adventures of Pinky and Perky 2nd Series:			
	A Blue back	1961	£3.00	—
	B Black back	1961	£3.00	—
50	British Birds and Their Eggs	1961	25p	£12.50
25	British Butterflies 1st Series	1963	80p	£20.00
25	Do You Know? 1st Series...	1962	£1.60	£40.00
25	Do You Know? 2nd Series	1962	£1.60	£40.00
50	Flags of All Nations	1963	£2.50	—
25	History of the Blue Lamp 1st Series	1961	80p	£20.00
25	History of the Blue Lamp 2nd Series	1961	80p	£20.00
30	Kings and Queens	1961	20p	£3.00
25	Modern Motor Cars	1959	£5.00	—
25	Modern Motor Cars of the World 1st Series...	1962	£5.00	—
25	Modern Motor Cars of the World 2nd Series	1962	£5.00	—
25	Red Indians 1st Series...	1960	80p	£20.00
25	Red Indians 2nd Series	1960	80p	£20.00
25	Top Secret 1st Series	1967	£3.20	—
25	Top Secret 2nd Series	1967	£3.20	—
	GEE'S FOOD PRODUCTS			
30	Kings and Queens	1961	60p	£18.00
16	See Britain by Coach	1955	20p	£2.50
	THE GEM LIBRARY			
MP15	Footballers Special Action Photo	1922	£5.00	—
MP6	Footballers Autographed Real Action Photo Series	1922	£5.00	—
MP4	Footballers Autographed Action Series	1923	£5.50	—
L16	Marvels of the Future	1929	£3.25	—
	GENERAL FOODS (South Africa)			
L50	Animals and Birds	1973	20p	£9.00
	GENERAL MILLS (Canada)			
LT6	Baseball Players (10 players per card)	1989	—	£5.00
	THE GIRLS FRIEND			
M6	Actresses (Silk)	1912	£10.00	—
	GIRLS MIRROR			
MP10	Actors and Actresses	c1922	£4.00	—
	GIRLS WEEKLY			
12	Flower Fortune Cards	1912	£15.00	—
	GLENGETTIE TEA			
25	Animals of the World	1964	20p	£3.00
25	Birds and Their Eggs	1970	24p	£6.00
25	The British Army, 1815:			
	A Black back	1976	24p	£6.00
	B Blue back	1976	24p	£6.00
25	British Locomotives	1959	20p	£3.00

Qty		Date	Odds	Sets

GLENGETTIE TEA (continued)

Qty		Date	Odds	Sets
25	Do You Know?	1970	20p	£2.50
25	Historical Scenes	1968	20p	£3.00
25	History of the Railway 1st Series	1974	20p	£3.50
25	History of the Railway 2nd Series	1974	20p	£3.50
25	International Air Liners	1963	50p	—
25	Medals of the World:			
	A Black back	1961	20p	£2.50
	B Blue back	1961	60p	£15.00
25	Modern Transport:			
	A Black back	1963	60p	£15.00
	B Blue back	1963	60p	£15.00
25	Naval Battles	1971	20p	£2.50
25	Rare British Birds	1967	20p	£5.00
25	Sovereigns, Consorts and Rulers of Great Britain, 1st Series	1970	£1.00	—
25	Sovereigns, Consorts and Rulers of Great Britain, 2nd Series	1970	£1.00	£25.00
25	Trains of the World	1966	20p	£5.00
25	Veteran and Vintage Cars	1966	80p	£20.00
25	Wild Flowers	1961	40p	£10.00

GLENTONS LTD

24	World's Most Beautiful Butterflies	c1920	£9.00	—

GLOUCESTERSHIRE C.C.C.

M12	Gloucestershire Cricketers of 1990	1990	30p	£3.50

J. GODDARD & SONS LTD

	Back 'Eighty'			
M3	Four Generations	c1925	£2.00	£6.00
M12	London Views	c1925	£2.00	£24.00
M12	Old Silver	c1925	£1.50	£18.00
M2	Use and Cleaning of Silverware I	c1925	£1.25	£2.50
	Back 'Eighty-five'			
M4	Cleaning a Silver Teapot	c1930	£4.00	£16.00
M12	Ports of the World	c1930	£2.50	—
M4	Silverware and Flowers I	c1930	£2.25	£9.00
M12	Views of Old Leicester	c1930	£4.50	—
	Back 'Ninety'			
M9	Old Silver at the Victoria and Albert Museum	c1935	£2.00	£18.00
M8	Silverware and Flowers II	c1935	£3.50	—
M8	Views of Leicester	c1935	£5.00	—
	Back '95'			
M12	Present Day Silverware	c1940	£2.00	£24.00
M6	Use and Cleaning of Silverware II	c1940	£4.00	—

GOLDEN CHICK

24	World's Most Beautiful Birds	c1920	£9.00	—

GOLDEN ERA

L7	A.J.S. Motor Cycles	1995	—	£3.00
L25	Aircraft of the First World War	1994	—	£7.50
L7	Alfa Romeo (Cars)	1998	—	£3.00
LT10	American Automobiles of the 1950s	2003	—	£4.50

Qty		Date	Odds	Sets
	GOLDEN ERA (continued)			
LT7	Anglia, Prefect, Popular Small Fords 1953-1967 ...	2005	—	£3.75
L7	Antique Dolls	1996	—	£3.00
L7	Ariel Motor Cycles	1995	—	£3.00
L7	Aston Martin (Cars)	1993	—	£3.00
L7	Aston Martin Post-War Competition Cars	2001	—	£3.00
L10	Austin Cars	1996	—	£3.75
L7	Austin Healey Motor Cars...	1995	—	£3.00
L9	BMW (Cars)	1999	—	£3.75
L7	BSA 1st Series (Motor Cycles)	1993	—	£3.00
L7	BSA 2nd Series (Motor Cycles)...	1999	—	£3.00
L10	British Buses of the 1950s	1999	—	£3.75
L10	British Buses of the 1960s	1999	—	£3.75
L10	British Lorries of the 1950s	2000	—	£3.75
EL4	British Lorries of the 1950s (numbered 081-084) ...	1999	—	£2.25
L10	British Lorries of the 1950s & 1960s	1999	—	£3.75
L10	British Lorries of the 1960s	2000	—	£3.75
L10	British Military Vehicles of WWII	2000	—	£3.75
L25	British Motor Cycles of the Fifties	1993	—	£7.50
L7	British Tanks of WWII	2000	—	£3.00
L10	British Trucks (1950s and 1960s)	2010	—	£3.75
L7	British Vans of The 1950s...	2002	—	£3.00
L7	British Vans of The 1960s...	2002	—	£3.00
LT10	Buses in Britain 1950s	2005	—	£4.50
LT10	Buses in Britain 1960s	2005	—	£4.50
L10	Bygone Buses (1950s and 1960s)	2010	—	£3.75
L7	Capri Mk1 1969-74	2007	—	£3.00
L7	Capri Mk3 1978-86	2007	—	£3.00
LT7	Capri Mk I Performance Models (1969-74)	2004	—	£3.75
LT7	Capri Mk II Performance Models (1974-78)...	2004	—	£3.75
LT7	Capri Mk III Performance Models (1978-86)	2004	—	£3.75
L25	Cats (Full Length)	1994	—	£7.50
L26	Cats (Heads)	1995	—	£7.50
LT7	Chevrolet Camaro 1967-69	2004	—	£3.75
L7	Citroen (Cars)...	2001	—	£3.00
L10	Classic American Motor Cycles	1998	—	£3.75
L7	Classic Bentley (Cars)	1997	—	£3.00
L26	Classic British Motor Cars	1992	—	£7.50
L25	Classic British Motor Cycles of the '50s & '60s ...	1993	—	£7.50
L7	Classic Citroen 2CV	2001	—	£3.00
LT10	Classic Corvette (Cars)	1994	—	£4.50
L7	Classic Ferrari (Cars)	1993	—	£7.00
L7	Classic Ferrari F1 1961-2000	2002	—	£3.00
L7	Classic Fiat	2002	—	£3.00
L7	Classic Honda (Motor Cycles)	1999	—	£3.00
EL4	Classic Jaguar Series 1 (numbered 153-156)...	2010	—	£2.25
L10	Classic Jeep	2002	—	£3.75
L7	Classic Kawasaki (Motor Cycles)	1999	—	£3.00
EL6	Classic Lambretta — The Golden Era of Scootering	2008	—	£3.00
L10	Classic Lorries (1950s and 1960s)	2010	—	£3.75
L7	Classic Lotus (Cars) 1st Series	1995	—	£3.00
L7	Classic Lotus (Cars) 2nd Series	1997	—	£3.00
L7	Classic MG (Cars) 1st Series	1992	—	£3.00
L7	Classic MG (Cars) 2nd Series	1994	—	£3.00
L7	Classic MG Sports Cars	1996	—	£3.00

Qty		Date	Odds	Sets
	GOLDEN ERA (continued)			
L10	Classic Mercedes	2000	—	£3.75
LT10	Classic Mini	2005	—	£4.50
L7	Classic Morgan Sports Cars	1997	—	£3.00
LT10	Classic Mustang (Cars)	1994	—	£6.00
L13	Classic Porsche Cars	1996	—	£4.50
L7	Classic Rally Cars of the 1970s.............	2001	—	£3.00
L7	Classic Rally Cars of the 1980s.............	2001	—	£3.00
EL6	Classic Riley	2008	—	£3.00
L7	Classic Rolls-Royce (Cars)	1997	—	£3.00
L7	Classic Rover (Cars)	1995	—	£3.00
L10	Classic Scooters	2000	—	£3.75
L7	Classic Suzuki	1999	—	£3.00
L10	Classic Tractors	1998	—	£3.75
L7	Classic T.V.R. (Cars)	1997	—	£3.00
L7	Classic Vauxhalls of the 1950s & 1960s	2002	—	£3.00
L7	Classic Volkswagen Karmann Ghia 1955-74	2002	—	£3.00
L7	Classic Volkswagen Transporter 1950-79	1999	—	£3.00
L7	Classic Volkswagen VW Beetle 1949-66............	1999	—	£3.00
L7	Classic Volkswagen VW Beetle 1967-80............	1999	—	£3.00
L7	Classic Volkswagen VW Golf GTI 1975-92	2002	—	£3.00
L7	Classic Volvo (Cars)	2003	—	£3.00
L13	Classic VW (Cars)	1993	—	£4.50
EL6	Classic VW Transporter	2008	—	£3.00
EL6	Classic Wolseley...................................	2008	—	£3.00
L7	Classic Yamaha	1999	—	£3.00
L7	Cobra The Sports Car 1962-1969	1996	—	£3.00
LT7	Consul, Zephyr, Zodiac Big Fords 1951-1971	2005	—	£3.75
L7	Cortina Mk1 1962-1966	2007	—	£3.00
L7	Daimler Classics	2004	—	£3.00
L7	Dolls	1996	—	£3.00
L7	Ducati (Motor Cycles)	1999	—	£3.00
L7	E-Type (Cars).......................................	1993	—	£3.00
L10	Eight Wheelers Classic British Lorries	2007	—	£3.75
L7	Escort Mk1 R S Models	2007	—	£3.00
L7	Escort Mk2 1975-80	2007	—	£3.00
L7	Escort Twin-cam, RS & Mexico 1969-80............	1999	—	£3.00
L7	Escort Works Rally Mk I, MK II	1999	—	£3.00
LT7	Escort Mk I The Performers	2004	—	£3.75
LT7	Escort Mk II The Performers	2004	—	£3.75
LT10	Famous Bombers (Aircraft)	1997	—	£4.50
LT10	Famous Fighters (Aircraft)	1997	—	£4.50
M20	Famous Footballers by Stubbs — Arsenal	2001	—	£5.00
M20	Famous Footballers by Stubbs — Aston Villa	2002	—	£5.00
M20	Famous Footballers by Stubbs — Chelsea	2001	—	£5.00
M20	Famous Footballers by Stubbs — Leeds	2001	—	£5.00
M20	Famous Footballers by Stubbs — Liverpool	2001	—	£5.00
M20	Famous Footballers by Stubbs — Manchester United	2001	—	£5.00
M20	Famous Footballers by Stubbs — Newcastle United	2002	—	£5.00
M20	Famous Footballers by Stubbs — Spurs............	2001	—	£5.00
M20	Famous Footballers by Stubbs — West Ham United	2002	—	£5.00
L7	Famous Fords — Capri Mk2 1974-78	2008	—	£3.00
L7	Famous Fords — Cortina Mk2 1966-70	2008	—	£3.00

GOLDEN ERA (continued)

Qty		Date	Odds	Sets
L10	Famous T.T. Riders (Motorcyclists)	1998	—	£3.75
L7	Ferrari 1950s & 1960s	2003	—	£3.00
L7	Ferrari 1970s & 1980s	2003	—	£3.00
L7	Ford and Fordson Tractors 1945-1970	2010	—	£3.00
L10	The Ford Capri (Cars)	1995	—	£3.75
L7	Ford Cortina Story 1962-82	2002	—	£3.00
L7	Ford Executive (Cars)	1994	—	£3.00
L10	Ford in the Sixties (Cars)	1996	—	£3.75
L7	Ford RS Models 1983-92	2001	—	£3.00
LT7	Ford Sierra — The Performers	2005	—	£3.75
L7	Ford XR Performance Models 1980-89	2001	—	£3.00
L10	Formula 1 (Grand Prix)	1996	—	£3.75
L10	F1 Champions 1991-2000	2001	—	£3.75
L7	German Military Vehicles of WWII	2001	—	£3.00
L7	Graham & Damon Hill (Grand Prix Drivers)	2000	—	£3.00
LT7	Granada-Consul and Granada MkI and MkII	2005	—	£3.75
L10	Grand Prix Greats	1996	—	£3.75
L26	Grand Prix The Early Years (Cars)	1992	—	£7.50
L10	Heavy Haulage (Lorries etc)	2000	—	£3.75
EL4	Jaguar At Le Mans (numbered 029-032)	1995	—	£2.25
L7	Jaguar Classic (Cars) 1st Series	1992	—	£3.00
L7	Jaguar Classic (Cars) 2nd Series	1993	—	£3.00
L7	Jaguar Classic (Cars) 3rd Series	1997	—	£3.00
L7	Jaguar Classics (Cars) 4th Series	2003	—	£3.00
EL4	Jaguar E-Type (numbered 149-152)	2010	—	£2.25
L7	Jaguar Modern Classics (Cars) 5th Series	2003	—	£3.00
L7	Jim Clark (Grand Prix Driver)	2000	—	£3.00
L7	Lambretta (Motor Cycles)	2000	—	£3.00
EL6	Lambretta Innocetti — The Golden Era of			
	Scootering	2008	—	£3.00
L10	Lambretta The World's Finest Scooter	2007	—	£3.75
EL6	Lambrettability — The Golden Era of Scootering	2008	—	£3.00
L7	Lancia (Cars)	1998	—	£3.00
L7	Land Rover 1st Series	1996	—	£3.00
EL4	Land Rover 1st Series (numbered 049-052)	1997	—	£4.00
L7	Land Rover 2nd Series	1996	—	£3.00
EL4	Land Rover 2nd Series (numbered 053-056)	1997	—	£4.00
L7	Land Rover 3rd Series	1996	—	£3.00
EL4	Land Rover 3rd Series (numbered 057-060)	1997	—	£4.00
L7	Land Rover Discovery	2001	—	£3.00
L7	Land Rover Legends Series 1	2000	—	£3.00
EL4	Land Rover Legends Series 1 (numbered 093-096)	2000	—	£2.25
L7	Land Rover Legends Series 2	2000	—	£3.00
EL4	Land Rover Legends Series 2 (numbered 097-100)	2000	—	£2.25
L7	Land Rover Legends Series 3	2000	—	£3.00
EL4	Land Rover Legends Series 3 (numbered 101-104)	2000	—	£2.25
L7	Land Rover, Ninety, One Ten & Defender	2000	—	£3.00
EL4	Land Rover Ninety, One Ten & Defender			
	(numbered 105-108)	2000	—	£2.25
L7	The Legend Lives On, Ayrton Senna (Grand Prix			
	Driver)	2000	—	£3.00
L10	London Buses of the Post-War Years	1997	—	£3.75
EL4	London Buses Post-War (numbered 069-072)	1999	—	£2.25
L10	London Buses of the Pre-War Years	1997	—	£3.75
EL4	London Buses Pre-War (numbered 065-068)	1999	—	£2.25

Qty		Date	Odds	Sets
	GOLDEN ERA (continued)			
L7	The London Taxi	2001	—	£3.00
L10	London's Country Buses	2000	—	£3.75
EL4	London's Country Buses (numbered 061-064)... ...	2000	—	£2.25
L7	Mansell (by Wayne Vickery)	1994	—	£3.00
L7	Matchless Motor Cycles	1995	—	£3.00
L7	Mercedes SL (Cars)	1994	—	£3.00
EL4	M.G. Greats (Cars) (numbered 033-036)	1995	—	£2.25
EL4	M.G.B. (Cars) (numbered 037-040)	1995	—	£2.25
L10	Micro & Bubble Cars	2000	—	£3.75
EL4	Midland Red Buses (numbered 117-120)	2000	—	£2.25
L7	Mini Cooper (Cars)	1994	—	£3.00
EL4	Mini Cooper (Cars) (numbered 001-004)	1994	—	£2.25
EL4	Mini Cooper (numbered 161-164)	2010	—	£2.25
L10	Mini Cooper The 1960's	2007	—	£3.75
L10	The Mini Legend (Cars)	1995	—	£3.75
L7	Mini Moke 1961-89	2007	—	£3.00
L10	Mini (Cars) — Special Edition	1999	—	£3.75
EL4	Mini Vans (numbered 025-028)	1995	—	£2.25
EL4	Monte Carlo Minis (Cars) (numbered 009-012) ...	1994	—	£2.25
L9	Morris Minor (Cars)	1993	—	£3.75
EL4	Morris Minor (Cars) (numbered 045-048)	1995	—	£2.25
L9	Morris Minor — Fifty Years (Cars)	1998	—	£3.75
EL4	Morris Minor (Vans) (numbered 005-008)	1994	—	£2.25
L10	Motorcycling Greats...	1997	—	£3.75
L10	Municipal Buses of The 1950s and 1960s	2007	—	£3.75
L7	Norton (Motor Cycles) 1st Series	1993	—	£3.00
L7	Norton (Motor Cycles) 2nd Series	1998	—	£3.00
L7	Old Teddy Bears	1995	—	£3.00
L10	On The Move Classic British Lorries	2004	—	£3.75
EL6	Original Vespa — The Golden Age of Scootering...	2009	—	£3.00
EL4	Police Vehicles (numbered 013-016)	1994	—	£2.25
LT7	Pontiac GTO 1964-74	2004	—	£3.75
L7	Porsche 356 (1950-65)	2003	—	£3.00
L7	Porsche 911 (1963-77)...	2003	—	£3.00
L7	Porsche 911 (1978-98)...	2003	—	£3.00
L7	Racing & Rallying Mini Coopers of the 60's...	2000	—	£3.00
LT7	Racing Legends (Formula 1 Drivers)	2004	—	£3.75
L7	Range Rover (Cars)	1996	—	£3.00
L7	The Ringmaster — Michael Schumacher	2002	—	£3.00
L10	Road Haulage Classic British Lorries	2004	—	£3.75
LT10	Rootes Sixties Classics (Cars)	2005	—	£4.50
EL4	Southdown Buses (numbered 121-124)	2000	—	£2.25
L7	Spitfire (Cars)	1994	—	£3.00
L7	Sporting Ford (Cars)	1992	—	£3.00
EL4	Sporting Mini Cooper (numbered 157-160)...	2010	—	£2.25
L7	Spridget — Austin Healey Sprite & MG Midget			
	1958-79	2002	—	£3.00
L13	Superbikes of the 70s	2000	—	£4.50
L7	Tanks of WWII	2000	—	£3.00
L7	Teddies	1997	—	£3.00
L7	Teddy Bears	1994	—	£3.00
EL4	Teddy Bears (numbered 021-024)	1995	—	£2.25
EL4	Teddy Bear Families (numbered 017-020)	1995	—	£2.25
L10	35 Years of the Mini 1959-1994...	1994	—	£3.75
LT7	Thunderbird American Classics 1955-63 (Cars) ...	2003	—	£4.00

Qty		Date	Odds	Sets
	GOLDEN ERA (continued)			
L10	Traction Engines	1999	—	£3.75
EL4	Traction Engines (numbered 109-112)	2000	—	£2.25
EL4	Tractors 1st Series (numbered 073-076)...	1999	—	£4.00
EL4	Tractors 2nd Series (numbered 077-080)	1999	—	£4.00
L7	Tractors of the Fifties	1999	—	£3.00
L7	Tractors of the Sixties	1999	—	£3.00
L7	TR Collection (Triumph Cars)	1992	—	£3.00
L7	Triumph (Motor Cycles) 1st Series...	1993	—	£3.00
L7	Triumph (Motor Cycles) 2nd Series	1998	—	£3.00
L10	Triumph Herald 1959-71	2007	—	£3.75
L7	Triumph Saloon Cars 1960s & 1970s...	2002	—	£3.00
L7	Triumph Spitfire 1962-80	2007	—	£3.00
L7	Triumph Stag Motor Cars	1995	—	£3.00
L7	Triumph TR2 and TR3 1953-61	2007	—	£3.00
L7	Triumph TR4, TR5 and TR6 1961-76	2007	—	£3.00
L7	Triumph Vitesse 1962-71	2007	—	£3.00
L7	U.S. Military Vehicles of WWII	2001	—	£3.00
L7	Velocette (Motor Cycles)	1993	—	£3.00
L7	Vespa (Motor Cycles)	2000	—	£3.00
L7	Vincent Motor Cycles	1995	—	£3.00
L7	Vintage Vespa 1958-1966	2005	—	£3.00
EL4	Volkswagen Beetle (numbered 085-088)	1999	—	£4.00
EL4	Volkswagen Transporter (numbered 089-092)	1999	—	£4.00
L7	VW Transporter 1956-1961	2005	—	£3.00
EL6	VW Transporter Bus 1950-67	2008	—	£3.00
L7	VW Transporter 1968-80 Bay Window Models... ...	2007	—	£3.00
EL6	VW Transporter Type 2	2008	—	£3.00
LT7	World Champions (Formula 1 Drivers)	2004	—	£3.75

GOLDEN FLEECE (Australia)

L36	Dogs	1967	55p	£20.00

GOLDEN GRAIN TEA

25	Birds	1963	£1.20	—
25	British Cavalry Uniforms of the 19th Century	1965	50p	£12.50
25	Garden Flowers	1965	20p	£3.50
25	Passenger Liners	1966	36p	£9.00

GOLDEN WONDER

24	Soccer All Stars	1978	50p	£12.00
	Album		—	£6.00
14	Space Cards (yellow background)	1978	20p	£2.50
14	Space Cards (coloured)	1979	20p	£2.50
24	Sporting All Stars	1979	20p	£4.00
	Album		—	£6.00
24	TV All Stars	1979	20p	£2.50
36	World Cup Soccer All Stars	1978	50p	£18.00
	Album		—	£6.00

GOLF GIFTS LTD

M24	Ryder Cup 1989	1991	—	£15.00

Qty		Date	Odds	Sets

GOOD TIMES CREATIONS

Qty		Date	Odds	Sets
13	Golf Legends	2012	—	£8.50
23	Great Britons (Olympic Athletes Post War Gold Medalists)	2012	—	£12.00
13	Ladies of Rock	2013	—	£8.50
13	Legends of Rock...	2012	—	£8.50
13	Silkmen Legends (Macclesfield Town F.C.)	2012	—	£8.50
13	Twelve Days of Christmas	2012	—	£8.50

GOODIES LTD

Qty		Date	Odds	Sets
50	Doctor Who and the Daleks	1969	£10.00	—
25	Flags and Emblems...	1961	20p	£3.00
25	Indian Tribes	1969	£5.40	—
25	Mini Monsters...	1970	£1.80	—
25	The Monkees 1st Series	1967	£1.20	£30.00
25	The Monkees 2nd Series	1968	£5.00	—
24	Olympics	1972	£3.00	—
25	Pirates	1970	£3.20	—
25	Prehistoric Animals	1969	£3.00	—
25	Robbers and Thieves	1971	£2.20	—
25	Vanishing Animals	1971	£2.00	—
25	Weapons Through the Ages	1970	£1.80	—
25	Wicked Monarchs	1973	£1.60	£40.00
25	Wide World/People of Other Lands	1968	£1.40	£35.00
25	Wild Life	1969	£1.80	—
25	World Cup '74...	1974	£3.00	—

D.W. GOODWIN & CO.

Qty		Date	Odds	Sets
36	Careers for Boys and Girls	c1930	£8.00	—
24	Extra Rhymes 2nd Series...	c1930	£14.00	—
	Flags of All Nations (12 different backs):			
36	Series A Home Nursing	c1930	£6.00	—
36	Series B Common Ailments and Their Cures ...	c1930	£6.00	—
36	Series C Tenants' Rights	c1930	£6.00	—
36	Series D Gardening Hints	c1930	£6.00	—
36	Series E Household Hints	c1930	£6.00	—
36	Series F Poultry Keeping	c1930	£6.00	—
36	Series G Beauty Aids	c1930	£6.00	—
36	Series H The World's Great Women	c1930	£6.00	—
36	Series I First Aid	c1930	£6.00	—
36	Series J Cookery Recipes...	c1930	£6.00	—
36	Series K Cookery Recipes	c1930	£6.00	—
36	Series L General Knowledge	c1930	£6.00	—
36	Jokes Series	c1930	£10.00	—
36	Optical Illusions	c1930	£12.00	—
36	Ships Series	c1930	£10.00	—
24	Wireless Series	c1930	£14.00	—
36	World Interest Series	c1930	£7.00	—
24	World's Most Beautiful Birds	c1930	£9.00	—
24	World's Most Beautiful Fishes	c1930	£9.00	—

W. GOSSAGE & SONS LTD

Qty		Date	Odds	Sets
48	British Birds and their Eggs	1924	£3.00	—
48	Butterflies and Moths	1925	£2.00	—

70

Qty		Date	Odds	Sets
	GOWERS & BURGONS			
25	British Birds and Their Nests...	1967	30p	£7.50
25	The Circus	1966	£2.40	—
25	Family Pets	1967	20p	£3.00
25	People and Places	1966	20p	£3.00
25	Prehistoric Animals	1967	£1.00	£25.00
25	Sailing Ships Through the Ages...	1963	£1.00	£25.00
25	Veteran and Vintage Cars	1965	£1.20	£30.00
25	Veteran Racing Cars	1963	£1.20	£30.00
	GRAFFITI INC. (USA)			
LT90	Goldeneye, James Bond 007	1997	—	£9.50
	GRAIN PRODUCTS (New Zealand)			
M20	Adventuring in New Zealand...	1982	—	£10.00
M20	American Holiday	1986	—	£10.00
M20	Amusement Parks	1987	—	£10.00
M20	European Holiday	1980	—	£10.00
M20	Farming in N.Z.	1986	—	£10.00
M20	Fish of the New Zealand Seas	1981	—	£15.00
M20	Hong Kong Highlights	1991	—	£10.00
M20	Horse and Pony World...	1978	—	£12.00
EL9	How to Cartoon	1989	—	£9.00
M20	New Zealand Police...	1984	—	£15.00
M20	Our Heritage on Parade	1980	—	£10.00
M20	Our Mighty Forests	1979	—	£15.00
M20	Passport Los Angeles	1990	—	£10.00
M20	Space Exploration	1986	—	£15.00
M20	Television in New Zealand	1983	—	£10.00
EL10	Vintage and Veteran Cars	1985	—	£10.00
M20	World of Bridges	1981	—	£15.00
	GRAMPUS PHOTOS			
M20	Film Favourites (of 1920s)	1993	—	£10.00
M20	Modern Beauties (topless pin-up girls)	1992	—	£15.00
	GRANDSTAND			
LT100	Scottish Footballers Nos 1-100	1993	20p	£10.00
LT102	Scottish Footballers Nos 101-202	1993	20p	£10.00
	GRANGER'S			
12	Dr. Mabuse	c1920	£11.00	—
	GRANOSE FOODS LTD			
M48	Adventures of Billy the Buck	1952	20p	£4.00
M16	Air Transport	1957	30p	£5.00
M16	Animal Life...	1957	20p	£3.00
25	Animals in the Service of Man	c1965	£3.00	—
M16	Aquatic and Reptile Life	1957	20p	£5.00
M48	King of the Air...	1956	60p	—
M48	Life Story of Blower the Whale	1956	60p	—
M48	Lone Leo the Cougar	1955	60p	—
M20	150 Years of British Locomotives	1980	75p	£15.00
M48	Silver Mane, The Timber Wolf	1955	25p	£12.50
M16	Space Travel	1957	60p	£10.00
M48	Tippytail the Grizzly Bear	1956	20p	£7.50
M16	Water Transport	1957	20p	£3.00
M16	World Wide Visits	1957	20p	£3.00

Qty		Date	Odds	Sets
	W. GRANT & SONS LTD			
25	Clan Tartans	1992	–	£15.00

	GREATER MANCHESTER POLICE			
L24	British Lions (Rugby League)	1992	–	£7.50
EL15	British Stamps	1986	30p	£4.50
L24	Riversiders Wigan R.L.F.C.	1990	30p	£7.50
L12	Rugby 13 Hall of Fame	1992	–	£6.00
L24	Wigan R.L.F.C. Simply the Best...	1996	–	£12.00
L24	Wigan Rugby League F.C. (As Safe As ...)	2001	–	£6.00

	D. GREEN			
15	Alexandra The Greats (Crewe Alexandra F.C. Footballers)...	2006	–	£4.50

	GREGG (New Zealand)			
M48	Aquatic Birds	1965	40p	£20.00
	Album		–	£12.00
M40	Birds (Land Birds)	1963	60p	–
M40	Introduced Birds	1967	60p	£24.00
M40	Native Birds of New Zealand...	1971	30p	£12.00
M35	Rare and Endangered Birds	1977	60p	–
M40	Remarkable Birds	1969	60p	£24.00
M35	Unusual Birds of the World	1981	60p	

	GUINNESS			
EL6	Famous Guinness Alice Posters	1951	£12.50	£75.00
EL6	Famous Guinness for Strength Posters	1951	£12.50	£75.00
EL6	Guinness Advertisements, Set A	1932	£18.00	–
EL6	Guinness Advertisements, Set B	1932	£18.00	–
EL6	Guinness Advertisements, Set C	1932	£18.00	–

	H.M.A.F. TOYS			
EL9	H.M. Armed Forces	2009	–	£9.00

	HADDEN'S			
24	World's Most Beautiful Butterflies	c1920	£10.00	–

	NICHOLAS HALL			
25	War Series	1915	£20.00	–

	B. HALLS			
M35	Cricket Sudocards	2006	–	£5.00
M25	Rowing Sudocards	2006	–	£4.00

	HALPIN'S WILLOW TEA			
	Aircraft of the World:			
25	A Standard Set	1958	20p	£2.50
M20	B Two Pictures per Card, 25 Subjects	1958	£1.00	£20.00
25	Nature Studies	1957	20p	£5.00

	T. P. K. HANNAH (Confectionery)			
25	Top Flight Stars (Sport)	1960	£3.40	–

Qty		Date	Odds	Sets
	THE HAPPY HOME			
M8	Child Studies (silks)	c1915	£16.00	—
M9	Flags (silks)	c1915	£8.00	—
K14	The Happy Home Silk Button (silks)	c1915	£8.00	—
M9	Our Lucky Flowers (silks)	c1915	£14.00	—
M12	Women on War Work (silks)	c1915	£10.00	—
	HARBOUR DIGITAL			
M12	Birds in Flight	1997	—	£6.00
30	Cars At the Turn of the Century	1996	—	£9.00
M18	Cricket Teams of the 1890s	1997	—	£9.00
12	England & South Africa Cricketers	1996	—	£8.00
12	European Locomotives	1996	—	£6.00
L38	Famous Cricketers 1895	2000	—	£10.00
24	Golden Oldies Extracts from Famous Cricketer 1890	1996	—	£10.00
M20	Harry Vardon's Golf Clinic...	1997	—	£6.00
24	Historic Hampshire	1996	—	£6.00
24	Jaguar Cars	1996	—	£9.00
20	More Golden Oldies — Cricketers	1995	60p	£12.00
30	The Old Fruit Garden	1995	40p	£12.00
20	The Operatic Stage	1996	—	£7.00
L18	The Romance of India	2000	—	£6.00
M10	The Sea Mens Dress	1997	—	£8.00
18	Ships That Battle the Seas	1996	—	£9.00
M12	World Boxers 3rd Series	1996	—	£6.00
	HARDEN BROTHERS & LINDSAY LTD			
50	Animals of the World	1959	40p	£20.00
	Album		—	£6.00
50	British Birds and Their Eggs	1960	£1.00	—
50	National Pets	1961	20p	£4.00
	Album		—	£6.00
	HAROLD HARE			
L16	Animals and Pets plus album	1960	—	£10.00
	HARRISON			
25	Beauties	c1910	£26.00	—
25	Types of British Soldiers	c1910	£40.00	—
	HAT-TRICK CARDS			
15	Burnley (Footballers of the 1960s)	2011	—	£5.50
10	Everton Heroes (Footballers of the 1960s)	2011	—	£5.00
10	Hat-Trick Football Cards 1960/70s (black and white)	2011	—	£4.50
10	Hat-Trick Football Cards 1st Series (1970s footballers) coloured	2011	—	£5.00
10	Hat-Trick Football Cards 2nd Series (1970s footballers) coloured	2011	—	£5.00
10	Hat-Trick Football Cards 3rd Series (1970s footballers) coloured	2011	—	£5.00
10	Hat-Trick Football Cards 4th Series (1970s footballers) coloured	2011	—	£5.00
10	Hat-Trick Football Cards 5th Series (1970s footballers) coloured	2011	—	£5.00

Qty		Date	Odds	Sets

HAT-TRICK CARDS (continued)

Qty		Date	Odds	Sets
10	Hat-Trick Football Cards 6th Series (1970s footballers) coloured	2011	—	£5.00
10	Hat-Trick Football Cards 7th Series (1970s footballers) coloured	2011	—	£5.00
10	Hat-Trick Football Cards 8th Series (1970s footballers) coloured	2013	—	£5.00
10	Hat-Trick Football Cards 9th Series (1970s footballers) coloured	2013	—	£5.00
10	Kick Off 1st Series (Footballers of the 1960/70s) ...	2012	—	£5.00
10	Kick Off 2nd Series (Footballers of the 1960/70s)	2012	—	£5.00

J. HAWKINS & SONS LTD

M30	The Story of Cotton	c1920	£6.00	—

HAYMAN

24	World's Most Beautiful Butterflies	c1920	£10.00	—

HEDNESFORD TOWN FOOTBALL CLUB

24	Hednesford Town Football Stars (including Information Sheets)	1986	25p	£6.00

HEINZ

EL1	Australian Cricket Team England	1964	—	£15.00

HERALD ALARMS

10	Feudal Lords	1986	—	£20.00
EL10	Feudal Lords	1986	—	£12.00

HERTFORDSHIRE POLICE

L12	Stamp Out Crime	1983	—	£6.00

HITCHMAN'S DAIRIES LTD

25	Aircraft of World War II			
	A Black back	1966	36p	£9.00
	B Blue back	1966	£1.00	£25.00
25	Animals of the World	1965	60p	£15.00
25	British Birds and their Nests	1966	£1.00	—
25	British Railways	1964	20p	£3.50
25	Buses & Trams:			
	A White card	1966	20p	£4.00
	B Cream card	1966	20p	£4.00
25	Merchant Ships of the World	1962	60p	£15.00
25	Modern Wonders	1965	40p	£10.00
25	Naval Battles	1971	20p	£5.00
25	People and Places	1971	24p	£6.00
25	Regimental Uniforms of the Past	1973	20p	£2.50
25	Science in the 20th Century	1966	30p	£7.50
25	The Story of Milk	1965	60p	£15.00
25	Trains of the World	1970	£1.00	—

F. HOADLEY LTD

24	World's Most Beautiful Birds	c1920	£12.00	—

Qty		Date	Odds	Sets
	HOADLEY'S CHOCOLATES LTD (Australia)			
50	The Birth of a Nation	c1940	£2.00	—
50	British Empire Kings and Queens	c1940	£1.80	—
?33	Cricketers (black and white)	1928	£17.00	—
36	Cricketers (brown)	1933	£12.00	—
50	Early Australian Series...........................	c1940	£2.00	—
50	Empire Games and Test Teams...................	c1940	£9.00	—
50	National Safety Council	c1937	£3.00	—
40	Test Cricketers	1936	£15.00	—
M36	Test Cricketers	1938	£15.00	—
50	Victorian Footballers 1st Series nd 1-50	c1940	£8.00	—
50	Victorian Footballers 2nd Series nd 51-100.........	c1940	£8.00	—
50	Victorian Footballers (action studies)	c1940	£8.00	—
50	Wild West Series.................................	c1940	£2.20	—
	HOBBYPRESS GUIDES			
20	Preserved Railway Locomotives	1983	—	£3.00
20	Preserved Steam Railways 1st Series	1983	—	£3.00
20	Preserved Steam Railways 2nd Series	1984	—	£4.00
20	The Worlds Great Cricketers.....................	1984	—	£6.00
	THOMAS HOLLOWAY LTD			
EL60	Natural History Series — Animals (full length)	c1900	£10.00	—
EL39	Natural History Series — Animals' Heads	c1900	£8.00	—
EL39	Natural History Series — Birds	c1900	£8.00	—
EL50	Pictorial History of the Sports and Pastimes of All Nations	c1900	£12.00	—
	HOME AND COLONIAL STORES LTD			
26	Advertising Alphabet (boxed letters)	1913	£7.00	—
26	Advertising Alphabet different series (unboxed letters)	1913	£14.00	—
M100	Flag Pictures	1915	£4.00	—
100	War Pictures	1915	£4.00	—
M40	War Pictures (Personalities)	c1915	£6.50	—
M40	War Pictures (Scenes)...........................	c1915	£6.50	—
	HOME COUNTIES DAIRIES TEA			
25	Country Life	1964	20p	£5.00
25	International Air Liners	1968	20p	£2.50
25	The Story of Milk................................	1965	20p	£4.50
	THE HOME MIRROR			
M4	Cinema Star Pictures (silks)	1919	£15.00	—
	HOME PUBLICITY LTD			
?98	Merry Miniatures	c1950	£12.00	—
	HOME WEEKLY			
12	Little Charlie Cards	c1915	£18.00	—
	HORNIMAN TEA			
EL10	Boating Ways	c1910	£20.00	—
EL12	British Birds and Eggs	c1910	£20.00	—
48	Dogs	1961	20p	£5.00

ILLUSTRATIONS

1 Breygent. Vampirella
2 Cards Inc. U.F.O. (TV Series)
3 Rockwell. Suffragettes
4 J.F. Sporting Collectibles. Cricketers 1919-1939 4th Series
5 Topps. Star Wars Episode 1 Series 1
6 G. Payne Tea. American Indian Tribes
7 Victoria Gallery. Olympic Greats
8 Hunter. Infantry Regimental Colours The Royal Irish Regiment 2nd Series
9 Walls. Moonfleet
10 Walls. Skateboard Surfer
11 Cadbury. Dangerous Animals
12 Wrights Biscuits. Mischief Goes To Mars
13 Dutton's Beers. Team of Sporting Heroes
14 Lychgate Press. Eloise
15 Primrose. Happy Howlers
16 Mister Softee's. Top 20
17 P. Neill. Liverpool Legends
18 Victoria Gallery. Deep Sea Diving
19 Northamptonshire County Cricket Club. Northamptonshire County Cricketers 1905-1985
20 Lingford. British War Leaders
21 Brooke Bond Tea. International Soccer Stars
22 Impel. Star Trek The Next Generation
23 Skybox. Toy Story
24 Brooke Bond Tea. The Secret Diary of Kevin Tipps
25 Victoria Gallery. Ashes Winning Captains
26 Golden Era. Famous Footballers Newcastle United
27 Warus. The Beatles — The Beatles EP Series
28 Royal Navy Submarine Museum. Pictorial History of R.N. Submarines
29 M.P. Cards. The Geisha Collection
30 Eclipse Enterprises. National Lampoon Loaded Weapon 1
31 Gallery of Legends. The British Open Golf Collection
32 Rockwell. Post War Wimbledon Men's Champions 1st Series
33 Rockwell. Early Allied Warplanes
34 Bassett. Looney Tunes (yellow border)
35 Rockwell. The Hornby Book of Trains
36 Reflections. St Pancras International

37 Walls. Do You Know
38 Primrose. Andy Pandy
39 My Weekly. Soldiers of the King
40 Trade Cards Europe. Newcastle United F.C.
41 Inkworks. The Phantom
42 Sporting Profiles. Movie Idols John Wayne Series 3
43 Yorkshire Framing Co. England World Cup 2006
44 Sporting Profiles. Olympic Posters Winter Games
45 Perikim Cards. The English Springer Spaniel
46 Faulkner. Golf Humour (reprint)
47 Perennial Music Co. Forever Gold Entertainment Legends
48 Brooke Bond Tea. British Costume
49 Phillips Tea. Army Badges Past & Present
50 Redsky. Doris Day
51 Rockwell. World War II Posters The Services
52 Topps UK. American Baseball 1988
53 Primrose. Popeye 3rd Series
54 Sporting Profiles. The Rolling Stones Concert Posters
55 Goodies. The Monkees 1st Series
56 Primrose. Dads Army
57 Cadbury Schweppes. Age of the Dinosaur
58 Prescott Pickup. Railway Locomotives
59 Priory Tea. Bridges
60 Cadbury Transport
61 Cadbury Strange But True
62 Elkes Biscuits. Do You Know
63 Brooke Bond Tea. African Wild Life
64 Facchino. How or Why
65 Express Weekly. The Wild West
66 Moseley. Historic Buildings
67 Typhoo Tea. Characters From Shakespeare
68 Facchino. Cinema Stars
69 Typhoo Tea. Important Industries of the British Empire
70 Dryfoods. Zoo Animals
71 Trucards. Sport
72 Walls. Magicards Prehistoric Animals
73 Trucards. World War II

1

2

3

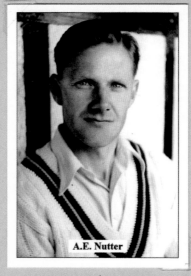

4

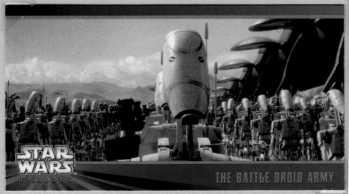

5

6

ΟΛΥΜΠΙΟΝΙΚΗΣ

SEBASTIAN COE

7

Regimental Colour
2nd Battalion The 18th (Royal Irish)
Regiment of Foot
1859-1903

8

9

10

Cadbury's
Dangerous Animals?

Polar Bear

16

11

12

DUTTON'S BEERS

BRIAN STATHAM CBE

13

ELOISE

14

WHY ARE FISH
WELL-EDUCATED?

15

16

LIVERPOOL LEGENDS
FIFTEEN OF THEIR GREATEST STARS

BILL SHANKLY
MANAGER 1959-1974

17

DEEP SEA DIVING

SINGLE TELEPHONE.

18

A. J. LAMB

19

LINGFORDS CUSTARD POWDER
LINGFORDS BAKING POWDER

HORTON

20

21

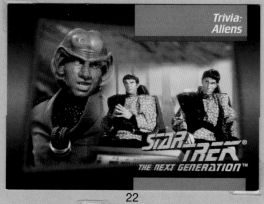

Trivia:
Aliens

STAR TREK
THE NEXT GENERATION™

22

23

Meet the Dolittles

DOLITTLE BROS.

24

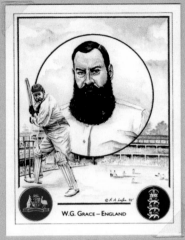

W.G. Grace – England

25

26

27

28

Wind's Whisper

29

30

S. SNEAD

31

BJORN BORG (SWEDEN)

32

33

34

35

36

37

38

39

40

41

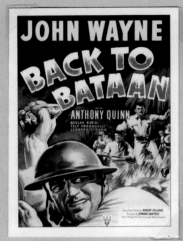

42

JERMAINE DEFOE

43

44

45

"Well forward."

Golf Humour c1900

46

47

48

49

50

51

52

53

54

55

56

57

58

59

60

61

62

63

65

66

OTHELLO   *Othello*

Covered with honour gained in battle
against the foes of Venice, Othello the
Moor married the fair Desdemona. She
loved her husband passionately but
Iago, former Lieutenant to the Moor,
caused unfounded suspicion to fall
upon her. In a fit of jealousy Othello
smothered Desdemona, subsequently,
learning her innocence, he put an end
to his own life.

Characters from Shakespeare.

Ty phoo Series of 25   No. 24

67

HOW DOES THE LEANING TOWER
OF PISA REMAIN STANDING !

64

GRACIE FIELDS
A.B.F.D.

68

Arms of
N. Rhodesia

Important Industries of the British Empire
NORTHERN RHODESIA : COPPER
In 1937, out of a total value of
exports amounting to £11,903,734,
Northern Rhodesia exported copper
to the value of £10,704,078.
168,813 tons of blister, or coarse,
copper were produced, and 28,724
tons of electrolytic copper. Other
valuable minerals found include
gold, silver, cobalt and zinc. Cattle
farming is also carried on in some
areas. Our picture shows a typical
Northern Rhodesian copper mine.
(Imperial Institute Diorama).

Ty phoo Series of 25   No. 16

69

70

71

72   73

Qty		Date	Odds	Sets

HORNIMAN TEA (continued)

Qty		Date	Odds	Sets
EL10	Naval Heroes	c1910	£20.00	—
48	Pets	1960	20p	£5.00
	Album		—	£8.00
48	Wild Animals	1958	20p	£5.00

HORSLEY'S STORES

Qty		Date	Odds	Sets
25	British Uniforms of the 19th Century	1968	40p	£10.00
25	Castles of Britain...	1968	£1.80	—
25	Family Pets	1968	50p	£12.50

HUDDERSFIELD TOWN F.C.

Qty		Date	Odds	Sets
M37	Huddersfield Town Players and Officials Season 1935-36	1936	£16.00	—

HULL CITY FOOTBALL CLUB

Qty		Date	Odds	Sets
L20	Footballers	1950	£12.00	—

HULL DAILY MAIL

Qty		Date	Odds	Sets
EL8	100 Years of Hull Public Transport	1980	—	£5.00

HUMBERSIDE POLICE

Qty		Date	Odds	Sets
EL36	East Yorkshire Scenes of Natural Beauty	1987	30p	£10.00

HUNT, CROP AND SONS

Qty		Date	Odds	Sets
15	Characters from Dickens	1912	£12.00	—

D.J. HUNTER

Infantry Regimental Colours:

Qty		Date	Odds	Sets
L7	The Argyll & Sutherland Highlanders 1st Series:			
	A Error Set with light yellow border	2008	—	£3.00
	B Corrected Set with orange border	2008	—	£3.00
L7	The Argyll & Sutherland Highlanders 2nd Series	2011	—	£3.00
L7	The Bedfordshire & Herefordshire Regiment ...	2009	—	£3.00
L7	The Black Watch 1st Series	2006	—	£3.00
L7	The Black Watch 2nd Series	2011	—	£3.00
L7	The Border Regiment	2005	—	£3.00
L7	The Buffs (Royal East Kent Regiment)	2005	—	£3.00
L7	The Cameronians (Scottish Rifles)	2009	—	£3.00
L7	The Cheshire Regiment	2006	—	£3.00
L7	The Coldstream Guards 1st Series...	2009	—	£3.00
L7	The Coldstream Guards 2nd Series ... ...'	2009	—	£3.00
L7	The Coldstream Guards 3rd Series	2009	—	£3.00
L7	The Connaught Rangers	2010	—	£3.00
L7	The Devonshire Regiment 1st Series	2006	—	£3.00
L7	The Devonshire Regiment 2nd Series...	2012	—	£3.00
L7	The Dorset Regiment 1st Series	2010	—	£3.00
L7	The Dorset Regiment 2nd Series	2012	—	£3.00
L7	The Duke of Cornwall's Light Infantry	2007	—	£3.00
L7	The Duke of Wellington's Regiment 1st Series ..	2006	—	£3.00
L7	The Duke of Wellington's Regiment 2nd Series	2011	—	£3.00
L7	The Durham Light Infantry 1st Series	2009	—	£3.00
L7	The Durham Light Infantry 2nd Series	2012	—	£3.00
L7	The East Lancashire Regiment 1st Series	2007	—	£3.00

D.J. HUNTER (continued)

Infantry Regimental Colours *continued*:

Qty		Date	Odds	Sets
L7	The East Lancashire Regiment 2nd Series … …	2012	—	£3.00
L7	The East Surrey Regiment … … … … … … …	2004	—	£3.00
L7	The East Yorkshire Regiment 1st Series … … .	2010	—	£3.00
L7	The East Yorkshire Regiment 2nd Series … …	2011	—	£3.00
L7	The Essex Regiment … … … … … … … … …	2007	—	£3.00
L7	The Gloucestershire Regiment 1st Series … …	2006	—	£3.00
L7	The Gloucestershire Regiment 2nd Series … …	2013	—	£3.00
L7	The Gordon Highlanders 1st Series … … … …	2004	—	£3.00
L7	The Gordon Highlanders 2nd Series … … … …	2013	—	£3.00
L7	The Green Howards… … … … … … … … … …	2010	—	£3.00
L7	The Grenadier Guards 1st Series … … … … …	2009	—	£3.00
L7	The Grenadier Guards 2nd Series … … … … …	2009	—	£3.00
L7	The Grenadier Guards 3rd Series … … … … …	2009	—	£3.00
L7	The Highland Light Infantry … … … … … … …	2007	—	£3.00
L7	The Irish Guards 1st Series … … … … … … …	2009	—	£3.00
L7	The Irish Guards 2nd Series … … … … … … …	2009	—	£3.00
L7	The King's Own Royal Regiment (Lancaster) 1st Series … … … … … … … … … … …	2005	—	£3.00
L7	The King's Own Royal Regiment (Lancaster) 2nd Series … … … … … … … … … …	2012	—	£3.00
L7	The King's Own Scottish Borderers 1st Series …	2004	—	£3.00
L7	The King's Own Scottish Borderers 2nd Series (includes errors and two number 3s but no number 4) … … … … … … … … … … … …	2013	—	£3.00
L7	The King's Own Yorkshire Light Infantry … … …	2009	—	£3.00
L7	The King's Regiment (Liverpool) … … … … … .	2005	—	£3.00
L7	The King's Shropshire Light Infantry 1st Series	2004	—	£3.00
L7	The King's Shropshire Light Infantry 2nd Series	2008	—	£3.00
L7	The Lancashire Fusiliers 1st Series:			
	A Error Set with 'Royal' in title … … … … …	2005	—	£3.00
	B Corrected Set without 'Royal' in title … …	2006	—	£3.00
L7	The Lancashire Fusiliers 2nd Series … … … …	2011	—	£3.00
L7	The London Regiment 1st Series … … … … …	2008	—	£3.00
L7	The London Regiment 2nd Series … … … … …	2008	—	£3.00
L7	The Loyal Regiment (North Lancashire) … … …	2009	—	£3.00
L7	The Manchester Regiment 1st Series … … … …	2005	—	£3.00
L7	The Manchester Regiment 2nd Series … … …	2012	—	£3.00
L7	The Middlesex Regiment (Duke of Cambridge Own) … … … … … … … … … … … … …	2007	—	£3.00
L9	Miscellaneous Colours … … … … … … … … …	2013	—	£3.00
L7	The North Staffordshire Regiment 1st Series …	2004	—	£3.00
L7	The North Staffordshire Regiment 2nd Series …	2008	—	£3.00
L7	The Northamptonshire Regiment 1st Series… …	2007	—	£3.00
L7	The Northamptonshire Regiment 2nd Series …	2013	—	£3.00
L7	The Oxfordshire & Buckinghamshire Light Infantry 1st Series … … … … … … … … …	2007	—	£3.00
L7	The Oxfordshire & Buckinghamshire Light Infantry 2nd Series … … … … … … … …	2011	—	£3.00
L7	The Prince of Wales's Leinster Regiment … … .	2010	—	£3.00
L7	The Queen's Own Cameron Highlanders 1st Series … … … … … … … … … … … … .	2006	—	£3.00
L7	The Queen's Own Cameron Highlanders 2nd Series… … … … … … … … … … … … …	2012	—	£3.00
L7	The Queen's Own Royal West Kent Regiment …	2005	—	£3.00

D.J. HUNTER (continued)

Infantry Regimental Colours *continued*:

Qty		Date	Odds	Sets
L7	The Queen's Royal Regiment (West Surrey) 1st Series	2004	—	£3.00
L7	The Queen's Royal Regiment (West Surrey) 2nd Series	2012	—	£3.00
L7	The Royal Berkshire Regiment	2010	—	£3.00
L7	The Royal Dublin Fusiliers	2010	—	£3.00
L7	The Royal Fusiliers (City of London Regiment)	2005	—	£3.00
L7	The Royal Hampshire Regiment	2008	—	£3.00
L7	The Royal Inniskilling Fusiliers 1st Series	2005	—	£3.00
L7	The Royal Inniskilling Fusiliers 2nd Series	2011	—	£3.00
L7	The Royal Irish Fusiliers	2008	—	£3.00
L7	The Royal Irish Regiment (18th Foot) 1st Series	2006	—	£3.00
L7	The Royal Irish Regiment (18th Foot) 2nd Series	2012	—	£3.00
L7	The Royal Irish Rifles	2010	—	£3.00
L7	The Royal Leicestershire Regiment 1st Series	2006	—	£3.00
L7	The Royal Leicestershire Regiment 2nd Series	2013	—	£3.00
L7	The Royal Lincolnshire Regiment	2006	—	£3.00
L7	The Royal Marines 1st Series	2008	—	£3.00
L7	The Royal Marines 2nd Series	2008	—	£3.00
L7	The Royal Munster Fusiliers	2010	—	£3.00
L7	The Royal Norfolk Regiment	2004	—	£3.00
L7	The Royal Northumberland Fusiliers	2005	—	£3.00
L7	The Royal Scots 1st Series	2004	—	£3.00
L7	The Royal Scots 2nd Series	2007	—	£3.00
L7	The Royal Scots Fusiliers 1st Series	2006	—	£3.00
L7	The Royal Scots Fusiliers 2nd Series	2012	—	£3.00
L7	The Royal Sussex Regiment	2007	—	£3.00
L7	The Royal Warwickshire Fusiliers	2005	—	£3.00
L7	The Royal Welch Fusiliers 1st Series	2008	—	£3.00
L7	The Royal Welch Fusiliers 2nd Series	2011	—	£3.00
L7	The Scots Guards 1st Series	2009	—	£3.00
L7	The Scots Guards 2nd Series	2009	—	£3.00
L7	The Scots Guards 3rd Series	2009	—	£3.00
L7	The Seaforth Highlanders 1st Series	2006	—	£3.00
L7	The Seaforth Highlanders 2nd Series	2012	—	£3.00
L7	The Seaforth Highlanders 3rd Series	2012	—	£3.00
L7	The Sherwood Foresters 1st Series	2004	—	£3.00
L7	The Sherwood Foresters 2nd Series	2007	—	£3.00
L7	The Somerset Light Infantry 1st Series	2010	—	£3.00
L7	The Somerset Light Infantry 2nd Series	2011	—	£3.00
L7	The South Lancashire Regiment	2007	—	£3.00
L7	The South Staffordshire Regiment 1st Series	2004	—	£3.00
L7	The South Staffordshire Regiment 2nd Series	2008	—	£3.00
L7	The South Wales Borderers 1st Series	2006	—	£3.00
L7	The South Wales Borderers 2nd Series	2011	—	£3.00
L7	The Suffolk Regiment 1st Series	2004	—	£3.00
L7	The Suffolk Regiment 2nd Series:			
	A Error Set with light yellow border	2008	—	£3.00
	B Corrected Set with orange border	2008	—	£3.00
L7	The Welch Regiment	2005	—	£3.00
L7	The Welsh Guards	2009	—	£3.00
L7	The West Yorkshire Regiment	2010	—	£3.00
L7	The Wiltshire Regiment 1st Series	2010	—	£3.00
L7	The Wiltshire Regiment 2nd Series	2011	—	£3.00

Qty		Date	Odds	Sets
	D. J. HUNTER (continued)			
	Infantry Regimental Colours *continued*:			
L7	The Worcestershire Regiment 1st Series	2004	—	£3.00
L7	The Worcestershire Regiment 2nd Series			
	(Error on No. 6 marked 1st Series)	2007	—	£3.00
L7	The York and Lancaster Regiment 1st Series ...	2009	—	£3.00
L7	The York and Lancaster Regiment 2nd Series ...	2011	—	£3.00
	R. HYDE & CO. LTD			
80	British Birds	1929	£2.25	—
80	Cage Birds	1930	£1.50	—
80	Canary Culture	1930	£1.30	—
?M22	Hyde's Cartoons	1908	£13.00	—
	IDEAL ALBUMS			
L25	Boxing Greats...	1991	—	£12.50
	IKON (Australia)			
LT81	Buffy The Story Continues	2003	—	£16.00
LT81	Buffy The Story So Far	2000	—	£16.00
LT81	Cricketer Australia 2003	2003	—	£15.00
	IMPEL (USA)			
LT150	An American Tail — Fievel Goes West	1991	—	£12.00
LT80	Laffs	1991	—	£8.00
LT160	Minnie 'N' Me	1991	—	£12.00
LT120	Star Trek The Next Generation	1992	—	£14.00
LT5	Star Trek The Next Generation Bonus Foreign			
	Language	1992	—	£5.00
LT160	Star Trek 25th Anniversary 1st Series	1991	—	£12.00
LT150	Star Trek 25th Anniversary 2nd Series	1991	—	£12.00
LT140	Terminator 2 — The Film	1991	—	£9.50
LT36	Trading Card Treats (Cartoon Characters)	1991	—	£8.00
LT90	U.S. Olympic Hall of Fame	1991	20p	£9.50
LT162	WCW Wrestling	1991	—	£12.00
	IMPERIAL PUBLISHING			
L20	American Golfers	1990	—	£8.50
L24	Birds of Britain	2000	—	£8.50
L6	Breeds of Cats	2000	—	£3.00
L6	Dogs — Airedale Terriers	1999	—	£3.00
L6	Dogs — Border Collies	1999	—	£3.00
L6	Dogs — Boxers	1999	—	£3.00
L6	Dogs — Bulldogs	1999	—	£3.00
L6	Dogs — Cocker Spaniels	1999	—	£3.00
L6	Dogs — Dachshunds	1999	—	£3.00
L6	Dogs — Dalmatians...	1999	—	£3.00
L6	Dogs — Dobermann	1999	—	£3.00
L6	Dogs — German Shepherds...	1999	—	£3.00
L6	Dogs — Golden Retrievers	1999	—	£3.00
L6	Dogs — Greyhounds	2000	—	£3.00
L6	Dogs — Jack Russell Terriers	1999	—	£3.00
L6	Dogs — Labrador Retrievers	1999	—	£3.00
L6	Dogs — Pekingese	1999	—	£3.00
L6	Dogs — Poodles...	1999	—	£3.00

Qty		Date	Odds	Sets
	IMPERIAL PUBLISHING (continued)			
L6	Dogs — Scottish Terriers	1999	—	£3.00
L6	Dogs — Staffordshire Bull Terriers	2000	—	£3.00
L6	Dogs — West Highland White Terriers	2000	—	£3.00
L6	Dogs — Yorkshire Terriers	1999	—	£6.00
L24	The History of The Olympic Games	1996	—	£12.00
L20	Native North Americans	1995	—	£8.50
L48	Olympic Champions	1996	—	£15.00
L18	Snooker Celebrities	1993	—	£12.00

IN LINE (USA)

Qty		Date	Odds	Sets
LT56	Motor Cycles	1993	—	£9.50

INDIAN MOTOCYCLE CO (USA)

Qty		Date	Odds	Sets
LT10	Indian Motorcycles	1993	—	£10.00

INKWORKS (USA)

Qty		Date	Odds	Sets
LT90	The Adventures of Pinocchio	1996	—	£9.50
LT81	Alias Season 1	2002	—	£11.00
LT81	Alias Season 2	2003	—	£10.00
LT81	Alias Season 3	2004	—	£9.50
LT81	Alias Season 4	2006	—	£9.50
LT90	Alien Legacy (The Four Films)	1998	—	£9.50
LT90	Alien v Predator — The Film	2004	—	£12.00
LT81	Aliens vs Predator Requiem	2007	—	£8.50
LT45	American Pride	2000	—	£5.00
LT90	Andromeda Season 1	2001	—	£9.50
LT90	Andromeda Reign of The Commonwealth	2004	—	£8.00
LT90	Angel Season 1	2000	—	£9.50
LT90	Angel Season 2	2001	—	£9.50
LT90	Angel Season 3	2002	—	£9.50
LT90	Angel Season 4	2003	—	£9.50
LT90	Angel Season 5	2004	—	£9.50
LT90	Buffy The Vampire Slayer Season 3	1999	—	£15.00
LT90	Buffy The Vampire Slayer Season 4	2000	—	£12.00
LT90	Buffy The Vampire Slayer Season 5	2001	—	£12.00
LT90	Buffy The Vampire Slayer Season 6	2002	—	£12.00
LT90	Buffy The Vampire Slayer Season 7	2003	—	£9.50
LT72	Buffy The Vampire Slayer Big Bads	2004	—	£12.00
LT72	Buffy The Vampire Slayer Connections	2003	—	£18.00
LT50	Buffy The Vampire Slayer Evolution	2002	—	£15.00
LT90	Buffy The Vampire Slayer Memories	2006	—	£8.50
LT81	Buffy The Vampire Slayer Men of Sunnydale	2005	—	£8.00
LT72	Buffy The Vampire Slayer Reflections	2000	—	£15.00
LT90	Buffy The Vampire Slayer 10th Anniversary	2007	—	£8.50
LT90	Buffy The Vampire Slayer Women of Sunnydale ...	2004	—	£9.50
LT72	Catwoman — The Movie	2004	—	£12.00
LT72	Charmed Season 1	2000	—	£9.50
LT72	Charmed Connections	2004	—	£11.00
LT72	Charmed Conversations	2005	—	£8.00
LT72	Charmed Destiny	2006	—	£8.00
LT72	Charmed Forever	2007	—	£8.00
LT72	Charmed The Power of Three	2003	—	£12.00
LT72	Family Guy Season 1	2005	—	£7.50
LT72	Family Guy Season 2	2006	—	£7.50
LT72	Firefly The Complete Collection	2006	—	£9.50

Qty		Date	Odds	Sets
	INKWORKS (USA) (continued)			
LT72	The 4400 Season 1	2006	–	£8.00
LT81	The 4400 Season 2	2007	–	£8.50
EL72	Godzilla – The Film	1998	–	£9.50
LT72	The Golden Compass – The Film...	2007	–	£9.50
LT72	Hell Boy – The Film	2004	–	£12.00
LT72	Hellboy Animated Sword of Storms	2006	–	£7.50
LT90	James Bond 007 3rd Series	1997	–	£20.00
LT72	Jericho Season 1	2007	–	£8.50
LT72	Jurassic Park III – The Movie	2001	–	£8.50
LT72	Looney Tunes Back in Action	2003	–	£9.50
LT90	Lost Season 1	2005	–	£8.50
LT90	Lost Season 2	2006	–	£8.50
LT90	Lost Season 3	2007	–	£8.50
LT81	Lost Revelations	2006	–	£8.00
LT90	Lost in Space – The Film	1998	–	£9.50
LT72	Lost in Space Archives...	1997	–	£8.00
LT9	Lost in Space Archives Movie Preview	1997	–	£4.00
LT90	Men in Black – The Film	1997	–	£9.50
LT81	Men In Black II – The Film	2002	–	£12.00
LT81	Mummy Returns – The Movie	2001	–	£9.50
LT72	The Osbournes	2002	–	£8.00
LT90	The Phantom – The Movie	1996	–	£9.50
LT90	Robots – The Movie	2005	–	£9.50
LT90	Roswell Season 1	2000	–	£9.50
LT72	Scooby Doo – The Movie	2002	–	£9.50
LT72	Scooby Doo 2 Monsters Unleashed	2004	–	£11.00
LT72	The Scorpion King – The Movie	2002	–	£12.00
LT72	Serenity – The Film	2005	–	£8.00
LT81	The Simpsons Anniversary Celebration	2000	–	£16.00
LT72	Simpsons Mania	2001	–	£12.00
LT90	Sleepy Hollow – The Movie...	1999	–	£9.50
LT72	Sliders (TV Sci-Fi Series)	1997	–	£9.50
LT90	Small Soldiers – The Film	1998	–	£9.50
LT90	Smallville Season 1	2002	–	£9.50
LT90	Smallville Season 2	2003	–	£14.00
LT90	Smallville Season 3	2004	–	£12.00
LT90	Smallville Season 4	2005	–	£9.50
LT90	Smallville Season 5	2007	–	£9.50
LT90	Smallville Season 6	2008	–	£9.50
LT72	The Sopranos Season 1	2005	–	£9.50
LT81	Spawn The Movie	1997	–	£9.50
LT90	Spawn The Toy Files	1999	–	£9.50
LT72	Spike The Complete Story (Buffy & Angel)	2005	–	£11.00
LT72	The Spirit – The Film	2008	–	£8.00
LT81	Starship Troopers – The Movie	1997	–	£9.50
LT90	Supernatural Season 1	2006	–	£9.50
LT90	Supernatural Season 2	2007	–	£8.50
LT81	Supernatural Season 3	2008	–	£9.50
LT72	Supernatural Connections	2008	–	£8.00
LT90	Titan A.E.	2000	–	£9.50
LT90	Tomb Raider – The Movie	2001	–	£9.50
LT81	Tomb Raider 2 – The Cradle of Life	2003	–	£9.50
LT90	Tomorrow Never Dies – James Bond 007	1997	–	£12.00
LT90	TV's Coolest Classics Volume One	1998	–	£9.50
LT72	Veronica Mars Season 1	2006	–	£9.50

Qty		Date	Odds	Sets
	INKWORKS (USA) (continued)			
LT81	Veronica Mars Season 2	2007	—	£9.50
LT81	Witchblade	2002	—	£9.50
LT90	The World Is Not Enough James Bond 007			
	the Movie	1999	20p	£12.00
LT90	The X Files Season 4 & 5...	2001	20p	£9.50
LT90	The X Files Season 6 & 7...	2001	—	£12.00
LT90	The X Files Season 8	2002	20p	£12.00
LT90	The X Files Season 9	2003	20p	£12.00
LT72	The X Files Connections	2005	—	£9.50
LT72	The X Files I Want to Believe — The Film	2008	—	£8.00

INTERNATIONAL HERITAGE

Qty		Date	Odds	Sets
L20	Squadrons and Aircraft of the RAF	1993	—	£12.00

INTREPID (Australia)

Qty		Date	Odds	Sets
LT100	Tennis — A.T.P. Tour	1996	—	£15.00
LT90	X-Files	1996	—	£9.50

IPC MAGAZINES LTD

Qty		Date	Odds	Sets
M25	Lindy's Cards of Fortune	1975	20p	£5.00
	My Favourite Soccer Stars (blue back):			
M32	Issued with 'Buster' including album	1970	£1.25	—
M32	Issued with 'Lion' including album	1970	£1.25	—
M32	Issued with 'Scorcher' including album	1970	£1.25	—
M32	Issued with 'Smash' including album	1970	£1.25	—
M32	Issued with 'Tiger' including album	1970	£1.25	—
	My Favourite Soccer Stars — (red back):			
M32	Issued with 'Buster and Jet' including album ...	1971	—	£26.00
M32	Issued with 'Lion and Thunder' including album	1971	—	£26.00
M32	Issued with 'Scorcher and Score' including			
	album	1971	—	£26.00
M32	Issued with 'Tiger' including album	1971	—	£26.00
M32	Issued with 'Valiant and TV21' including album	1971	—	£26.00

JOHN IRWIN & SON

Qty		Date	Odds	Sets
12	Characters from Dickens' Works	1912	£17.00	—
6	Characters from Shakespeare	c1910	£17.00	—

J. F. SPORTING COLLECTIBLES

Qty		Date	Odds	Sets
LT24	Abbeys, Monasteries & Priorys in The 20th Century	2011	—	£16.00
LT24	Academy Award Winners (Film Stars)	2010	—	£16.00
LT24	Ali — His Fights, His Opponents	2004	—	£16.00
LT24	The Armies of India	2010	—	£16.00
LT24	Association Footballers 1950s 1st Series	2013	—	£16.00
LT15	Australian Cricketers 1930	1999	—	£10.00
LT28	Australian Rugby League Tourists 1948	2002	—	£21.00
LT36	Battle of The Roses Pre War Personalities			
	(Cricketers)	2003	—	£27.00
LT24	Belle Vue Speedway Aces	2001	—	£16.00
LT24	Birds in Britain and Their Eggs 1st Series	2013	—	£16.00
LT24	Boer War Officers	2008	—	£16.00
LT25	Boxers World Champions	2000	—	£16.00
L24	British Yeomanry Uniforms	2004	—	£16.00

Qty		Date	Odds	Sets
	J. F. SPORTING COLLECTIBLES (continued)			
LT24	Bygone Railway Stations and Architecture	2012	–	£16.00
LT24	Castles in Britain in the 20th Century 1st Series ...	2009	–	£16.00
LT24	Castles in Britain in the 20th Century 2nd Series ..	2010	–	£16.00
LT25	Centenarians Cricket's 100 100s Club	2008	–	£18.00
LT24	Classic Movies of the 1930s 1st Series	2013	–	£16.00
LT24	Classic Steam Locos 1st Series	2007	–	£16.00
LT24	Classic Steam Locos 2nd Series	2008	–	£16.00
LT24	Country Seats in the 19th Century in Great Britain & Ireland	2013	–	£16.00
LT24	Cowboy Film & TV Stars	2011	–	£16.00
LT24	Cricket England One Cap Winners	2011	–	£16.00
LT24	Cricket Parade 1940/50s	2001	–	£24.00
LT24	Cricket Personalities 1940/50s 1st Series	2000	–	£16.00
LT24	Cricket Personalities 1940/50s 2nd Series	2003	–	£16.00
LT24	Cricket Personalities 1940/50s 3rd Series	2004	–	£16.00
LT24	Cricket Personalities 1940/50s 4th Series	2005	–	£16.00
LT24	Cricket Personalities 1940/50s 5th Series	2006	–	£16.00
LT24	Cricket Personalities 1940/50s 6th Series	2007	–	£16.00
LT24	Cricket Personalities 1940/50s 7th Series	2009	–	£16.00
LT24	Cricket Personalities 1940/50s 8th Series	2013	–	£16.00
LT24	Cricket Personalities 1960s 1st Series	2007	–	£16.00
LT24	Cricket Personalities 1960s 2nd Series	2007	–	£16.00
LT24	Cricket Personalities 1960s 3rd Series	2008	–	£16.00
LT24	Cricket Personalities 1960s 4th Series	2010	–	£16.00
LT24	Cricketers From Overseas 1919-1939 1st Series ...	2009	–	£16.00
LT36	Cricketers From Overseas 1940/50s 1st Series ...	2005	–	£27.00
LT36	Cricketers From Overseas 1960s	2007	–	£27.00
LT24	Cricketers in Action 1940/50s 1st Series	2004	–	£16.00
LT24	Cricketers in Action 1940/50s 2nd Series	2005	–	£16.00
LT24	Cricketers In Action 1940/50s 3rd Series	2005	–	£16.00
LT24	Cricketers In Action 1940/50s 4th Series	2006	–	£16.00
LT24	Cricketers in Action 1960s 1st Series	2007	–	£16.00
LT24	Cricketers in Action 1960s 2nd Series	2007	–	£16.00
LT24	Cricketers in Action 1960s 3rd Series	2008	–	£16.00
LT24	Cricketers The Golden Age Pre Great War 1st Series	2009	–	£16.00
LT24	Cricketers The Golden Age Pre Great War 2nd Series	2010	–	£16.00
LT24	Cricketers The Golden Age Pre Great War 3rd Series	2010	–	£16.00
LT24	Cricketers The Golden Age Pre Great War 4th Series	2011	–	£16.00
LT24	Cricketers The Golden Age Pre Great War 5th Series	2011	–	£16.00
LT24	Cricketers The Golden Age Pre Great War 6th Series	2012	–	£16.00
LT24	Cricketers 1919-1939 1st Series	2008	–	£16.00
LT24	Cricketers 1919-1939 2nd Series	2008	–	£16.00
LT24	Cricketers 1919-1939 3rd Series	2008	–	£16.00
LT24	Cricketers 1919-1939 4th Series	2009	–	£16.00
LT24	Cricketers 1919-1939 5th Series	2009	–	£16.00
LT24	Cricketers 1919-1939 6th Series	2010	–	£16.00
LT24	Cricketers 1919-1939 7th Series	2011	–	£16.00
LT24	Cricketers 1919-1939 8th Series	2013	–	£16.00
LT24	The Empire's Air Power World War II	2007	–	£16.00

Qty		Date	Odds	Sets
	J. F. SPORTING COLLECTIBLES (continued)			
LT24	Families in First Class Cricket	2011	—	£16.00
LT24	Famous British Film & Stage Stars 1920-40s			
	1st Series	2009	—	£16.00
LT24	Famous Film Stars 1940/50s 1st Series	2008	—	£16.00
LT24	Famous Film Stars 1940/50s 2nd Series	2009	—	£16.00
LT24	Famous Film Stars 1940/50s 3rd Series	2009	—	£16.00
LT36	Famous Footballers Pre-Great War 1st Series... ...	2003	—	£27.00
LT36	Famous Footballers Pre-Great War 2nd Series ...	2005	—	£27.00
LT20	Famous Heavyweight Fights...	2007	—	£12.50
LT24	Film Stars of The World 1930s 1st Series	2009	—	£16.00
LT24	Film Stars of The World 1930s 2nd Series	2013	—	£16.00
LT24	Films and Their Stars 1940/50s...	2012	—	£16.00
LT36	Football Stars of the Seventies	2000	—	£27.00
LT36	Football Wartime Guests	2011	—	£27.00
LT24	Footballers In Action 1940/50s 1st Series	1999	—	£16.00
LT36	Forties Favourites in Action (Footballers) 1st Series	2004	—	£27.00
LT36	Forties Favourites in Action (Footballers) 2nd Series	2005	—	£27.00
LT36	Forties Favourites in Action (Footballers) 3rd Series	2005	—	£27.00
LT36	Forties Favourites in Action (Footballers) 4th Series	2006	—	£27.00
LT36	Forties Favourites in Action (Footballers) 5th Series	2007	—	£27.00
LT24	Gentlemen v Players Pre-War Personalities			
	(Cricketers) 1st Series	2003	—	£16.00
LT24	Gentlemen v Players Pre-War Personalities			
	(Cricketers) 2nd Series...	2004	—	£16.00
LT24	Gentlemen v Players Pre-War Personalities			
	(Cricketers) 3rd Series	2007	—	£16.00
LT24	George Formby Tribute	2011	—	£16.00
LT24	Golf Personalities 1940/50s	2005	—	£16.00
LT24	Music Hall Artistes	2013	—	£16.00
LT24	Ocean Steamers Through The Ages	2010	—	£16.00
LT24	Popular Footballers 1919-1939 1st Series	2002	—	£16.00
LT24	Popular Footballers 1919-1939 2nd Series	2002	—	£16.00
LT24	Popular Footballers 1919-1939 3rd Series	2002	—	£16.00
LT36	Popular Footballers 1919-1939 4th Series	2002	—	£27.00
LT36	Popular Footballers 1919-1939 5th Series	2003	—	£27.00
LT36	Popular Footballers 1919-1939 6th Series	2006	—	£27.00
LT36	Popular Footballers 1919-1939 7th Series	2007	—	£27.00
LT36	Popular Footballers 1919-1939 8th Series	2007	—	£27.00
LT36	Popular Footballers 1919-1939 9th Series	2008	—	£27.00
LT36	Popular Footballers 1919-1939 10th Series...	2009	—	£27.00
LT36	Popular Footballers 1919-1939 11th Series...	2012	—	£27.00
LT36	Popular Footballers 1960s 1st Series...	1999	—	£27.00
LT36	Popular Footballers 1970s 1st Series...	2001	—	£27.00
LT36	Popular Footballers 1970s 2nd Series	2001	—	£27.00
LT36	Popular Footballers 1970s 3rd Series...	2002	—	£27.00
LT36	Popular Footballers 1970s 4th Series...	2004	—	£27.00
LT36	Popular Footballers 1970s 5th Series...	2004	—	£27.00
LT24	Rugby League Stars 1940/50s 1st Series	2002	—	£16.00
LT24	Rugby League Stars In Action 1940/50s...	2007	—	£16.00
	Scottish Clan Tartans 1st Series:			
L24	A Titled Scottish Clan Tartans	2002	—	—
LT24	B Titled Scottish Tartans...	2012	—	£16.00
L24	Scottish Clan Tartans 2nd Series	2003	—	£16.00
LT24	Seaside Piers in England and Wales in The 20th			
	Century 1st Series	2009	—	£16.00

Qty		Date	Odds	Sets
	J. F. SPORTING COLLECTIBLES (continued)			
LT24	Seaside Piers in England and Wales in The 20th			
	Century 2nd Series	2010	−	£16.00
LT24	Sheffield Tigers Speedway Post-War Legends... ...	2001	−	£16.00
LT24	Sherlock Holmes Film Stars	2011	−	£16.00
LT24	Silent Movie Stars 1st Series	2009	−	£16.00
LT24	Silver Screen Actors 1930s	2012	−	£16.00
LT24	Silver Screen Actresses 1930s	2009	−	£16.00
L24	Soldiers of Queen Victoria's Army 1837-1901			
	1st Series	2004	−	£16.00
L24	Soldiers of Queen Victoria's Army 1837-1901			
	2nd Series	2007	−	£16.00
LT24	Speedway All-Time Greats 1st Series	1999	−	£16.00
LT24	Speedway All-Time Greats 2nd Series	1999	−	£16.00
LT24	Speedway All-Time Greats 3rd Series	2000	−	£16.00
LT24	Speedway Personalities In Action 1st Series	2000	−	£16.00
LT24	Speedway Personalities In Action 2nd Series	2000	−	£16.00
LT24	Speedway Riders From Overseas 1st Series	2006	−	£16.00
LT24	Stars of Bradford Speedway	2004	−	£16.00
LT30	Stars of Football 1940s	2002	−	£21.00
LT24	Stars of London Speedway	2002	−	£16.00
LT24	Stars of Midland Speedway 1st Series	2006	−	£16.00
LT36	Stars of Scottish Football Pre-Great War			
	1st Series	2004	−	£27.00
LT25	Stars of Scottish Speedway	2002	−	£17.50
LT20	Tennis Stars 1950/60s	2007	−	£13.00
LT24	Test Cricketers 1950s/60s 1st Series	2013	−	£16.00
L24	Uniforms of The Royal Regiment of Artillery	2003	−	£16.00
LT28	Victorian Cricket Personalities	2000	−	£20.00
LT24	Victorian Cricketers	2012	−	£16.00
LT24	Victorian Railway Stations	2011	−	£16.00
LT15	Wembley Speedway Stars 1st Series...	1999	−	£10.00
LT21	Wembley Speedway Stars 2nd Series	2000	−	£16.00
LT24	Western Films and Their Stars	2013	−	£16.00
L24	World Heavyweight Boxing Champions	1999	−	£16.00
LT20	World Heavyweight Championship Contenders ...	2000	−	£12.00
LT24	World War II Films and Their Stars	2013	−	£16.00
	JACOB & CO.			
EL24	Banknotes that Made History	1975	20p	£2.50
	Album		−	£3.50
EL6	Build Your Own Prize	1972	£3.00	£18.00
EL16	Circus	c1970	£3.00	−
EL8	Doodles	1970	£3.00	−
32	Famous Picture Cards from History	1978	20p	£3.00
EL18	Happy Families	1967	£3.00	−
EL6	Nursery Rhymes	1969	£3.00	−
M30	School of Dinosaurs	1994	−	£9.00
EL10	Through the Looking Glass	1971	£3.00	−
25	Vehicles of All Ages	1924	£2.60	£65.00
25	Zoo Series:			
	A (brown back)	1924	£1.80	£45.00
	B (green back)	1924	£1.40	£35.00
	M.V. JASINSKI (USA)			
LT36	Flash Gordon 1st Series	1990	−	£15.00

M.V. JASINSKI (USA) (continued)

LT36	Flash Gordon's Trip to Mars 2nd Series	1991	—	£15.00
LT36	Flash Gordon Conquers the Universe 3rd Series ...	1992	—	£15.00

JENSEN PRINT

10	Soccer Stars (1960s Footballers) 1st Series	1998	—	£4.50
10	Soccer Stars (1960s Footballers) 2nd Series	1998	—	£4.50

JERMYN'S

25	National Heroes	c1975	£2.40	—

JESK CONFECTIONERY

25	Buses and Trams	1959	£1.20	£30.00

JIFFI

M64	Kama Sutra	1989	—	£50.00

JONDER (UK)

L53	Doctor Who — Playing Cards	1996	—	£20.00

R.L. JONES & CO. LTD

24	Jet Aircraft of the World	1957	20p	£4.00

JUNIOR EXPRESS WEEKLY

25	Jeff Hawke & Space Gen.	1956	£3.00	—

JUNIOR PASTIMES

52	Popular English Players	c1960	£3.50	—
52	Popular Players (Footballers)	c1960	£7.00	—
52	Popular Railway Engines	c1960	£2.40	—
M80	Star Pix	c1960	£1.80	—

JUST SEVENTEEN (Periodical)

M17	Advertisement Stickers	1985	—	£2.50

K.P. FOODS

K30	Flintstones, Wackey Races, Tom & Jerry	1996	—	£15.00
20	Wonderful World of Nature	1983	75p	£15.00

KADLE KARDS

10	Who (Doctor Who)	2007	—	£4.50

KANE PRODUCTS LTD

50	British Birds and Their Eggs	1960	60p	£30.00
25	Cricket Clubs & Badges	1957	20p	£3.00
L50	Disc Stars	1959	£1.60	£80.00
M50	Disc Stars	1960	£3.00	—
50	Dogs	1955	£3.00	—
L72	Film Stars	1955	£2.00	—
50	Flags of All Nations	1959	30p	£15.00
25	Football Clubs and Colours	1957	20p	£3.50
50	Historical Characters	1957	25p	£12.50
25	International Football Stars	1958	£1.20	£30.00
30	Kings and Queens	1959	50p	£15.00
L30	Kings and Queens	1959	50p	£15.00

Qty		Date	Odds	Sets

KANE PRODUCTS LTD (continued)

Qty		Date	Odds	Sets
25	Modern Motor Cars	1959	70p	£17.50
50	Modern Racing Cars	1954	50p	£25.00
25	National Pets Club 1st Series	1958	24p	£6.00
25	National Pets Club 2nd Series	1958	£2.40	—
25	1956 Cricketers 1st Series	1956	80p	£20.00
25	1956 Cricketers 2nd Series	1956	80p	£20.00
25	Red Indians 1st Series...	1957	£1.00	£25.00
25	Red Indians 2nd Series	1958	£1.00	£25.00
25	Roy Rogers Colour Series	1958	£2.40	£60.00
25	Roy Rogers Series	1957	£4.00	—
50	Space Adventure...	1955	70p	£35.00
50	20th Century Events	1959	£1.50	—
K50	Wild Animals	1954	20p	£4.00

KARDOMAH

Qty		Date	Odds	Sets
K50	Wild Animals	c1920	£5.00	—
K50	Wonders of the Deep	c1920	£5.00	—

M. & S. KEECH

Qty		Date	Odds	Sets
15	Australian Cricket Team 1905	1986	—	£4.00
15	English Cricketers 1902	1987	—	£6.00

KEEPSAKE (USA)

Qty		Date	Odds	Sets
LT72	The Blue and the Gray — Civil War Art by Kunstler	1997	—	£16.00
LT72	Wild West by Mort Kunstler	1996	—	£9.50

JAMES KEILLER & SON LTD

Qty		Date	Odds	Sets
ELP18	Film Favourites	c1925	£10.00	—
25	Scottish Heritage...	c1970	40p	£10.00

KELLOGG COMPANY OF GREAT BRITAIN LTD

Qty		Date	Odds	Sets
K16	Animals — 3D	c1968	£3.50	—
M56	Crunchy Nut Corn Flakes Playing Cards...	1986	—	£4.00
12	Famous Firsts...	1963	20p	£2.50
M20	Gardens to Visit	1987	30p	£6.00
	Album		—	£15.00
16	History of British Military Aircraft	1963	£1.25	£20.00
12	International Soccer Stars	1961	£1.00	£12.00
M8	International Soccer Tips	c1978	£5.00	—
40	Motor Cars:			
	A Black and white	1949	£3.50	—
	B Coloured	1949	£6.00	—
M20	Olympic Champions	1991	£1.50	—
K8	Prehistoric Monsters and the Present...	1985	£1.50	£12.00
16	Ships of the British Navy	1962	£1.25	£20.00
12	The Story of the Bicycle	1960	£3.25	—
	Story of the Locomotive 1st Series:			
16	A Inscribed 'A Series of 16'...	1962	£1.50	£24.00
12	B Inscribed 'A Series of 12'...	1962	£4.00	—
16	The Story of the Locomotive 2nd Series:			
	A Inscribed 'Series 2'...	1965	£1.50	£24.00
	B Without 'Series 2'	1965	£3.50	—
16	Veteran Motor Cars	1962	£1.00	£16.00

Qty		Date	Odds	Sets
	KELLOGG (Canada)			
M32	Dinosaur Stickers	1992	–	£5.00
	General Interest Set 1:			
M15	Aeroplanes	c1937	£2.00	–
M15	Campcraft	c1937	£2.00	–
M15	Firearms...	c1937	£2.00	–
M15	People of the World	c1937	£2.00	–
M15	Ships of War	c1937	£2.00	–
M15	Sports Records	c1937	£2.00	–
M30	Sports Tips	c1937	£2.00	–
M15	Strange Animals	c1937	£2.00	–
M15	Vehicles of War	c1937	£2.00	–
	General Interest Set 2:			
M15	Aeroplanes	c1938	£2.00	–
M15	Denizens of the Deep	c1938	£2.00	–
M15	Dogs	c1938	£2.00	–
M15	Great Deeds in Canada	c1938	£2.00	–
M15	History of Flight	c1938	£2.00	–
M30	Sports Tips	c1938	£2.00	–
M15	Things to Make	c1938	£2.00	–
M15	Tricks...	c1938	£2.00	–
M15	Uniforms...	c1938	£2.00	–
	General Interest Set 3:			
M15	Aeroplanes	c1939	£2.00	–
M15	Boats	c1939	£2.00	–
M15	First Aid Tips	c1939	£2.00	–
M15	Historic Automobiles...	c1939	£2.00	–
M15	Picture Puzzles	c1939	£2.00	–
M15	Sports History	c1939	£2.00	–
M30	Sports Tips	c1939	£2.00	–
M15	Strange Birds	c1939	£2.00	–
M15	Things to Make	c1939	£2.00	–
	KENT COUNTY CONSTABULARY			
L24	England World Cup Squad	1982	£2.50	–
L30	England World Cup Squad	1986	£2.50	–
L30	Olympic Athletes	1988	£1.50	£45.00
	KENT COUNTY CRICKET CLUB			
50	Cricketers of Kent	1985	–	£9.00
	KENTUCKY FRIED CHICKEN			
M20	Star Wars Episode 1	1999	38p	£7.50
	KICK OFF CARDS			
10	Kick Off (Footballers of the 1970s)...	2011	–	£5.00
	KIDDY'S FAVOURITES LTD			
52	New Popular Film Stars	c1950	£4.00	–
52	Popular Boxers	c1950	£2.50	–
52	Popular Cricketers	c1950	£3.50	–
65	Popular Film Stars	c1950	£5.00	–
52	Popular Footballers	c1950	£3.50	–
52	Popular Olympics	c1950	£3.00	–

Qty		Date	Odds	Sets

KIDDY'S FAVOURITES LTD (continued)
'Popular' Players (Footballers):

Qty		Date	Odds	Sets
75	A Five red hearts at top of front	c1950	£7.00	—
52	B Three red shamrocks at top of front	1949	£3.50	—
52	'Popular' Speedway Riders	c1950	£3.50	—

KILPATRICKS BREAD (USA)
LT33	Star Trek The Motion Picture	1979	—	£12.00

KIMBALL (USA)
LT12	The Space Shuttle	1992	—	£6.00

KING FEATURES (USA)
LT50	Beetle Bailey	1995	—	£9.50
LT50	Blondie (Comic Strip)	1995	—	£9.50

KINGS, YORK (Laundry)
K25	Flags of all Nations (silks)...	1954	£3.00	—
30	Kings and Queens of England	1954	20p	£5.00

KING'S LAUNDRIES LTD (Walthamstow)
25	Famous Railway Engines	c1955	£5.00	—
25	Modern British Warplanes	1953	£4.00	—
25	Modern Motor Cycles	c1955	£4.00	—
25	Radio and Television Stars	c1955	£4.00	—

KING'S SPECIALITIES
26	Alphabet Rhymes	c1915	£12.00	—
24	'Don'ts' or Lessons in Etiquette	c1915	£11.00	—
25	Great War Celebrities & Warships	c1915	£12.00	—
25	Heroes of Famous Books	1914	£11.00	—
25	King's Discoveries	c1915	£11.00	—
25	King's Servants	c1915	£11.00	—
24	Proverbs	c1915	£11.00	—
37	Unrecorded History	c1915	£11.00	—
100	War Pictures	c1915	£12.00	—
25	Where King's Supplies Grow...	1913	£11.00	—

KITCHEN SINK (USA)
LT90	The Crow — City of Angels — The Film	1996	—	£9.50
LT90	Universal Monsters of the Silver Screen	1996	—	£12.00

KLENE (GUM)
L50	Footballers (Val Footer Gum)	1936	£35.00	—
L80	Shirley Temple and Film Stars (Nos 1 to 80)	1935	£6.00	—
L70	Shirley Temple (black and white) (Nos 81 to 100 & 161 to 210))	1935	£7.00	—
L80	Shirley Temple (coloured) title in blue (Nos 81 to 160)	1935	£7.00	—
L60	Shirley Temple (coloured) title in black (Nos 101 to 160)	1935	£7.00	—

J. KNIGHT (Hustler Soap)
20	Animals of the World (cut outs):			
	A Corner officially cut...	1925	£1.25	£25.00
	B Uncut card	1925	£1.50	£30.00

J. KNIGHT (Hustler Soap) (continued)

Qty		Date	Odds	Sets
20	Animals of the World 2nd Series (cut outs):			
	A Corner officially cut...	1925	£1.25	£25.00
	B Uncut card	1925	£1.50	£30.00
20	Animals of the World 3rd Series (cut outs):			
	A Corner officially cut...	1925	£1.25	£25.00
	B Uncut card	1925	£1.50	£30.00
30	Regimental Nicknames:			
	A Corner officially cut...	1925	£2.25	—
	B Uncut card	1925	£2.75	—

KNOCKOUT

Qty		Date	Odds	Sets
20	Super Planes of Today...	c1960	30p	£6.00

KNORR

Qty		Date	Odds	Sets
L6	Great Trains of Europe...	1983	£5.00	—

KRAFT CHEESE

Qty		Date	Odds	Sets
12	Historic Military Uniforms	1971	20p	£2.50
	Album		—	£4.00

KROME (USA)

Qty		Date	Odds	Sets
LT50	Betty Boop 1st Series	1996	—	£20.00
LT45	Betty Boop 2nd Series	1997	—	£20.00
LT100	Bloom County Outland Chromium	1995	—	£12.00
LT50	Creed Chromium From Lightning Comics	1996	—	£12.00

LACEY'S CHEWING GUM

Qty		Date	Odds	Sets
50	Footballers...	c1925	£32.00	—
40	Uniforms	c1925	£22.00	—

F. LAMBERT & SONS LTD (Tea)

Qty		Date	Odds	Sets
25	Before our Time	1961	20p	£2.50
25	Birds & Their Eggs	1960	£1.00	£25.00
25	Butterflies & Moths	1966	24p	£6.00
25	Cacti	1962	20p	£2.50
25	Car Registration Numbers 1st Series	1959	40p	£10.00
25	Car Registration Numbers 2nd Series	1960	£1.20	—
25	Football Clubs and Badges	1958	20p	£4.00
25	Game Birds and Wild Fowl	1964	60p	£15.00
25	Historic East Anglia	1963	20p	£2.50
25	Interesting Hobbies	1965	60p	£15.00
25	Passenger Liners	1965	60p	£15.00
25	Past and Present	1964	20p	£2.50
25	People and Places	1966	20p	£5.00
25	Pond Life	1964	50p	£12.50
25	Sports and Games	1964	20p	£5.00

LAMPORT AND HOLT

Qty		Date	Odds	Sets
L1	TSS Vandyck and TSS Voltaire:			
	A Criss Cross border	1925	—	£12.00
	B Chain border	1925	—	£25.00

LANCASHIRE CONSTABULARY

Qty		Date	Odds	Sets
L12	Austin Rover Motor Cars	1987	50p	£6.00

Qty		Date	Odds	Sets
	LANCASHIRE CONSTABULARY (continued)			
11	History of the Police	1989	25p	£2.50
24	Lancashire Police File	1986	50p	£12.00

LATARCHE

L25	Skiing Through the Ages	1994	—	£7.50

LEAF GUM CO. (USA)

L72	Star Trek	1967	—	—

LEAF SALES CONFECTIONERY LTD

L50	Cliff Richard	1961	£3.50	—
EL50	Do You Know?	1961	50p	£25.00
EL90	Famous Artists	1963	£2.20	—
EL50	Famous Discoveries and Adventures	1961	£2.40	—
EL40	The Flag Game	1960	60p	£24.00
EL50	Footballers (Portraits and Caricatures)	1961	£2.40	—
EL50	Totem Pole Talking Signs	1960	80p	£40.00

LEEDS POLICE

L20	Leeds Rugby League F.C.	1992	—	£6.00
L20	Leeds Rugby League F.C.	1993	—	£6.00
L20	Leeds Rugby League F.C.	1994	—	£6.00
L20	Leeds Rugby League F.C.	1995	—	£6.00

LEESLEY (USA)

LT100	Big Foot (Trucks)	1988	—	£9.50

LEGENDS

L20	British Rock Legends	1993	—	£9.00

LEICESTER MERCURY

LT40	Leicester City Footballers	2003	—	£30.00

LEVER BROS

20	British Birds and Their Nests ('Sunlight Soap')	1961	20p	£3.00
152	Celebrities, white borders large and small	1905	£4.00	—
M39	Celebrities, black border	1905	£7.00	—

LIEBIG

We publish a separate Liebig catalogue listing around 1500 different series issued throughout Europe from 1872 to 1973. The prices in the 2009 catalogue will remain valid until further notice.

2009 Edition ... ... £4.50 post free

LIFEGUARD PRODUCTS (Soap etc.)

25	British Butterflies	1955	20p	£5.00

LIME ROCK (USA)

LT40	Dallas Cowboys Cheerleaders	1992	—	£6.00
LT110	Dream Machines Nos 1-110 (Motoring)	1991	—	£15.00
LT55	Dream Machines Nos 111-165 (Motoring & Powerboats)	1992	—	£9.50
LT110	Heroes of the Persian Gulf	1991	—	£9.50
LT49	Los Angeles Raiderettes Cheerleaders	1992	—	£6.00

Qty		Date	Odds	Sets
	LIME ROCK (USA) (continued)			
LT31	Miami Dolphins Cheerleaders	1992	—	£6.00
LT36	New Orleans Saintsations Cheerleaders...	1992	—	£6.00
LT44	Pro Cheerleaders (basketball)	1991	—	£6.00
LT55	Space Art	1993	—	£9.50

JOSEPH LINGFORD & SON LTD (Baking Powder)

36	British War Leaders	1950	£1.65	£60.00

LIPTON LTD (Tea)

50	Conquest of Space	1962	80p	—
60	Flags of the World	1966	20p	£12.00
	Album		—	£6.00

LIPTON TEA (Canada)

48	Animals and Their Young	1991	60p	£30.00

LIPTON TEA (Overseas)

EL30	Birds of Prey (Arabic text)...	c1970	—	£25.00

J. LIVINGSTONE

11	Flags, Arms and Types of Nations	c1905	£25.00	—

LOBO (Portugal)

L12	David Bowie 1993 Calendar Back	1992	—	£5.00
L12	Iron Maiden (Pop Group) 1990 Calendar Back ...	1989	—	£5.00
L16	Iron Maiden (Pop Group) 1992 Calendar Back ...	1991	—	£5.00
L12	Michael Jackson 1992 Calendar Back	1991	—	£5.00
L12	Mick Jagger (Rolling Stones) 1992 Calendar Back	1991	—	£5.00

LOCAL AUTHORITIES CATERERS ASSOCIATION

5	British Sporting Personalities	1997	—	£2.50

LODGE PLUGS LTD

M20	Vintage Cars	c1950	£12.00	—

LONGLEAT HOUSE

25	Longleat House	1966	20p	£2.50

LOS ANGELES POLICE (USA)

EL30	Dodgers Baseball Players	1988	—	£10.00

LOT-O-FUN

MP4	Sports Champions	1922	£6.00	—

G.F. LOVELL & CO. LTD

?31	British Royalty Series	1911	£35.00	—
36	Football Series	1910	£65.00	—
25	Photos of Football Stars	1928	£24.00	—

B. LUND

6	Rugby Union Six Nations 2000	2000	—	£1.25
6	Rugby Union Six Nations 2001	2001	—	£1.25
8	Rugby Union World Cup 1999	1999	—	£1.50

Qty		Date	Odds	Sets
	LYCHGATE PRESS			
10	Amazing World	2004	—	£3.50
10	The Beatles	2002	—	£4.00
12	The Beatles 1963	2005	—	£4.75
10	Eloise (Adult Fantasy Art)............................	2001	—	£4.00
10	Hendrix (Jimi)	2010	—	£5.00
10	Images of the Great War 1st Series	2013	—	£5.00
10	Images of the Great War 2nd Series	2013	—	£5.00
10	Images of the Great War 3rd Series	2013	—	£5.00
10	Images of the Great War 4th Series	2013	—	£5.00
10	Kings of Comedy......................................	2005	—	£4.00
10	Rock'N'Roll Greats	2005	—	£4.50
10	60's Soccer Stars	2006	—	£4.50
L25	Soccer Gallery (Footballers of the 1960s)	2000	—	£10.00
18	Tottenham (Footballers)	2000	—	£6.50
10	The Wonderful World of Inventions	2004	—	£4.00
	J. LYONS			
48	Australia	1959	20p	£7.50
L16	Catweazle Magic Cards	1971	40p	£6.00
32	HM Ships 1902-1962:			
	A Descriptive Back	1962	25p	£8.00
	B Advertisement Back	1962	40p	£12.00
	Illustrated Map of the British Isles:			
M35	A Set of 35	1959	£1.00	—
M1	B Key card	1959	—	£2.00
EL6	150th Anniversary of the Postage Stamp	1990	40p	£2.50
K100	Tricks and Puzzles	1926	£3.50	—
48	What Do You Know?	1957	20p	£4.00
24	Wings Across the World:			
	A Descriptive Back	1961	25p	£6.00
	B Advertisement Back	1961	40p	£10.00
24	Wings of Speed:			
	A Descriptive Back	1960	20p	£5.00
	B Advertisement Back	1960	32p	£8.00
	LYONS MAID (Ice Cream)			
40	All Systems Go	1967	£2.00	—
M20	Banknotes	1974	—	£10.00
M12	Beautiful Butterflies	1974	—	£6.00
25	Birds and Their Eggs	1963	£1.00	—
40	British Wildlife.......................................	1970	£1.25	£50.00
M20	County Badge Collection	1974	—	£5.00
EL12	Did You Know?	1975	—	£6.00
40	European Adventure	1969	£1.50	—
40	Famous Aircraft	1965	50p	£20.00
	Album		—	£6.00
40	Famous Cars	1966	£2.00	—
40	Famous Locomotives	1964	£2.50	—
48	Famous People	1962	£1.00	£50.00
M12	Farmyard Stencils	1977	—	£8.00
M14	Flowers	c1976	—	£28.00
EL12	Horses in the Service of Man	1984	—	£4.00
40	International Footballers	1971	£5.00	—
40	Into the Unknown	1968	£1.50	£60.00
15	Jubilee Kings and Queens of England	1977	£2.00	—

Qty		Date	Odds	Sets
	LYONS MAID (Ice Cream) (continued)			
EL10	Junior Champs	1983	—	£3.50
50	100 Years of Motoring	1961	£1.20	—
40	On Safari	1969	£1.20	—
40	Pop Scene...	1970	£2.50	—
40	Pop Stars	1969	£2.50	—
M10	Pop Stars (shaped)	1975	50p	£5.00
40	Soccer Stars	1970	£4.00	—
40	Space Age Britain	1968	£1.50	—
40	Space Exploration	1963	£2.00	—
25	Space 1999	1976	£5.40	—
25	Star Trek	1980	£5.40	—
50	Train Spotters...	1962	60p	£30.00
40	Views of London	1967	90p	£36.00
	M.P. CARDS			
L12	The Geisha Collection	1997	—	£10.00
L14	Nishikigo — Koi Carp	1997	—	£15.00
L6	The Staffordshire Bull Terrier...	1996	—	£6.00
	MAC FISHERIES			
L12	Gallery Pictures	1924	£1.50	£18.00
L14	Japanese Colour Prints	1924	£1.50	—
L12	Poster Pointers	1925	£1.25	£16.00
L12	Sporting Prints	1923	£4.50	—
	Wm. McEWAN & CO. LTD			
25	Old Glasgow	1929	£12.00	—
	McVITIE & PRICE			
8	The European War Series	1915	£17.00	—
	MADISON CONFECTIONERY PRODUCTS LTD			
L48	Disc Jockey 1st Series...	1957	£2.50	—
L48	Disc Jockey 2nd Series	1958	£1.60	£80.00
L50	Recording Stars	c1960	£1.80	—
	THE MAGNET LIBRARY			
MP6	Football Teams (11.11.22 to 16.12.22)	1922	£5.00	—
MP4	Football Teams (2.2.23 to 24.2.23)...	1923	£5.00	—
MP15	Footballers	1922	£4.00	—
	MAINSTREAM PUBLISHING			
13	The Story of Newcastle United's No. 9 Heroes ...	2004	—	£6.00
	MANCHESTER EVENING NEWS			
L30	Manchester City & United Footballers	1976	£3.00	—
	MANOR BREAD (USA)			
LT33	Star Trek The Motion Picture	1979	—	£15.00
	R. MARCANTONIO LTD			
50	Interesting Animals (black and white)	1953	20p	£4.00

Qty		*Date*	*Odds*	*Sets*

MARKET-SCENE LTD (New Zealand)

Qty		Date	Odds	Sets
M21	Super Stars of Wrestling 1st Series	1989	£1.00	—
M21	Super Stars of Wrestling 2nd Series	1989	£1.00	—
M21	Super Stars of Wrestling 3rd Series	1990	£1.00	—

A.T. MARKS

Qty		Date	Odds	Sets
14	Australian Cricketers 1893	1993	—	£3.00
8	Buses in Luton	1991	—	£2.50
M35	Cricket (1900 Period) unnumbered	1994	—	£5.00
M16	Cricket (1900 Period) 1st Series nos 1-16	1994	—	£3.00
M16	Cricket (1900 Period) 2nd Series nos 17-32	1995	—	£3.00
M16	Cricket (1900 Period) 3rd Series nos 33-48.........	1995	—	£3.00
M8	Cricket (1900 Period) 4th Series nos 49-56.........	1995	—	£2.50
12	Derbyshire Cricketers 1895	1993	—	£3.00
13	Essex Cricketers 1895	1993	—	£3.00
11	Gloucestershire Cricketers 1892	1990	—	£2.50
13	Gloucestershire Cricketers 1894	1993	—	£3.00
13	Hampshire Cricketers 1895	1993	—	£3.00
11	Kent Cricketers 1892	1991	—	£3.00
14	Kent Cricketers 1897	1993	—	£3.00
13	Kent Cricketers 1909	1991	—	£3.00
12	Lancashire Cricketers 1892	1992	—	£3.00
14	Lancashire Cricketers 1895	1993	—	£3.00
13	Leicestershire Cricketers 1895	1993	—	£3.00
11	Middlesex Cricketers 1892	1990	—	£2.50
12	Middlesex Cricketers 1895	1993	—	£3.00
12	Middlesex Cricketers 1903	1990	—	£2.50
11	Northamptonshire Cricketers 1912...................	1990	—	£3.00
13	Nottinghamshire Cricketers 1895	1992	—	£3.00
12	Somerset Cricketers 1894	1992	—	£3.00
11	Surrey Cricketers 1892	1990	—	£3.00
13	Surrey Cricketers 1896	1993	—	£3.00
11	Sussex Cricketers 1892	1990	—	£3.00
15	Sussex Cricketers 1895	1993	—	£3.00
12	Warwickshire Cricketers 1895	1992	—	£3.00
12	Yorkshire Cricketers 1892.................................	1991	—	£3.00
17	Yorkshire Cricketers 1898.................................	1993	—	£3.00
12	Yorkshire Cricketers 1903.................................	1990	—	£2.50

MARLOW CIVIL ENGINEERING

Qty		Date	Odds	Sets
25	Famous Clowns	1990	—	£30.00

MARS CONFECTIONS LTD

Qty		Date	Odds	Sets
25	Ceremonies of the Coronation:			
	A Caption on front in black, back in black	1937	£1.80	—
	B Caption on front in blue, back in black	1937	£1.20	£30.00
	C Caption on front in blue, back in blue	1937	£4.60	—
50	Famous Aeroplanes, Pilots and Airports	1938	£1.80	£90.00
50	Famous Escapes	1937	£1.50	£75.00
50	Famous Film Stars	1939	£1.60	£80.00
25	Wonders of the 'Queen Mary'	1936	£1.80	£45.00

JAMES MARSHALL (GLASGOW) LTD

Qty		Date	Odds	Sets
30	Colonial Troops	1900	£35.00	—
10	Recipes/House Hints	c1930	£5.00	—
10	Recipes (coloured)	c1930	£5.00	—

96

Qty		Date	Odds	Sets
	THE MASTER VENDING CO. LTD (Chewing Gum)			
L25	A Bombshell for the Sheriff	1959	£1.00	£25.00
L16	Cricketer Series, New Zealand	1958	£1.25	£20.00
L50	Did You Know? (Football Cards)	1959	£1.50	—
L50	Football Tips (2 printings)	1958	£1.80	—
L100	Jet Aircraft of the World:			
	A Send 3/6 for 20 page album	1958	£2.00	—
	B Send for details of the Album	1958	£2.00	—
	C German Text	1958	£2.50	—
L25	Taxing the Sheriff	1959	£1.00	£25.00
L36	Tommy Steele...	1960	£3.50	—
	MASTERS			
L12	Food From Britain	1986	20p	£2.50
	MATCH WEEKLY			
M36	Euro Football	1988	—	£2.50
L31	FA Cup Facts File	1986	25p	£7.50
	MATCHBOX INT. LTD			
75	Matchbox Models	1985	60p	£45.00
	MATCHDAY CARDS			
EL18	Stockport County F.C. 2010-11	2010	—	£6.00
EL16	Stockport County F.C. 2011-12	2011	—	£6.00
	MAXILIN MARKETING CO. LTD			
25	Motor Cars...	1951	20p	£5.00
	MAXX (UK)			
LT76	British Athletics nos 1-76	1992	20p	£10.00
LT74	British Athletics nos 77-150	1992	20p	£10.00
	MAYNARDS LTD			
12	Billy Bunter Series	c1920	£22.00	—
8	European War Series	c1915	£17.00	—
17	Football Clubs	1932	£35.00	—
18	Girl Guides...	c1920	£17.00	—
50	Girls of All Nations	1924	£5.00	—
12	Strange Insects	c1920	£5.00	—
12	Wonders of the Deep	c1920	£6.00	—
	World's Wonder Series:			
12	A Numbered...	c1920	£5.00	—
10	B Unnumbered	c1920	£6.00	—
	MAYPOLE			
25	War Series	1915	£10.00	—
	MAZAWATTEE (Tea)			
L39	Kings and Queens	c1905	£4.50	—
	MEADOW DAIRY CO.			
50	War Series	1914	£9.00	—

Qty		Date	Odds	Sets
	MELOX			
L50	Famous Breeds of Dogs	1937	£7.00	—
M32	Happy Families (Dogs)...	1937	£8.00	—

MERCURY HOUSE CONSUMER PUBLICATIONS LTD

L4	PM Car Starter ('Popular Motoring')	1972	60p	£2.50

MERLIN

LT120	Football Premier League	1994	—	£10.00
LT88	Football Premier League	1996	—	£18.00
LT161	Football Premier League Gold	1997	—	£25.00
LT150	Football Premier League Gold	1998	—	£20.00
LT150	Football Premier League Gold	1999	—	£20.00
LT20	Football Premier League Gold Club Badges Nos A1 to A20	1999	—	£15.00
LT10	Football Premier League Gold World Cup Super-stars etc. Nos B1 to B10	1999	—	£15.00
LT105	Football Premier League Gold	2000	—	£15.00
LT20	Football Premier League Gold — Top Scorers... ...	2000	—	£12.00
LT20	Football Premier League Gold — Key Players... ...	2000	—	£12.00
LT80	Rugby League Footballers Nos 1-80	1991	20p	£9.00
LT80	Rugby League Footballers Nos 81-160	1991	20p	£9.00
LT100	Shooting Stars (Footballers) Nos 1-100	1991	20p	£10.00
LT100	Shooting Stars (Footballers) Nos 101-200	1991	20p	£10.00
LT100	Shooting Stars (Footballers) Nos 201-300	1991	20p	£10.00
LT96	Shooting Stars (Footballers) Nos 301-396	1991	20p	£10.00
LT125	Star Wars Trilogy	1997	20p	£15.00
LT96	World Wrestling Federation Gold Series Part 1 ...	1992	20p	—
LT96	World Wrestling Federation Gold Series Part 2 ...	1992	20p	—
LT75	World Wrestling Federation Stars Nos 1-75...	1991	20p	—
LT75	World Wrestling Federation Stars Nos 76-150	1991	20p	—

MERRYSWEETS LTD

L48	Telegum TV Stars	1958	£1.60	—
L48	World Racing Cars	1959	£3.00	—

GEOFFREY MICHAEL PUBLISHERS LTD

40	Modern Motor Cars (booklets)	1953	£1.50	—

MIDLAND CARTOPHILIC BRANCH

L24	Silhouettes of Veteran & Vintage Cars	1991	—	£6.00

MIDLAND COUNTIES

M20	Banknotes	1974	—	£12.50
M12	Farmyard Stencils	1977	—	£4.00
M24	Kings of the Road	1977	—	£8.00
EL10	Steam Power	1978	—	£5.00

MIDLAND COUNTIES & CADBURY

12	Action Soldiers	1976	35p	£4.00

MILK MARKETING BOARD

25	Prehistoric Animals	1964	24p	£6.00

Qty		Date	Odds	Sets
	MILLERS (Tea)			
25	Animals and Reptiles	1962	20p	£3.00
	MINUTE MAID/UPPER DECK (USA)			
LT25	World Cup All Stars (Football)	1994	—	£10.00
	ROBERT R. MIRANDA LTD			
50	150 Years of Locomotives:			
	A White lettering on black panel	1957	20p	£6.00
	B Black lettering on white background	1958	20p	£5.00
50	100 Years of Motoring	1955	20p	£5.00
25	Ships Through the Ages	1958	40p	£10.00
50	Strange Creatures	1960	20p	£6.00
	MIS-SPENT YOUTH			
L55	Toon Traders (Newcastle Utd. Footballers)	1996	—	£12.00
	MISTER SOFTEE LTD (Ice Cream)			
M12	Beautiful Butterflies	1977	60p	£7.00
M20	County Badge Collection	1976	25p	£5.00
L12	Did You Know?	1976	35p	£4.00
25	Do You Know?	1961	£3.50	—
L20	Famous Sports Trophies (shaped)	1975	—	£12.00
M12	Farmyard Stencils	1977	40p	£5.00
M24	1st Division Football League Club Badges	1972	—	£8.00
L12	Horses in the Service of Man	1977	£1.25	£15.00
M24	Kings of the Road (car radiator badges)	1977	30p	£7.50
20	Mister Softee's TOP 20	1963	70p	£14.00
EL12	Mister Softee TOP 10 ('Record Mirror' blue printed back — no address)	1964	50p	£6.00
EL12	First 12 Subjects: Mister Softee's Top Ten (black printing on back 'Win a Big Prize')	1965	£1.50	£18.00
EL12	Second 12 Subjects:			
	A Mister Softee's Top Ten — address '350 King Street'	1966	£5.00	—
	B Lord Neilson's Star Cards, address '350 King Street'	1966	£2.00	—
EL12	Third 12 Subjects: Lord Neilson's Star Cards — no address...	1967	£1.50	£18.00
EL24	Lord Neilson's Star Cards ('Disc and Music Echo') unnumbered	1968	£1.50	£36.00
EL24	Mister Softee's Pop Parade ('Disc and Music Echo') numbered	1969	£1.25	£30.00
EL24	Lord Neilson's Star Cards ('Disc and Music Echo') numbered	1969	£1.75	—
M24	Mister Softee Pop Discs (circular card)	1973	£1.25	£30.00
L24	Lord Neilson Star Discs (circular card)	1970	£1.50	£36.00
15	Moon Mission	1962	£2.30	—
M10	Pop Stars (star shaped)	1975	—	£10.00
M20	Stamp in a Million	1976	—	£10.00
L10	Steam Power	1978	30p	£3.00
M4	Super Human Heroes	1979	—	£2.50
25	TV Personalities	1962	£3.00	—
EL12	Your World	1963	20p	£3.00

Qty		Date	Odds	Sets
	MISTER SOFTEE & CADBURY			
12	Action Soldiers	1976	40p	£5.00
	MITCHAM FOODS LTD			
25	Aircraft of Today	1960	20p	£5.00
25	Aquarium Fish 1st Series	1957	£2.00	£50.00
25	Aquarium Fish 2nd Series	1957	20p	£3.00
50	Butterflies and Moths (issued in pairs)	1959	£1.20	—
25	Footballers	1956	£3.00	—
50	Mars Adventure	c1960	£6.00	—
25	Motor Racing	1957	£2.00	£50.00
	MOBIL OIL CO. LTD			
EL36	The Story of Grand Prix Motor Racing	1970	55p	£20.00
25	Veteran and Vintage Cars	1963	£2.40	£60.00
24	Vintage Cars	1966	20p	£5.00
	MODERN BOY			
16	Fighting Planes of the World	1936	£4.50	—
32	Mechanical Wonders of 1935	1935	£2.50	—
	MOFFAT BROS			
L100	Cinema Artistes	1914	£12.00	—
	MOFFAT (B. & G. LTD)			
EL102	Money That Made History	1971	20p	£9.00
	MOLASSINE (Vims)			
50	Dogs (full length)			
	A Title boxed	1963	£1.50	—
	B Title unboxed	1963	£1.50	—
50	Dogs (head and shoulder)	1964	£2.00	—
25	Dogs at Work	1971	20p	£3.50
12	Dogs of All Countries	1925	£9.00	—
50	Puppies	1966	£2.00	—
	MONTAGU MOTOR MUSEUM			
M24	Veteran & Vintage Cars 1st Series	1961	£3.50	—
M24	Veteran & Vintage Cars 2nd Series	1961	£5.00	—
	MONTY GUM			
M54	Bay City Rollers (Playing Card inset)	1978	60p	£32.00
L72	Daily Fables	1969	33p	£25.00
M94	Dallas	1981	—	£12.00
LT50	Elvis	1978	—	£80.00
M98	Flags + 2 varieties (nos. 59 and 92 not issued) ...	c1980	—	£7.00
L56	Footballers (Playing Card inset)	1961	£3.00	—
M54	Hitmakers (Playing Card inset)	1978	50p	—
M72	Kojak	1975	—	£36.00
M54	Kojak (Playing Card inset) black back	1976	50p	£27.00
M56	Kojak (Playing Card inset) red back	1976	70p	—
L55	Motor Cars (Playing Card inset) Symbols 36-38mm apart	1960	£1.75	—
L56	Motor Cars (Playing Card inset) Symbols 33-34mm apart	1960	£1.50	—

Qty		Date	Odds	Sets
	MONTY GUM (continued)			
M64	Space Alpha 1999	1978	50p	£32.00
L56	Vintage Cars	1962	£1.40	—
L52	World Aircraft (Playing Card inset)	c1960	£3.00	—
	MORLEY LTD			
10	The Morley Circus	c1960	£3.00	—
	MORNING FOODS LTD			
1	Advertisement Card...	c1955	—	£5.00
P25	British Planes:			
	A Unnumbered	1953	60p	£15.00
	B Numbered...	1953	£7.00	—
P50	British Trains	1952	£7.00	—
25	British Uniforms	1954	24p	£6.00
12	The Cunard Line:			
	A Black back	1957	20p	£2.50
	B Blue back	1957	35p	£4.00
50	Modern Cars	1954	40p	£20.00
50	Our England	1955	20p	£6.00
25	Test Cricketers	1953	£2.40	—
25	World Locomotives:			
	A Black back	1956	20p	£3.00
	B Blue back	1956	£1.00	£25.00
	E.D.L. MOSELEY			
M25	Historical Buildings	1956	20p	£3.00
	MOTOR ART (USA)			
LT110	Iditarod (Sled Dog Race Across Alaska)	1992	—	£9.50
	MOTOR CYCLE NEWS			
M24	Best of British Motor Cycling (including poster)	1988	—	£2.50
	MOTOR MAGAZINE			
24	The Great British Sports Car (including album) ...	1988	25p	£6.00
	MOTOR SPORT CHARITY MEMORABILIA			
50	Formula 1 World Championship	1999	—	£10.00
	MURCO PETROLEUM			
50	Airlines of the World	1978	—	£4.00
	R.S. MURRAY & CO.			
9	Alphabet Cards	c1930	£25.00	—
	MUSEUM OF BRITISH MILITARY UNIFORMS			
25	British Cavalry Uniforms	1987	—	£7.50
25	Military Maids	1987	—	£7.50
25	Warriors Through the Ages	1987	—	£7.50
	MUSGRAVE BROTHERS LTD			
25	Birds	1961	£1.00	£25.00
25	Into Space	1961	30p	£7.50

Qty		Date	Odds	Sets
MUSGRAVE BROTHERS LTD (continued)				
25	Modern Motor Cars	1963	70p	£17.50
25	Pond Life	1963	50p	£12.50
25	Products of the World	1961	20p	£4.00
25	Tropical Birds	1965	30p	£7.50
25	Wild Flowers	1961	60p	£15.00
MUSICAL COLLECTABLES				
25	Gilbert & Sullivan 1st Series	1995	—	£6.00
25	Gilbert & Sullivan 2nd Series	1995	—	£6.00
MY WEEKLY				
M9	Battle Series (silk)	1916	£8.00	—
M12	Floral Beauties (silk)	c1915	£8.00	—
M15	Language of Flowers (silk)	c1915	£8.00	—
M51	Lucky Emblems (silk)	c1915	£9.00	—
M6	Lucky Flowers (silk)	c1915	£12.00	—
M12	Our Soldier Boys (silk)	c1915	£8.00	—
M14	Soldiers of the King (silk)	c1915	£8.00	—
M6	Sweet Kiss Series (silk)	c1915	£8.00	—
M6	War Heroes (silk)	c1915	£8.00	—
NABISCO FOODS LTD				
K5	Aces in Action	1980	£4.00	—
M24	Action Shots of Olympic Sports	1980	£2.00	—
L4	Adventure Books	1970	£6.00	—
EL20	Champions of Sport	1961	£3.00	—
EL6	Eagle Eye	1979	—	£2.50
12	ET — The Extra-Terrestrial	1982	40p	£5.00
M24	Footballers	1970	£3.00	—
EL8	Football Tactics (England Soccer Stars)	1977	—	£12.00
EL12	Freshwater Fishes of Britain	1974	—	£15.00
M10	History of Aviation	1970	£2.50	£25.00
K4	Johan Cruyff Demonstrates	1980	£5.00	—
EL10	Kevin Keegan's Keep Fit with the Stars	1977	—	£12.00
EL6	Kevin Keegan's Play 'N' Score	1977	—	£7.00
EL10	Motor Show	1960	£3.00	—
L6	World Super Stars and Sporting Trophies	1980	£4.00	—
NAC (USA)				
LT100	Branson on Stage (TV Music Show)	1992	—	£8.00
NASSAR (Gold Coast)				
25	Transport — Present and Future	1955	20p	£5.00
NATIONAL GALLERY				
EL24	Masterpieces	1978	—	£6.00
NATIONAL SPASTICS SOCIETY				
24	Famous County Cricketers (booklet)	1958	£2.00	£50.00
24	Famous Footballers	1958	80p	£20.00
NECA				
LT24	Beetlejuice The Movie	2001	—	£6.00

Qty		Date	Odds	Sets
	NEEDLERS			
13	Military Series...	1916	£25.00	—
	PHILIP NEILL			
15	Arsenal Double Legends of 1970/71	2002	—	£5.50
15	Arsenal 79 (A Tribute To The Classic FA Cup			
	Winners of 1979)	2009	—	£5.50
15	Aston Villa F.C. European Champions 81/82	2013	—	£6.00
10	Bizarre Club Shirts (Football)	2001	—	£4.00
15	Blackburn Rovers Heroes & Legends...	2009	—	£5.50
12	Brazil '70 (Football)	2005	—	£4.75
10	Brazilliant — The Story of Pele (Footballer)...	2001	—	£4.00
20	British Internationals 1950-2 (Football)	1999	—	£7.00
15	The Busby Babes 1st Series (Manchester			
	United F.C.)	2002	—	£5.50
15	The Busby Babes 2nd Series (Manchester			
	United F.C.)	2005	—	£5.50
L8	Celtic '67 The Lisbon Lions (Footballers)	2003	—	£4.25
15	Chelsea F.C. 1970 (F.A. Cup Winners)	2008	—	£5.50
10	Chelsea's Top Ten Goalscorers	2013	—	£5.00
15	Claret Heroes of The 1970s (Burnley F.C.)	2008	—	£5.50
10	Classic Kits (Football Team Colours)	2001	—	£4.00
15	Classic Soccer Strips	2006	—	£5.50
10	Crystal Palace Heroes and Legends (Footballers)	2012	—	£5.00
15	Derby County Champions of 1971/72...	2007	—	£5.50
L10	Elvis in Pictures	2003	—	£5.75
15	England World Cup Winners 1966	2006	—	£5.50
10	England's Top Goal Scorers	2002	—	£4.00
10	Everton Heroes and Legends	2012	—	£5.00
20	Favourite Footballers Pre 1st & 2nd World War			
	1st Series	2009	—	£7.00
20	Favourite Footballers Pre 1st & 2nd World War			
	2nd Series	2009	—	£7.00
20	Favourite Footballers Pre 1st & 2nd World War			
	3rd Series	2009	—	£7.00
20	Favourite Footballers Pre 1st & 2nd World War			
	4th Series	2009	—	£7.00
25	Fergie's Heroes 2003/04 — Manchester United			
	Footballers	2003	—	£7.50
10	Football Heroes (Stars of the 1960s)	2001	—	£4.00
10	Football in the Fifties	2001	—	£4.00
10	Football League Stars	2005	—	£3.75
25	Football Stars of the '20s and '30s...	2004	—	£5.25
15	Football Stars of The Seventies 1st Series	2002	—	£5.50
15	Football Stars of The Seventies 2nd Series...	2003	—	£5.50
15	Footballer of the Year (1948-1965)...	1999	—	£5.50
10	Footy Star (Soccer Stars of the 1950s)	2008	—	£4.00
12	Forest Kings of Europe 1979 (Nottingham			
	Forest F.C.)...	2005	—	£4.50
10	George Formby 50th Anniversary Issue	2011	—	£5.50
10	Greavsie — A Tribute to Jimmy Greaves			
	(Footballer)	2001	—	£4.00
10	Hotshot Football (Soccer Stars of the 1960s)	2008	—	£4.00
10	International Stars of Yesteryear 1st Series			
	(Footballers)	2000	—	£4.00

Qty		Date	Odds	Sets
	PHILIP NEILL (continued)			
10	International Stars of Yesteryear 2nd Series (Football)	2001	—	£4.00
15	Ipswich Town F.C. (UEFA Cup Winners 1981)	2008	—	£5.50
15	Kings of Europe (Manchester United F.C.)	1999	—	£5.50
15	Leeds United The Revie Era	2002	—	£5.50
12	The Lisbon Lions (Celtic European Cup Winning Legends)	1999	—	£4.50
15	Liverpool F.C. Champions League 2005	2005	—	£5.50
15	Liverpool F.C. Kings of Europe 1977	2005	—	£5.50
15	Liverpool Legends (Footballers)	2000	—	£5.50
15	Maine Road Heroes (Manchester City Footballers)	2003	—	£5.50
15	Manchester City's Euro Kings of '70	2006	—	£5.50
15	Manchester United Classic Kits	2004	—	£5.50
15	Moscow Magic (Manchester United Champions League Winners)	2008	—	£5.50
15	Newcastle Heroes — Post War Toon Legends	2004	—	£5.50
10	Nicole Kidman	1999	—	£4.00
15	Premiership Burnley Tribute To The Turf Moor Play-off Heroes	2009	—	£6.00
15	Rangers Euro Kings of '72	2006	—	£5.50
20	Red Legends (Manchester United Footballers)	1998	—	£5.50
10	Scottish Footballers of the 1930s	2000	—	£4.00
10	Scottish Internationals (1960s Footballers)	2002	—	£4.00
15	70's Soccer Stars	2003	—	£5.50
10	Soccer in the 60s 1st Series	1999	—	£4.00
10	Soccer in the 60s 2nd Series	2000	—	£4.00
15	Soccer Portraits of the 1950s Series 1	2008	—	£5.00
15	Soccer Portraits of the 1960s Series 1	2008	—	£5.00
15	Soccer Portraits of the 1970s Series 1	2008	—	£5.00
10	Soccer Selection (Footballing Greats)	2004	—	£4.00
10	Soccer 70 (1970s Footballers)	2002	—	£4.00
10	Soccer Sketch (Footballers of 50s and 60s)	2010	—	£4.50
10	Soccer Stars of The 50s	2001	—	£4.00
10	Soccer Stars of The 60s	2001	—	£4.00
15	Stamford Bridge Superstars — Chelsea F.C.	2006	—	£5.50
10	Striker Soccer Cards (of the '70s) 1st Series	2009	—	£5.00
10	Striker Soccer Cards (of the '70s) 2nd Series	2009	—	£5.00
15	Sunderland FA Cup Winners of 1973	2008	—	£5.50
L18	Super Reds (Manchester United Footballers)	1998	—	£7.50
10	Ten of the Best — George Best (Footballer)	2000	—	£4.00
10	10 Select Manchester United Footballers	2011	—	£5.50
10	Third Lanark Favourites (Footballers)	2009	—	£5.00
15	Tottenham Double Winners 1960-61	2004	—	£5.50
10	Tottenham Heroes & Legends	2012	—	£5.00
25	United Legends (Manchester United Footballers)	2000	—	£7.50
15	United '68 (Manchester United F.C.)	2006	—	£5.50
12	Villa Cup Winners 1957 (Aston Villa F.C.)	2005	—	£4.50
10	Vintage Football of the 1900s	2005	—	£4.00
15	Vintage Soccer Heroes	2005	—	£5.00
L7	Visions of Marilyn Munroe	2003	—	£4.25
15	West Ham United Cup Winning Sides of 1964 and 1965	2007	—	£5.50
15	Wolves Heroes and Legends (Wolverhampton Wanderers F.C.)	2011	—	£6.00

Qty		Date	Odds	Sets
	PHILIP NEILL (continued)			
10	World Cup Heroes and Legends 1st Series (Football)	2009	—	£5.00
10	World Cup Heroes and Legends 2nd Series (Football)	2010	—	£5.00
10	World Soccer Heroes 1st Series	2009	—	£5.00
10	World Soccer Heroes 2nd Series.................	2009	—	£5.00
10	World Soccer Stars (1960s to 1980s)............	2013	—	£5.00
	NEILSON'S			
50	Interesting Animals	1954	20p	£4.00
	THE NELSON LEE LIBRARY			
MP15	Footballers........................	1922	£4.50	—
MP6	Modern British Locomotives	1922	£6.50	—
	NESTLE (Chocolate)			
EL12	Animal Bar (wrappers)........................	1970	—	£2.50
49	Happy Families	1935	£1.00	—
100	Stars of the Silver Screen, Vol I........................	1936	£1.80	—
50	Stars of the Silver Screen, Vol II	1937	£2.20	—
136	This England	1936	£1.20	—
156	Wonders of the World, Vol I	1932	£1.00	—
144	Wonders of the World, Vol II	1933	£1.00	—
288	Wonders of the World, Vol III	1934	£1.00	—
	NEW ENGLAND CONFECTIONERY (USA)			
M12	Real Airplane Pictures	c1930	£3.00	£36.00
	NEW SOUTH WALES CRICKET ASSOCIATION (Australia)			
L20	The Blues — N.S.W. Cricketers 1998-99 (inscribed 'Toyota')	1998	—	£6.00
L20	The Blues — N.S.W. Cricketers 1999-2000 (without 'Toyota')	1999	—	£6.00
	NEW SOUTH WALES FIRE SERVICE (Australia)			
L10	Fire Appliances and Equipment 1st Series	1980	75p	—
L10	Fire Appliances and Equipment 2nd Series	1981	75p	—
L10	Fire Appliances and Equipment 3rd Series	1982	75p	—
L10	Fire Appliances and Equipment 4th Series	1983	75p	—
L10	Fire Appliances and Equipment 5th Series	1984	75p	—
L10	Fire Appliances and Equipment 7th Series	1986	75p	—
L10	Fire Appliances and Equipment 8th Series	1987	75p	£7.50
L10	Fire Appliances and Equipment 9th Series	1988	75p	£7.50
L10	Fire Appliances and Equipment 10th Series	1989	75p	£7.50
L10	Fire Appliances and Equipment 11th Series	1990	75p	£7.50
	NEWMARKET HARDWARE			
L24	Some of Britain's Finest (Motor) Bikes	1993	—	£6.00
	NEWS CHRONICLE			
L12	Cricketers — England v S Africa 1955	1955	£15.00	—
	Football Players:			
L13	Barrow RFC	1955	£2.00	—
L14	Blackburn Rovers FC	1955	£2.00	—

Qty		Date	Odds	Sets

NEWS CHRONICLE (continued)
Football Players *continued*:

Qty		Date	Odds	Sets
L12	Bradford City FC	1955	£2.00	–
L11	Chesterfield FC	1955	£2.00	–
L12	Everton FC (no stars at base)	1955	£2.00	–
L10	Everton FC (two stars at base)	1955	£2.00	–
L15	Manchester City FC	1955	£2.00	–
L12	Newcastle United FC	1955	£3.00	–
L14	Rochdale Hornets RFC...	1955	£2.00	–
L13	Salford RFC	1955	£2.00	–
L17	Stockport County FC	1955	£2.00	–
L13	Sunderland FC	1955	£2.50	–
L13	Swinton RFC	1955	£2.00	–
L11	Workington Town FC	1955	£2.00	–
L11	York City FC	1955	£2.00	–
L12	The Story of Stirling Moss	1955	£10.00	–

NEWTON, CHAMBERS & CO.

EL18	Izal Nursery Rhymes 1st Series	c1930	£4.00	–
EL18	Izal Nursery Rhymes 2nd Series	c1930	£4.00	–

NEW ZEALAND MEAT PRODUCERS BOARD

EL6	New Zealand Pastoral Scenes	c1930	50p	£3.00
M25	Scenes of New Zealand Lamb	c1930	£4.00	–

NINETY MINUTES

20	Ninety Minutes Footballers of the 1950s 1st Series	2009	–	£9.00
20	Ninety Minutes Footballers of the 1950s 2nd Series	2009	–	£9.00
20	Ninety Minutes Footballers of the 1950s 3rd Series	2010	–	£7.50
20	Ninety Minutes Footballers of the 1950s 4th Series	2010	–	£7.50
20	Ninety Minutes Footballers of the 1950s 5th Series	2010	–	£7.50

NORTHAMPTONSHIRE COUNTY CRICKET CLUB

30	Northamptonshire County Cricket 1905-1985	1985	50p	£15.00

NORTHERN CONFECTIONS LTD

48	Aeroplanes...	c1955	£5.00	–

NORTHERN CO-OPERATIVE SOCIETY LTD

25	Birds	1963	£1.20	–
25	History of the Railways 1st Series	1964	50p	£12.50
25	History of the Railways 2nd Series	1964	70p	£17.50
25	Passenger Liners	1963	20p	£3.00
25	Then and Now	1963	30p	£7.50
25	Tropical Birds	1967	44p	£11.00
25	Weapons of World War II	1962	80p	£20.00
25	Wonders of the Deep	1966	20p	£3.50

NORTH'S BREAD (New Zealand)

LT16	Canterbury Crusaders (Rugby Union)	1997	–	£5.00
	Album		–	£5.00

NORTHUMBRIA POLICE

EL21	Sunderland AFC (Footballers)	1991	–	£12.00

106

Qty		Date	Odds	Sets

NORTON'S

Qty		Date	Odds	Sets
25	Evolution of The Royal Navy...	c1965	£1.60	—

NUGGET POLISH CO.

Qty		Date	Odds	Sets
EL30	Allied Series	c1910	£15.00	—
50	Flags of all Nations	c1925	£5.00	—
EL40	Mail Carriers and Stamps...	c1910	£14.00	—

NUMBER ONE MAGAZINE

Qty		Date	Odds	Sets
EL5	Get Fit And Have Fun	1991	—	£2.50

NUNBETTA

Qty		Date	Odds	Sets
25	Motor Cars...	1955	£10.00	—

NUNEATON F C

Qty		Date	Odds	Sets
L30	Nuneaton Borough Footballers	1995	—	£10.00
L30	Nuneaton Football Greats...	1992	—	£15.00

O'CARROLL KENT LTD

Qty		Date	Odds	Sets
50	Railway Engines	c1955	£4.50	—

OCTUS SPORTS (USA)

Qty		Date	Odds	Sets
LT44	Rams NFL Cheerleaders	1994	—	£6.00

ODLING & WILLSON

Qty		Date	Odds	Sets
25	Bygone Locomotives	1999	—	£10.00

N. OLDHAM

Qty		Date	Odds	Sets
13	Golf Legends	2005	—	£6.00

TONY L. OLIVER

Qty		Date	Odds	Sets
1	Advert Card for German Orders & Decorations ...	1963	—	£2.50
25	Aircraft of World War II...	c1970	£5.00	—
50	German Orders and Decorations	1963	£2.50	—
50	German Uniforms	1971	25p	£12.50
M25	Vehicles of the German Wehrmacht	c1970	£1.20	£30.00

ORBIS LTD

Qty		Date	Odds	Sets
EL90	Dinosaurs	1992	20p	£10.00

ORBIT ADVERTISING

Qty		Date	Odds	Sets
15	Engines of the London & North Eastern Railway ...	1986	—	£4.00
20	Famous Douglas Aeroplanes	1986	—	£10.00
28	Great Rugby Sides New Zealand Tourists 1905 ...	1986	20p	£4.00
16	New Zealand Cricketers of 1958	1988	—	£7.00

OVALTINE

Qty		Date	Odds	Sets
25	Do You Know?	1968	32p	£8.00

O.V.S. TEA CO.

Qty		Date	Odds	Sets
K25	Modern Engineering	1955	30p	£7.50

Qty		Date	Odds	Sets

OXO LTD

Qty		Date	Odds	Sets
K?	Advertisement Cards	c1925	£8.00	—
K20	British Cattle	1924	£4.50	£90.00
15	Bull Series	1927	£3.00	£45.00
K24	Feats of Endurance	1926	£3.00	£75.00
K20	Furs and their Story	1924	£3.00	£60.00
K36	Lifeboats and their History	1925	£3.25	
K30	Mystery Painting Pictures	1928	£3.00	£90.00
EL6	Oxo Cattle Studies	c1920	£35.00	—
25	Oxo Recipes	1936	£2.80	—

P.C.G.C. (Gum)

LT88	War Bulletin	1966	£1.75	—

P.M.R. ASSOCIATES LTD

25	England The World Cup Spain '82	1982	20p	£3.00

P.Y.Q.C.C. (USA)

LT100	Great Guns	1993	—	£15.00

PACIFIC TRADING (USA)

LT110	American Soccer Players 1987-88	1987	—	£10.00
LT110	American Soccer Players 1988-89	1989	—	£10.00
LT110	American Soccer Players 1989-90	1990	—	£10.00
LT220	American Soccer Players 1990-91	1990	—	£15.00
LT110	American Soccer Players NPSL 1992/93	1993	20p	£15.00
LT110	Bingo — The Film	1991	—	£8.00
LT110	The College Years Saved By the Bell (TV Show) ...	1994	—	£7.50
LT110	Eight Men Out — The Film	1998	—	£9.50
LT110	Gunsmoke (1950-60s TV Show)	1993	—	£9.50
LT110	I Love Lucy (TV Series)	1991	—	£12.00
LT110	Operation Desert Shield (Gulf War)	1991	—	£9.50
LT110	Total Recall — The Movie	1990	—	£9.50
LT110	Where Are They	1992	—	£9.50
LT110	The Wizard of Oz	1991	—	£15.00
LT110	World War II	1992	—	£9.50

H.J. PACKER LTD

K30	Footballers	c1930	£50.00	—
50	Humorous Drawings	1936	£4.00	—

PAGE WOODCOCK

20	Humorous Sketches	c1905	£25.00	—

PALMER MANN & CO. LTD

Sifta Sam Salt Package Issues

24	Famous Cricketers	c1953	£20.00	—
24	Famous Footballers	c1954	£20.00	—
12	Famous Jets	c1955	£12.00	—
12	Famous Lighthouses	c1956	£12.00	—

PALS

M8	Famous Footballers Fineart Supplements	1922	£9.00	—
MP12	Football Series	1922	£4.50	—

Qty		Date	Odds	Sets

PANINI (UK)

Cards:

Qty		Date	Odds	Sets
LT150	Disney's Aladdin	1994	20p	£15.00
LT45	England Football Stars Gold Collection	1996	—	£15.00
LT100	Footballers 92 Nos 1-100	1991	20p	—
LT100	Footballers 92 Nos 101-200	1991	20p	—
LT100	Footballers 92 Nos 201-300	1991	20p	—
LT122	Footballers 92 Nos 301-422	1991	20p	—
	Sticker sets complete with albums:			
M180	The Adventures of the Animals of Farthing Wood...	1995	—	£22.00
M255	Care Bears News	1987	—	£22.00
M120	ET — The Extra Terrestrial	1982	—	£22.00

PANINI (USA and Canada)

Cards:

Qty		Date	Odds	Sets
LT100	Antique Cars 1st Series	c1995	—	£9.50
EL72	Austin Powers	1998	—	£12.00
LT198	Barbie and Friends	1992	—	£12.00
LT100	Dream Cars 1st Series	1991	—	£9.50
LT100	Dream Cars 2nd Series	1992	—	£9.50
LT90	The Lion King — Walt Disney Film	1995	—	£9.50
EL108	NSYNC (Pop Group) (Nos 34 & 100 blurred as issued)	1999	—	£12.00
LT100	Wildlife in Danger	c1993	—	£9.50
LT100	Wings Of Fire (Military Aircraft etc)	1992	—	£9.50
	Sticker Sets complete with albums:			
M240	Star Trek — The Next Generation (Factory Set) ...	1993	—	£12.00

PARAMINT CARDS

Qty		Date	Odds	Sets
10	Arthur Askey — Comedy Heroes	2012	—	£5.00
10	Football Stars (of the 1970s) 1st Series	2012	—	£5.00
10	Football Stars (of the 1970s) 2nd Series...	2012	—	£5.00
10	Football Stars (of the 1970s) 3rd Series	2012	—	£5.00
10	Football Stars (of the 1970s) 4th Series	2012	—	£5.00
10	Football Stars (of the 1970s) 5th Series	2012	—	£5.00
10	Gracie Fields From Rochdale to Capri	2012	—	£5.00
10	Margaret Rutherford	2012	—	£5.00
10	Norman Wisdom — Comedy Heroes	2012	—	£5.00
10	Scottish Football Stars (1970s footballers)	2011	—	£5.00

PARAMOUNT LABORATORIES LTD

Qty		Date	Odds	Sets
50	Fifty Years of Flying	1954	90p	£45.00
50	Motor Cars	1954	£1.75	—
50	Railways of the World:			
	A 'Paramount Sweets':			
	(i) Correct numbering	1955	50p	£25.00
	(ii) Incorrect numbering	1955	£1.00	—
	B 'Paramount Laboratories Ltd'	1955	80p	£40.00

PARRS

Qty		Date	Odds	Sets
L20	Famous Aircraft	1953	£6.00	—

JAMES PASCALL LTD

Qty		Date	Odds	Sets
48	Boy Scouts Series (multi-backed)	c1910	£12.00	—
24	British Birds	1925	£3.50	—

Qty		Date	Odds	Sets
	JAMES PASCALL LTD (continued)			
30	Devon Ferns	1927	£2.00	—
30	Devon Flowers:			
	A Without Red Overprint	1927	£2.00	—
	B With Red Overprint...	1927	£4.00	—
24	Devon Worthies	1927	£2.50	—
18	Dogs	1924	£4.50	—
10	Felix the Film Cat	c1920	£30.00	—
15	Flags and Flags with Soldiers (with bow, cord)			
	(multi-backed)	c1910	£15.00	—
15	Flags and Flags with Soldiers (without bow, cord)			
	(multi-backed)	c1910	£15.00	—
30	Glorious Devon	1929	£2.00	—
36	Glorious Devon 2nd Series:			
	A Marked 2nd Series	1929	£2.00	—
	B Marked Aids for Mothers	1929	£7.00	—
36	Glorious Devon (Ambrosia black back)	c1930	£2.00	—
2	King George V and Queen Mary (multi-backed) ...	c1915	£30.00	—
44	Military Series (multi-backed)	c1910	£20.00	—
20	Pascall's Specialities (multi-backed)	c1920	£20.00	—
12	Royal Navy Cadet Series (multi-backed)...	c1915	£20.00	—
8	Rulers of the World	c1910	£30.00	—
68	Town and Other Arms (multi-backed)	c1910	£12.00	—
50	Tricks and Puzzles	c1920	£10.00	—
13	War Portraits	c1915	£24.00	—
	J. PATERSON & SON LTD			
M48	Balloons...	1964	90p	£45.00
	PATRICK GARAGES			
	The Patrick Collection (Motor Cars):			
M24	A Without Coupon	1986	60p	£15.00
EL24	B With Coupon	1986	£1.00	£25.00
	GEORGE PAYNE (Tea)			
25	American Indian Tribes			
	A Cream Card	1962	£1.00	£25.00
	B White Card	1962	£1.00	£25.00
25	British Railways	1962	20p	£5.00
	Characters from Dickens' Works:			
12	A Numbered	c1912	£15.00	—
6	B Unnumbered	c1912	£15.00	—
25	Dogs' Heads	1963	50p	£12.50
25	Mickey Mouse Pleasure Cruise	c1920	£30.00	—
25	Science in the 20th Century	1963	20p	£3.00
	PENGUIN BISCUITS			
EL10	Home Hints	c1974	£2.50	—
EL10	Making the Most of Your Countryside	1975	£2.50	—
EL10	Pastimes	c1972	£2.50	—
EL12	Penguin Farm Animal Series...	c1968	£2.50	—
EL10	Penguin Zoo Animal Series	c1968	£2.50	—
EL10	Playday	c1974	£2.50	—
EL12	Wildlife	1973	£2.50	—

Qty		Date	Odds	Sets
	PENNY MAGAZINE			
M12	Film Stars	c1930	£4.00	—
	PEPSI (UK)			
L7	Star Wars Episode 1 The Phantom Menace	1999	—	£5.00
	PEPSI (Thailand)			
LT8	Britney Spears	2002	—	£8.00
LT32	World Football Stars	2002	—	£7.50
	PEPSICO FOODS (Saudi Arabia)			
M22	World Soccer	1998	30p	£7.00
	PERENNIAL MUSIC			
M45	Forever Gold Entertainment Legends...	2000	—	£11.00
	PERFETTI GUM			
40	Famous Trains	1983	£3.25	—
	PERIKIM			
L7	Dogs — The Boxer	2001	—	£3.00
L7	Dogs — The Bull Terrier	2005	—	£3.00
L7	Dogs — The Bulldog	2005	—	£3.00
L7	Dogs — The Cocker Spaniel...	2001	—	£3.00
L7	Dogs — The Dalmatian	2005	—	£3.00
L7	Dogs — The Dobermann	2001	—	£3.00
L7	Dogs — The English Springer Spaniel	2001	—	£3.00
L7	Dogs — The German Shepherd	2001	—	£3.00
L7	Dogs — The Golden Retriever	2001	—	£3.00
L7	Dogs — The Irish Setter	2005	—	£3.00
L7	Dogs — The Jack Russell	2001	—	£3.00
L7	Dogs — The King Charles Cavalier	2005	—	£3.00
L7	Dogs — The Rottweiler	2005	—	£3.00
L7	Dogs — The Rough Collie	2005	—	£3.00
L7	Dogs — The Staffordshire Bull Terrier	2005	—	£3.00
L7	Dogs — The West Highland	2005	—	£3.00
L7	Dogs — The Yorkshire Terrier	2005	—	£3.00
L13	Nursery Rhymes	1996	—	£5.00
	PETER MAX (USA)			
LT6	Peter Max Posters	1994	—	£3.00
	PETERKIN			
M8	English Sporting Dogs	c1930	£13.00	—
	PETPRO LTD			
35	Grand Prix Racing Cars (64 × 29mm)	1966	30p	£10.00
	THE PHILATELIC POSTCARD PUBLISHING CO. LTD			
EL10	Philatelic Anniversary Series	1983	—	£4.50
	PHILLIPS TEA			
25	Army Badges, Past and Present	1964	20p	£3.50
25	British Birds and Their Nests...	1971	£1.60	—
25	British Rail	1965	30p	£7.50

Qty		Date	Odds	Sets

PHILOSOPHY FOOTBALL

Qty		Date	Odds	Sets
L20	Philosopher Footballers	1998	—	£12.00

PHOTAL

EL2	Duncan Edwards (Footballer)	2001	—	£5.00
EL4	Manchester United F.C. 1967 Series 1	2001	—	£8.00
EL10	Manchester United F.C. 1968 Series 2 Nos 1-10 ...	2001	—	£15.00
EL10	Manchester United F.C. 1968 Series 2 Nos 11-20	2001	—	£15.00
EL6	Northern Footballing Knights...	2001	—	£12.00
EL10	Sir Tom Finney (Footballer)	2001	—	£16.00

PHOTO ANSWERS MAGAZINE

EL12	Holiday Fax	1990	—	£3.00

PHOTO PRECISION

EL20	Fighting Aircraft of World War II...	1978	—	£5.00
EL10	Flowers	1979	—	£2.50
EL10	Old English Series	1979	—	£2.50
EL10	Traction Engines	1979	—	£2.50
EL12	Vintage Cars	1975	—	£2.50
EL10	Wild Birds	1979	—	£2.50
EL10	Wild Life	1979	—	£2.50

PILOT

32	Aeroplanes and Carriers	1937	£3.25	—
32	Football Fame Series	1935	£4.00	—

GEO. M. PITT

25	Types of British Soldiers	1914	£25.00	—

PIZZA HUT

EL12	Football Skill Cards	c1995	—	£6.00

PLANET LTD

L50	Racing Cars of the World	1959	£3.00	—

PLANTERS NUT AND CHOCOLATE CO. (USA)

M25	Hunted Animals	1933	£3.00	£75.00

PLAY HOUR

M24	Zoo plus album	c1960	—	£9.00

PLAYER PARADE

20	Player Parade (Footballers of the 50s) 1st Series .	2010	—	£7.50
20	Player Parade (Footballers of the 50s) 2nd Series .	2011	—	£7.50

PLAYERS INTERNATIONAL

LT40	Boxing Personalities — Ringlords	1991	—	£5.00

PLUCK

MP27	Famous Football Teams	1922	£4.00	—

PLYMOUTH COUNTY COUNCIL

EL20	Endangered Species	1985	—	£5.00

Qty		Date	Odds	Sets

POLAR PRODUCTS LTD (BARBADOS)

Qty		Date	Odds	Sets
25	International Air Liners	c1970	60p	£15.00
25	Modern Motor Cars	c1970	80p	£20.00
25	Tropical Birds	c1970	60p	£15.00
25	Wonders of the Deep	c1970	50p	£12.50

POLYDOR

Qty		Date	Odds	Sets
16	Polydor Guitar	1975	50p	£8.00

PONY MAGAZINE

Qty		Date	Odds	Sets
EL26	Horse & Pony Breeds (Trumps Cards)	2008	—	£6.00

H. POPPLETON & SONS

Qty		Date	Odds	Sets
50	Cricketers Series.......................................	1926	£27.00	—
16	Film Stars	1928	£8.00	—
9	War Series	c1915	£27.00	—
12	Wembley Empire Exhibition Series	c1920	£27.00	—

POPULAR GARDENING

Qty		Date	Odds	Sets
EL6	Colour Schemes With Garden Flowers	1939	£2.00	—

PORTFOLIO INTERNATIONAL (USA)

Qty		Date	Odds	Sets
LT50	Endless Summer (Pin Up Girls).....................	1993	—	£9.50
LT50	Portfolio (Pin Up Girls)	1992	—	£9.50
LT50	Portfolio (Pin Up Girls)	1993	—	£9.50
LT36	Portfolio's Secret (Pin Up Girls) (No. 12 unissued, 2 different No. 15s)	1994	—	£9.50

PoSTA

Qty		Date	Odds	Sets
25	Modern Transport	1957	20p	£5.00

PRESCOTT CONFECTIONERY

Qty		Date	Odds	Sets
L36	Speed Kings	1966	75p	£27.00

PRESCOTT — PICKUP

Qty		Date	Odds	Sets
EL60	Action Portraits of Famous Footballers	1979	—	£15.00
EL60	Interregnum (Military)	1978	—	£20.00
EL64	Our Iron Roads (Railways)	1980	—	£12.00
EL60	Queen and People	1977	—	£12.00
EL60	Railway Locomotives:			
	A Post Card back	1976	—	£12.00
	B Textback	1978	—	£12.00
50	Railway Locomotives	1978	25p	£12.50
EL12	The Royal Wedding	1981	—	£9.00
EL60	Sovereign Series No. 1 Royal Wedding	1981	—	£20.00
EL60	Sovereign Series No. 2 30 Years of Elizabeth II ...	1982	—	£15.00
EL30	Sovereign Series No. 3 — Charles & Diana in the Antipodes	1983	—	£8.00
EL15	Sovereign Series No. 3 — Charles & Diana in Canada	1983	—	£4.00
EL70	Sovereign Series No. 4 — Royal Family............	1982	—	£15.00
EL63	Sovereign Series No. 6 — Papal Visit	1982	—	£10.00
EL63	Sovereign Series No. 7 — Falklands Task Force ...	1982	—	£25.00

Qty		Date	Odds	Sets

PRESCOTT – PICKUP (continued)

Qty		Date	Odds	Sets
EL63	Sovereign Series No. 8 — War in the South			
	Atlantic	1983	—	£20.00
EL60	Tramcars & Tramways	1977	—	£15.00
EL60	Tramcyclopaedia...	1979	—	£18.00

PRESS PASS (USA)

Qty		Date	Odds	Sets
LT100	Elvis Is (Elvis Presley)	2008	—	£20.00
LT110	Royal Family	1993	20p	£9.50

PRESTON DAIRIES

Qty		Date	Odds	Sets
25	Country Life	1966	20p	£2.50

PRICE'S PATENT CANDLE CO. LTD

Qty		Date	Odds	Sets
EL12	Famous Battles	c1910	£12.00	—

W.R. PRIDDY

Qty		Date	Odds	Sets
80	Famous Boxers	1992	—	£10.00

PRIMROSE CONFECTIONERY CO. LTD

Qty		Date	Odds	Sets
24	Action Man...	1976	£3.20	—
50	Amos Burke, Secret Agent:			
	A With 'printed in England'	1970	£1.00	£50.00
	B Without 'printed in England'	1966	£1.20	—
50	Andy Pandy	1960	40p	£20.00
50	Bugs Bunny	1964	£1.20	£60.00
50	Burke's Law	1966	£5.00	—
25	Captain Kid	1975	£5.00	—
50	Chitty Chitty Bang Bang:			
	A Thick card	1969	£1.00	£50.00
	B Paper thin card	1969	40p	£20.00
50	Cowboy	1961	20p	£10.00
25	Cup Tie Quiz	1973	20p	£3.00
25	Dad's Army...	1973	80p	£20.00
50	Famous Footballers (FBSI) back	1961	40p	£20.00
50	Flintstones	1963	£1.00	—
25	Football Funnies	1974	30p	£7.50
25	Happy Howlers	1975	20p	£4.00
50	Joe 90:			
	A Thick card	1969	£2.00	—
	B Paper thin card	1970	£1.70	—
50	Krazy Kreatures from Outer Space:			
	A Thick card	1970	60p	£30.00
	B Thin card	1972	20p	£6.00
	C Paper thin card	1972	20p	£5.00
50	Laramie	1964	£1.60	£80.00
50	Laurel & Hardy:			
	A Thick card	1968	£3.00	—
	B Thin card	1972	£1.60	£80.00
	C Paper thin card	1972	£1.20	£60.00
22	Mounties (Package Issue)	1960	£6.00	—
50	Popeye 1st Series	1960	£6.00	—
50	Popeye 2nd Series	1960	£5.50	£275.00
50	Popeye 3rd Series	1961	25p	£12.50

Date   *Odds*   *Sets*

PRIMROSE CONFECTIONERY CO. LTD (continued)

50 Popeye 4th Series:
    A   Back headed '4th Series Popeye No. ...'
        a) Address 'Argyle Avenue', Album clause

Qty	Item	Date	Odds	Sets
	'send only 9d ...'	1963	25p	£12.50
	B Back headed 'Popeye ... 4th Series'			
	Address 'Farnham Road'			
	A Thick card	1970	30p	£15.00
	B Thin card	1970	25p	£12.50
50	Queen Elizabeth 2 (The Cunard Liner):			
	A Cream card	1969	£1.00	£50.00
	B White card	1969	90p	£45.00
50	Quick Draw McGraw, Series Q.1	1965	£1.50	£75.00
50	Space Patrol:			
	A Thick card	1968	25p	£12.50
	B Thin card	1968	20p	£10.00
50	Space Race	1969	20p	£6.00
12	Star Trek	1971	65p	£7.50
50	Superman:			
	A Thick card	1968	80p	–
	B Paper thin card	1972	50p	£25.00
50	Yellow Submarine	1968	£5.00	–
50	Z Cars Album send only 9d	1964	25p	£12.50
50	Z Cars Album send only 1/- (different Series)	1968	50p	£25.00

A.S. PRIOR (Fish and Chips)

Qty	Item	Date	Odds	Sets
25	Evolution of the Royal Navy	c1965	£1.40	–

S. PRIOR (Bookshop)

Qty	Item	Date	Odds	Sets
25	British Uniforms of the 19th Century	c1965	£1.40	–

PRIORY TEA & COFFEE CO. LTD

Qty	Item	Date	Odds	Sets
1	Advert Card Set Completion Offer	1966	–	£10.00
50	Aircraft	1961	£1.20	–
	Album		–	£6.00
50	Birds	1963	£1.00	–
24	Bridges	1959	20p	£3.00
50	Cars	1964	60p	£30.00
	Album		–	£6.00
24	Cars	1958	£4.00	–
50	Cycles and Motorcycles	1960	£2.00	–
24	Dogs	1957	20p	£3.50
24	Flowering Trees	1959	20p	£3.00
24	Men at Work	1959	20p	£2.50
24	Out and About	1957	40p	£10.00
24	People in Uniform	1957	£2.00	–
24	Pets	1957	20p	£3.00
50	Wild Flowers	1961	80p	£40.00
	Album for Cars (24) and Flowering Trees			
	combined		–	£15.00

PRISM LEISURE

Qty	Item	Date	Odds	Sets
L30	George Formby	1993	–	£15.00
L12	Patsy Cline (Country Singer)	1993	–	£10.00

PRO SET (UK)

Qty		Date	Odds	Sets
LT100	Bill & Ted's Excellent Adventure	1992	20p	£9.00
LT100	Football Fixtures/Footballers	1991	20p	£10.00
LT110	Footballers 1990-91 Nos 1-110	1990	20p	£9.00
LT110	Footballers 1990-91 Nos 111-220	1990	20p	£9.00
LT108	Footballers 1990-91 Nos 221-328	1990	20p	£9.00
LT115	Footballers 1991-92 Nos 1-115	1991	20p	£9.00
LT115	Footballers 1991-92 Nos 116-230	1991	20p	£9.00
LT125	Footballers 1991-92 Nos 231-355	1992	20p	£9.00
LT124	Footballers 1991-92 Nos 356-479	1992	20p	£9.00
LT100	Footballers — Scottish 1991-92	1991	20p	£8.00
LT100	Guinness Book of Records	1992	20p	£7.50
LT75	Super Stars Musicards (Pop Stars) Nos 1-75	1991	20p	£7.50
LT75	Super Stars Musicards (Pop Stars) Nos 76-150 ...	1991	20p	£7.50
LT100	Thunderbirds	1992	20p	£8.00

PRO SET (USA)

Qty		Date	Odds	Sets
LT150	American Football World League	1991	—	£12.00
LT95	Beauty and The Beast	1992	—	£8.00
LT90	The Little Mermaid (Disney Film) + 37 Bonus Cards	1991	—	£12.00
LT160	NFL Super Bowl XXV	1991	—	£15.00
LT100	PGA Golf	1990	—	£12.00
LT285	PGA Golf Tour	1991	—	£25.00
LT100	PGA Golf nos E1-E20, 1-80	1992	20p	£10.00
LT100	PGA Golf nos 81-180	1992	20p	£10.00
LT100	PGA Golf nos 181-280	1992	20p	£10.00
LT50	Petty Family Racing (Motor Racing)	1991	—	£7.00
LT100	Yo MTV Raps Musicards Nos 1-100	1991	—	£8.00
LT50	Yo MTV Raps Musicards Nos 101-150	1991	—	£6.00
LT95	The Young Indiana Jones Chronicles	1992	20p	£8.00
LT8	The Young Indiana Jones Chronicles Hidden Treasures	1992	30p	£2.50
LT11	The Young Indiana Jones Chronicles 3-D	1992	20p	£2.50

PRO TRAC'S (USA)

Qty		Date	Odds	Sets
LT100	Formula One Racing Series 1 Nos 1-100	1991	—	£15.00
LT100	Formula One Racing Series 1 Nos 101-200	1991	—	£15.00

PROMATCH

Qty		Date	Odds	Sets
LT200	Premier League Footballers 1st Series	1996	—	£22.00
LT110	Premier League Footballers 2nd Series (10 numbers unissued)	1997	—	£22.00
LT200	Premier League Footballers 3rd Series	1998	—	£18.00
LT198	Premier League Footballers 4th Series (Number 163 not issued, 2 different Number 162s)	1999	—	£18.00

PROPERT SHOE POLISH

Qty		Date	Odds	Sets
25	British Uniforms	1955	24p	£6.00

PUB PUBLICITY

Qty		Date	Odds	Sets
M45	Inns of East Sussex	1975	20p	£7.00

PUBLICATIONS INT (USA)

Qty		Date	Odds	Sets
M100	Micro Machines 1st Series (Cars, etc)	1989	—	£10.00
M100	Micro Machines 2nd Series (Cars, etc)	1989	—	£10.00

Qty		Date	Odds	Sets
	PUKKA TEA CO. LTD			
50	Aquarium Fish	1960	£1.00	£50.00
	PURITY PRETZEL CO. (USA)			
M56	US Air Force Planes, US Navy Planes, Ships of the US Navy...	c1930	£1.50	—
	PYREX			
EL16	The Pyrex Guide to Simple Cooking	1975	20p	£2.50
	QUADRIGA			
M126	Snooker Kings	1985	—	£20.00
	Album		—	£6.00
	QUAKER OATS			
EL12	Armour Through the Ages...	1963	£1.25	£15.00
M4	Famous Puffers	1978	£5.00	—
M54	Historic Arms of Merry England	c1938	£1.50	—
EL8	Historic Ships	1965	£4.00	—
15	Honey Monster Crazy Games	1982	£1.50	—
M16	Jeremy's Animal Kingdom	1970	£1.50	—
L8	Legends of Batman	1995	£1.50	—
12	Monsters of the Deep	1984	£2.00	—
M6	Nature Trek	1976	40p	£2.50
EL12	Prehistoric Animals	1964	£5.00	—
EL12	Space Cards	1963	£5.00	—
EL12	Vintage Engines	1964	£5.00	—
	Package Issues:			
	Quaker Cards blue border issues:			
L36	British Landmarks	1961	£1.25	—
L36	Great Moments of Sport	1961	£3.00	—
L36	Household Hints	1961	£1.25	—
L36	Phiz Quiz	1961	£1.50	—
L36	Railways of the World	1961	£3.00	—
L36	The Story of Fashion	1961	£2.00	—
	Quaker Quiz Cards yellow border issues:			
M12	British Customs	1961	£1.50	—
M12	Famous Explorers	1961	£1.50	—
M12	Famous Inventors	1961	£2.00	—
M12	Famous Ships	1961	£2.00	—
M12	Famous Women	1961	£1.50	—
M12	Fascinating Costumes	1961	£1.25	—
M12	Great Feats of Building...	1961	£1.25	—
M12	History of Flight	1961	£2.00	—
M12	Homes and Houses	1961	£1.25	—
M12	On the Seashore	1961	£1.50	—
M12	The Wild West...	1961	£2.00	—
M12	Weapons & Armour	1961	£2.00	—
	Sugar Puffs Series (text back):			
12	Exploration & Adventure	1974	£1.50	—
12	National Maritime Museum	1974	£1.50	—
12	National Motor Museum	1974	£1.50	—
12	Royal Air Force Museum	1974	£1.50	—
12	Science & Invention	1974	£1.50	—

Qty		Date	Odds	Sets
	QUEENS			
30	Kings and Queens of England	1955	£1.20	£36.00
	QUORN SPECIALITIES LTD			
25	Fish and Game	1963	£6.00	—
	RADIO FUN			
20	British Sports Stars	1956	25p	£5.00
	RADIO REVIEW			
L36	Broadcasting Series	1935	£5.00	—
EL20	Broadcasting Stars	c1935	£5.00	—
	RAIL ENTHUSIAST			
EL48	British Diesel and Electric Railway Engines...	1984	—	£6.00
	RAILWAY TAVERN			
L12	Preserved British Locomotives	2000	—	£7.50
12	Steam Locomotives...	1999	—	£10.00
	RAINBO BREAD (USA)			
LT33	Star Trek The Motion Picture	1979	—	£9.50
	RAINBOW PRESS			
L26	Grand Prix The Early Years (Cars)...	1992	—	£12.50
	RALEIGH BICYCLES			
M48	Raleigh, The All Steel Bicycle	1957	£1.50	£75.00
	RED AND GREEN			
20	Football Heroes (1950s Footballers) 1st Series	2009	—	£9.00
20	Football Heroes (1950s Footballers) 2nd Series... ..	2010	—	£7.50
20	Football Heroes (1950s Footballers) 3rd Series	2010	—	£7.50
	RED HEART			
EL6	Cats	1954	—	£40.00
EL6	Dogs 1st Series	1955	—	£40.00
EL6	Dogs 2nd Series	1955	—	£40.00
EL6	Dogs 3rd Series	1956	—	£40.00
	RED LETTER, RED STAR WEEKLY			
L99	Fortune Cards	c1930	£3.50	—
EL8	Good Luck Song Cards	c1930	£3.00	—
L98	Midget Message Cards	1915	£2.50	—
L12	Red Letter Message Cards	c1920	£3.20	—
	RED ROSE RADIO			
EL6	Disc Jockeys from Gold AM	1992	—	£4.00
EL5	Disc Jockeys from Rock FM	1992	—	£3.00
	RED, WHITE & BLUE PRINT			
15	Aston Villa European Champions 81/82	2010	—	£6.50

Qty		Date	Odds	Sets

REDDINGS TEA COMPANY

Qty		Date	Odds	Sets
25	Castles of Great Britain	1965	£2.00	£50.00
25	Cathedrals of Great Britain	1965	£2.00	£50.00
25	Heraldry of Famous Places	1966	£2.00	£50.00
48	Ships of the World	1963	20p	£7.00
25	Strange Customs of the World:			
	A Text back	1969	20p	£2.50
	B Advertisement back	1969	£5.00	—
24	Warriors of the World 1st Series	1962	£2.00	£50.00
24	Warriors of the World 2nd Series	1962	£2.00	£50.00
24	Warriors of the World with Ships of the World			
	fronts	1963	£7.00	—

REDDISH MAID CONFECTIONERY

Qty		Date	Odds	Sets
K50	Famous International Aircraft	1963	£3.00	—
K25	Famous International Athletes	1965	£8.00	—
25	International Footballers of Today	1966	£8.00	—

REDSKY

Qty		Date	Odds	Sets
10	Audrey Hepburn	2011	—	£5.00
10	Ava Gardner	2012	—	£5.00
10	Brigitte Bardot	2011	—	£5.00
10	Claudia Cardinale	2011	—	£5.00
10	Doris Day	2011	—	£5.00
10	Elizabeth Taylor	2011	—	£5.00
10	Grace Kelly	2012	—	£5.00
10	Ingrid Bergman	2011	—	£5.00
10	Jane Russell	2012	—	£5.00
10	Jayne Mansfield	2011	—	£5.00
10	Lauren Bacall	2011	—	£5.00
10	Rita Hayworth	2011	—	£5.00
10	Sophia Loren	2011	—	£5.00
10	Susan Hayward	2011	—	£5.00

REDSTONE (USA)

Qty		Date	Odds	Sets
LT50	Dinosaurs	1993	20p	£8.00

REEVES LTD

Qty		Date	Odds	Sets
25	Cricketers	1912	£30.00	—

REFLECTIONS

Qty		Date	Odds	Sets
12	Nottingham Heritage/Poster	1996	—	£2.25
12	Nottingham Trams	2004/07	—	£2.25
4	Nottingham Trams	2008/10	—	£1.25
6	Nottinghamshire Towns 1st Series	1999	—	£1.25
4	Nottinghamshire Towns 2nd Series	2009	—	£1.25
6	Railways Around Nottingham	1996	—	£1.25
4	Rugby Union World Cup 2003	2003	—	£1.00
6	Sporting Occasions	2002	—	£1.25
6	St Pancras International (Railway Station)	2008	—	£1.25
6	Steam Around Britain 1st Series Nos 1-6 (Railways)	1999	—	£1.25
6	Steam Around Britain 2nd Series Nos 7-12			
	(Railways)	2001	—	£1.25
6	Steam Around Britain 3rd Series Nos 13-18			
	(Railways)	2003	—	£1.25

REFLECTIONS (continued)

6	Steam Around Britain 4th Series Nos 19-24 (Railways)	2005	–	£1.25
6	Steam Around Britain 5th Series Nos 25-30 (Railways)	2008	–	£1.25
6	Steam Around Britain 6th Series Nos 31-36 (Railways)...	2009	–	£1.25
6	Steam Around Britain 7th Series Nos. 37-42 (Railways)	2012	–	£1.25

REGENT OIL

L25	Do You Know?	1964	20p	£2.50

RICHARDS COLLECTION

25	Soccer Stars of Yesteryear 1st Series	1995	–	£8.75
25	Soccer Stars of Yesteryear 2nd Series	1997	–	£8.75
25	Soccer Stars of Yesteryear 3rd Series	1997	–	£8.75
25	Soccer Stars of Yesteryear 4th Series	1998	–	£5.00
5	Soccer Stars of Yesteryear 5th Series	2002	–	£2.50
20	Sporting Stars by Jos Walker (Cricketers)	1997	–	£5.00
21	Stars of the Past (Football)	1994	–	£8.75

RINGSIDE TRADING (USA)

LT80	Ringside Boxing	1996	–	£15.00

RINGTONS LTD (Tea)

25	Aircraft of World War II...	1962	£2.40	–
25	British Cavalry Uniforms of the 19th Century	1971	£1.20	£30.00
25	Do You Know?	1964	20p	£2.50
25	Fruit of Trees and Shrubs...	1963	20p	£2.50
25	Head Dresses of the World	1973	20p	£2.50
25	Historical Scenes	1964	20p	£4.00
25	Old England	1964	20p	£2.50
25	People and Places	1964	20p	£2.50
25	Regimental Uniforms of the Past	1966	24p	£6.00
25	Sailing Ships Through the Ages...	1964	24p	£6.00
25	Ships of the Royal Navy	1963	40p	£10.00
25	Sovereigns, Consorts and Rulers of Great Britain, 1st Series	1961	30p	£7.50
25	Sovereigns, Consorts and Rulers of Great Britain, 2nd Series	1961	30p	£7.50
25	Then and Now	1970	£1.20	–
25	Trains of the World	1970	20p	£3.00
25	The West	1968	20p	£5.00

RISCA TRAVEL AGENCY

25	Holiday Resorts	1966	£1.00	£25.00

RITTENHOUSE ARCHIVES (USA)

LT81	Art and Images of Star Trek The Original Series ..	2005	–	£9.50
LT120	Babylon 5 The Complete Series	2002	–	£16.00
LT72	Battlestar Galactica	2005	–	£9.50
LT72	Battlestar Galactica Colonial Warriors	2005	–	£8.00
LT72	Battlestar Galactica The Complete Series	2004	–	£11.00
LT81	Battlestar Galactica Season 1	2006	–	£8.00

Qty		Date	Odds	Sets
	RITTENHOUSE ARCHIVES (USA) (continued)			
LT72	Battlestar Galactica Season 2	2007	—	£8.00
LT63	Battlestar Galactica Season 3	2008	—	£8.00
LT63	Battlestar Galactica Season 4	2009	—	£8.00
LT72	The Chronicles of Riddick...	2004	—	£9.50
LT81	The Complete Avengers 1963-Present	2007	—	£12.00
LT72	Conan Art of The Hyborian Age...	2004	—	£11.00
LT50	D C Legacy	2007	—	£9.00
LT100	The Dead Zone	2004	—	£12.00
LT90	Die Another Day James Bond 007...	2002	—	£15.00
LT100	The Fantasy Worlds of Irwin Allen...	2003	—	£9.50
LT72	Farscape Season 1	2001	—	£9.50
LT72	Farscape Season 2	2001	—	£8.00
LT72	Farscape Season 3	2002	—	£9.50
LT72	Farscape Season 4	2003	—	£8.00
LT72	Farscape Through The Wormhole	2004	—	£8.00
LT72	Game of Thrones Season I	2012	—	£8.00
LT88	Game of Thrones Season 2	2013	—	£8.50
LT72	Hercules and Xena The Animated Adventures	2005	—	£9.50
LT120	Hercules The Legendary Journeys...	2001	—	£9.50
LT72	Heroes Archives	2010	—	£8.00
LT126	Highlander The Complete Series	2003	20p	£18.00
LT70	Iron Man The Film	2008	—	£8.00
LT66	James Bond 007 Archives	2009	—	£8.50
LT189	James Bond 007 The Complete Series	2007	—	£18.00
LT110	James Bond 007 Dangerous Liaisons	2006	—	£9.50
LT60	James Bond 007 40th Anniversary...	2002	—	£18.00
LT19	James Bond 007 40th Anniversary — Bond Extras	2002	—	£10.00
LT19	James Bond 007 40th Anniversary — Bond Villains	2002	—	£12.00
LT99	James Bond 50th Anniversary Series 1 (only odd			
	numbers issued)	2012	—	£9.50
LT99	James Bond 50th Anniversary Series 2 (only even			
	numbers issued)	2012	—	£9.50
LT81	James Bond 007 Heroes and Villains	2010	—	£8.00
LT63	James Bond 007 In Motion (3-D)	2008	—	£9.50
LT66	James Bond 007 Mission Logs	2011	—	£8.00
LT100	James Bond 007 Quotable Series	2004	—	£9.50
LT72	Lost Archives	2010	—	£8.00
LT108	Lost Seasons 1 Thru 5	2009	—	£9.50
LT90	Lost In Space (The Complete Series)	2005	—	£9.50
LT81	The Outer Limits Sex, Cyborgs & Science Fiction	2003	—	£8.00
LT81	Six Feet Under	2004	20p	£8.50
LT72	Six Million Dollar Man	2004	—	£9.50
LT72	Spiderman Archives...	2009	—	£8.00
LT79	Spiderman III — The Film	2007	—	£8.00
LT90	Star Trek Celebrating 40 Years	2006	—	£9.50
LT189	Star Trek Deep Space Nine The Complete Series	2003	—	£18.00
LT108	Star Trek Deep Space Nine Quotable Series	2007	—	£9.50
LT81	Star Trek Enterprise Season I	2002	—	£12.00
LT81	Star Trek Enterprise Season 2	2003	—	£12.00
LT72	Star Trek Enterprise Season 3	2004	—	£9.50
LT72	Star Trek Enterprise Season 4	2005	—	£9.50
LT81	Star Trek Movie	2009	—	£8.00
LT60	Star Trek Movies In Motion (3-D)	2008	—	£15.00
LT90	Star Trek Movies The Complete Series	2007	—	£9.50
LT90	Star Trek Movies Quotable Series...	2010	—	£8.00

RITTENHOUSE ARCHIVES (USA) (continued)

Qty		Date	Odds	Sets
LT72	Star Trek Nemesis	2002	20p	£9.50
LT90	Star Trek The Next Generation Complete Series 1 (1987-1991) (Nos 1 to 88, 177 & 178)	2011	—	£8.00
LT90	Star Trek The Next Generation Complete Series 2 (1991-1994) (Nos 89 to 176, 179 & 180)	2012	—	£9.50
LT100	Star Trek The Next Generation Heroes and Villains	2013	—	£9.50
LT110	Star Trek The Next Generation Quotable Series ...	2005	—	£9.50
LT110	Star Trek The Original Series Archives	2009	—	£9.50
LT110	Star Trek The Original Series 40th Anniversary 1st Series	2006	—	£9.50
LT110	Star Trek The Original Series 40th Anniversary 2nd Series	2008	—	£9.50
LT100	Star Trek The Original Series Heroes and Villains	2013	—	£9.50
EL24	Star Trek The Original Series in Motion (3D)	1999	—	£20.00
LT110	Star Trek The Original Series Quotable	2004	—	£12.00
LT81	Star Trek The Remastered Original Series	2010	—	£8.00
LT183	Star Trek Voyager The Complete Series...	2002	—	£18.00
LT72	Star Trek Voyager Quotable Series	2012	—	£8.00
LT63	Stargate Atlantis Season 1	2005	—	£8.00
LT72	Stargate Atlantis Season 2	2006	—	£7.50
LT81	Stargate Atlantis Seasons 3 and 4	2008	—	£8.00
LT72	Stargate SG1 Season 1 to 3	2001	—	£9.50
LT72	Stargate SG1 Season 4	2002	—	£8.00
LT72	Stargate SG1 Season 5	2002	20p	£9.50
LT72	Stargate SG1 Season 6	2004	—	£9.50
LT3	Stargate SG1 Season 6 Checklist Corrected Cards	2004	—	£2.00
LT72	Stargate SG1 Season 7	2005	—	£8.00
LT81	Stargate SG1 Season 8	2006	—	£7.50
LT72	Stargate SG1 Season 9	2007	—	£7.50
LT72	Stargate SG1 Season 10	2008	—	£8.00
LT90	Stargate SG1 Heroes	2009	—	£8.50
LT72	Stargate Universe SG-U Season 1	2010	—	£8.00
LT98	Trueblood (TV Series)	2012	—	£9.50
LT72	Twilight Zone 1st Series	1999	—	£9.50
LT72	Twilight Zone 2nd Series	2000	—	£9.50
LT8/9	Twilight Zone 2nd Series Challenge Game (Minus 'S')	2000	—	£2.50
LT72	Twilight Zone 3rd Series	2002	—	£9.50
LT72	Twilight Zone 4th Series	2005	—	£9.50
LT79	Twilight Zone 50th Anniversary	2009	—	£8.50
LT72	Warehouse 13	2010	—	£8.00
LT63	Women of James Bond in Motion (3-D)	2003	—	£20.00
LT81	The Women of Star Trek	2010	—	£8.00
EL32	Women of Star Trek in Motion (3-D)	1999	—	£25.00
LT70	Women of Star Trek Voyager Holofex Series	2001	—	£16.00
LT72	X-Men Origins Wolverine	2009	—	£9.50
LT72	X-Men The Last Stand	2006	—	£8.00
LT72	Xena Warrior Princess Season 4 and 5	2001	—	£9.50
LT72	Xena Warrior Princess Season 6	2001	—	£9.50
LT63	Xena Warrior Princess Art & Images	2004	—	£9.50
LT72	Xena Warrior Princess Beauty & Brawn (No 70 not issued)	2002	20p	£9.50
LT72	Xena Warrior Princess Dangerous Liaisons	2007	—	£9.50
LT135	Xena Warrior Princess Quotable Series	2003	—	£15.00

Qty		Date	Odds	Sets

RITTENHOUSE ARCHIVES (USA) (continued)

Qty		Date	Odds	Sets
LT9	Xena Warrior Princess Quotable Series			
	Words from the Bard	2003	—	£4.00

RIVER GROUP (USA)

LT150	Dark Dominion	1993	—	£12.00
LT150	Plasm O	1993	—	£12.00
LT31	Splatter Bowl	1993	—	£6.00

RIVER WYE PRODUCTIONS

LT81	D-Day Commemorative Series	2005	—	£20.00
LT72	Hammer Horror Behind The Screams	2004	—	£20.00
LT9	Laurel and Hardy Babes At War (Limited Edition)...	2006	—	£12.00
LT90	Laurel & Hardy 70th Anniversary	1997	—	£20.00
LT72	Laurel & Hardy Millennium 2000 Celebration	2000	—	£18.00
LT72	Sherlock Holmes	2002	—	£25.00

THE 'RK' CONFECTIONERY CO. LTD

32	Felix	1922	£40.00	—

ROB ROY

L20	Manchester United Footballers	1995	—	£15.00

ROBERTSON LTD (Jam)

1	Advertisement Gollywog:			
	A Shaped figure	c1960	—	£4.00
	B Medium card 60 × 47mm...	c1960	—	£4.00
10	Musical Gollywogs:			
	A Shaped figure	c1960	£4.00	—
	B Medium card 60 × 47mm...	c1960	£4.00	—
10	Sporting Gollywogs			
	A Shaped figure	c1960	£4.00	—
	B Medium card 60 × 47mm...	c1960	£4.00	—

ROBERTSON & WOODCOCK LTD

50	British Aircraft Series	1930	£3.00	—

C. ROBINSON ARTWORKSHOP

L16	Plymouth Argyle FA Cup Squad 1983-84	1984	—	£8.00

ROBINSON'S BARLEY WATER

EL30	Sporting Records	1983	20p	£5.00

ROBINSON BROS. & MASTERS

25	Tea from the Garden to the House...	c1930	£12.00	—

ROCHE & CO. LTD

K50	Famous Footballers...	1927	—	£750.00
	49/50 (— No. 21)	1927	£12.00	—

THE ROCKET

MP11	Famous Knock-Outs	1923	£9.00	—

ROCKWELL

			Date	Odds	Sets
	Airship The Story of the R101:				
10	A	Standard size	2003	—	£4.50
L10	B	Large size	2003	—	£6.50
	Arsenal Goalscorers The Modern Era:				
10	A	Standard size	2010	—	£4.50
L10	B	Large size	2010	—	£7.00
	Bodyline — The Fight For The Ashes 1932-33:				
10	A	Standard size	2005	—	£4.50
L10	B	Large size	2005	—	£6.50
	Britain's Lost Railway Stations:				
10	A	Standard size	2005	—	£4.50
L10	B	Large size	2005	—	£6.50
	British Armoured Vehicles of World War II:				
10	A	Standard size	2001	—	£4.50
L10	B	Large size	2001	—	£6.50
	British Fighting Jets:				
10	A	Standard size	2003	—	£4.50
L10	B	Large size	2003	—	£6.50
	British Warplanes of the Second World War:				
10	A	Standard size	2000	—	£4.50
L10	B	Large size	2000	—	£6.50
10	Bygone Chingford		1998	—	£4.50
10	Bygone Highams Park		1998	—	£4.50
	Children's Book Illustrators of The Golden Age:				
10	A	Standard size	2005	—	£4.50
L10	B	Large size	2005	—	£6.50
L7	Classic Chelsea F.C.		2005	—	£5.00
L7	Classic Everton F.C.		2005	—	£5.00
	Classic Football Teams Before The First World War:				
10	A	Standard size	2000	—	£4.50
L10	B	Large size	2000	—	£6.50
	Classic Football Teams of the 1960s:				
10	A	Standard size	1999	—	£4.50
L10	B	Large size	1999	—	£6.50
	Classic Gunners (Arsenal F.C.):				
7	A	Standard size	2010	—	£4.50
L7	B	Large size	2001	—	£5.00
L7	Classic Hammers (West Ham United F.C.)		2003	—	£5.00
L7	Classic Liverpool F.C.		2005	—	£5.00
L7	Classic Reds (Manchester United F.C.)		2003	—	£5.00
	Classic Sci-Fi 'B' Movies:				
10	A	Standard size	2007	—	£4.50
L10	B	Large size	2007	—	£6.50
	Classic Spurs (Tottenham Hotspur F.C.):				
7	A	Standard size	2010	—	£4.50
L7	B	Large size	2002	—	£5.00
	Cunard In The 1950s:				
10	A	Standard size	2003	—	£4.50
L10	B	Large size	2003	—	£6.50
	Early Allied Warplanes:				
10	A	Standard size	2000	—	£4.50
L10	B	Large size (79 × 62mm)	2000	—	£6.50
LT10	C	Large size (89 × 64mm)	2000	—	£7.50

Qty			Date	Odds	Sets
	ROCKWELL (continued)				
	Early Balloon Flight:				
10	A	Standard size	2001	—	£4.50
L10	B	Large size	2001	—	£6.50
	Early Locomotives Series One:				
10	A	Standard size	2005	—	£4.50
L10	B	Large size	2005	—	£6.50
	Early Locomotives Series Two:				
10	A	Standard size	2005	—	£4.50
L10	B	Large size	2005	—	£6.50
	Family Cars of the 1950s:				
10	A	Standard size	2000	—	£4.50
L10	B	Large size (79 × 62mm)	2000	—	£6.50
LT10	C	Large size (89 × 64mm)	2000	—	£7.50
	Flying So High — West Ham United F.C. 1964-66:				
10	A	Standard size	2005	—	£4.50
L10	B	Large size	2005	—	£6.50
	German Armoured Vehicles of World War II:				
10	A	Standard size	2001	—	£4.50
L10	B	Large size (79 × 62mm)	2001	—	£6.50
LT10	C	Large size (89 × 64mm)	2001	—	£7.50
	German Warplanes of the Second World War:				
10	A	Standard size	2000	—	£4.50
L10	B	Large size (79 × 62mm)	2000	—	£6.50
LT10	C	Large size (89 × 64mm)	2000	—	£7.50
	The Great Heavyweights (Boxers):				
10	A	Standard size	2002	—	£4.50
L10	B	Large size	2002	—	£6.50
	The Great Middleweights (Boxers):				
10	A	Standard size	2002	—	£4.50
L10	B	Large size	2002	—	£6.50
	Heath Robinson At The Seaside:				
10	A	Standard size	2010	—	£4.50
L10	B	Large size	2010	—	£7.00
	Heath Robinson Sporting Eccentricities:				
10	A	Standard size	2010	—	£4.50
L10	B	Large size	2005	—	£7.00
	Heath Robinson Urban Life:				
10	A	Standard size	2010	—	£4.50
L10	B	Large size	2005	—	£7.00
	The Hornby Book of Trains:				
10	A	Standard size	2005	—	£4.50
L10	B	Large size	2005	—	£6.50
	Hurricane Flying Colours:				
10	A	Standard size	2002	—	£4.50
L10	B	Large size	2002	—	£6.50
	Images of World War One:				
10	A	Standard size	1999	—	£4.50
L10	B	Large size (79 × 62mm)	1999	—	£6.50
LT10	C	Large size (89 × 64mm)	1999	—	£7.50
	Lost Warships of WWII:				
10	A	Standard size	2002	—	£4.50
L10	B	Large size	2002	—	£6.50
	Meccano The Aviation Covers:				
10	A	Standard size	2006	—	£4.50
L10	B	Large size	2006	—	£6.50

ROCKWELL (continued)

Meccano The Railway Covers:

Qty			Date	Odds	Sets
10	A	Standard size … … … … … … … … … …	2006	–	£4.50
L10	B	Large size … … … … … … … … … … … .	2006	–	£6.50

Mighty Atoms The All Time Greats (Boxers):

10	A	Standard size … … … … … … … … … …	2004	–	£4.50
L10	B	Large size… … … … … … … … … … …	2004	–	£6.50

Modern Family Cars:

15	A	Standard size … … … … … … … … …	2001	–	£7.00
L15	B	Large size (79 × 62mm) … … … … … …	2001	–	£10.00
LT15	C	Large size (89 × 64mm) … … … … … …	2001	–	£11.00

The 1948 Australians (Cricketers):

10	A	Standard size … … … … … … … … … … ..	2006	–	£4.50
L10	B	Large size … … … … … … … … … … … .	2006	–	£6.50

Olympic, Titanic, Britannic (Liners):

25	A	Standard size … … … … … … … … … …	2001	–	£9.50
L25	B	Large size… … … … … … … … … … …	2001	–	£11.00

Post War Wimbledon Ladies Champions 1st Series:

10	A	Standard size … … … … … … … … … …	2004	–	£4.50
L10	B	Large size… … … … … … … … … … …	2004	–	£6.50

Post-War Wimbledon Ladies Champions 2nd Series:

10	A	Standard size … … … … … … … … … …	2005	–	£4.50
L10	B	Large size… … … … … … … … … … …	2005	–	£6.50

Post War Wimbledon Men's Champions 1st Series:

10	A	Standard size … … … … … … … … … …	2004	–	£4.50
L10	B	Large size… … … … … … … … … … …	2004	–	£6.50

Post-War Wimbledon Men's Champions 2nd Series:

10	A	Standard size … … … … … … … … … …	2005	–	£4.50
L10	B	Large size… … … … … … … … … … …	2005	–	£6.50

Relegated to History England's Lost Football Grounds:

10	A	Standard size … … … … … … … … … …	2004	–	£4.50
L10	B	Large size… … … … … … … … … … …	2004	–	£6.50

Solar System:

10	A	Standard size … … … … … … … … … …	2001	–	£4.50
L10	B	Large size… … … … … … … … … … …	2001	–	£6.50

Spitfire Flying Colours:

10	A	Standard size … … … … … … … … … …	1999	–	£4.50
L10	B	Large size (79 × 62mm) … … … … … …	1999	–	£6.50
LT10	C	Large size (89 × 64mm) … … … … … …	1999	–	£7.50

Spurs Great Post-War Goalscorers Series 1 (Tottenham Hotspur F.C.):

10	A	Standard size … … … … … … … … … …	2007	–	£4.50
L10	B	Large size… … … … … … … … … … …	2007	–	£6.50

Spurs Great Post-War Goalscorers Series 2 (Tottenham Hotspur F.C.):

10	A	Standard size … … … … … … … … … …	2007	–	£4.50
L10	B	Large size… … … … … … … … … … …	2007	–	£6.50

Spurs 1960-1963 — The Glory Years (Tottenham Hotspur F.C.):

10	A	Standard size … … … … … … … … … …	2005	–	£4.50
LT10	B	Large size… … … … … … … … … … …	2005	–	£6.50

Suffragettes:

10	A	Standard size … … … … … … … … … …	2005	–	£4.50
L10	B	Large size… … … … … … … … … … …	2005	–	£6.50

Qty				Date	Odds	Sets
		ROCKWELL (continued)				
	The Titanic Series:					
25	A	Standard size		1999	—	£9.50
L25	B	Large size (79 × 62mm)		1999	—	£11.00
LT25	C	Large size (89 × 64mm)		1999	—	£12.00
	Twopenny Tube Edwardian Sketches of The Central					
	Railway:					
10	A	Standard size		2010	—	£4.50
L10	B	Large size		2010	—	£7.00
L7	World Cup 1966			2005	—	£5.00
	World War I Posters:					
10	A	Standard size		2001	—	£4.50
L10	B	Large size...		2001	—	£6.50
	World War II Posters — The Home Front:					
10	A	Standard size		2001	—	£4.50
L10	B	Large size...		2001	—	£6.50
	World War II Posters — Industry:					
10	A	Standard size		2005	—	£4.50
L10	B	Large size...		2007	—	£6.50
	World War II Posters — Morale:					
10	A	Standard size		2005	—	£4.50
L10	B	Large size...		2007	—	£6.50
	World War II Posters — The Services:					
10	A	Standard size		2001	—	£4.50
L10	B	Large size...		2001	—	£6.50

ROGERSTOCK

		Date	Odds	Sets
LT13	American Cars of the 1950s	2007	—	£6.50
LT13	American Cars of the 1960s	2007	—	£6.50
LT13	Ferrari — Classic Ferrari Models 1958-92	2007	—	£6.50
LT13	Jaguar — Classic Jaguar Models 1950-96	2007	—	£6.50

ROLLS-ROYCE MOTORS

		Date	Odds	Sets
L25	Bentley Motor Cars 1st Series:			
	A Original Issue Thin frameline back	1985	£2.40	£60.00
	B Inscribed 'Second Edition' thin frameline back	1987	£2.00	£50.00
L25	Bentley Motor Cars 2nd Series thick frameline to			
	two sides	1987	£2.00	£50.00
L25	Rolls Royce Motor Cars 1st Series:			
	A Original Issue Thin frameline back	1985	—	£60.00
	B Inscribed 'Second Edition' thin frameline back	1987	£2.00	£50.00
L25	Rolls Royce Motor Cars 2nd Series thick frameline			
	to two sides	1987	—	£50.00

ROSSI'S ICES

		Date	Odds	Sets
M48	Flags of the Nations	1975	20p	£6.00
25	History of Flight 1st Series	1966	60p	£15.00
25	History of Flight 2nd Series	1966	60p	£15.00
25	World's Fastest Aircraft	1966	60p	£15.00

D. ROWLAND

		Date	Odds	Sets
L20	Arsenal F.C. 2002-03	2004	—	£15.00
25	Association Footballers Series 1	1999	—	£12.50
25	Association Footballers Series 2	1999	40p	£10.00

Qty				Date	Odds	Sets
	D. ROWLAND (continued)					
25	Association Footballers Series 3			1999	—	£7.50
25	Association Footballers Series 4			1999	—	£7.50
25	Association Footballers Series 5			1999	30p	£7.50
20	Boxers Series 1			1999	—	£7.00
20	Boxing Legends Series 1			1999	—	£7.00
L20	Chelsea F.C. 2002-03			2004	—	£12.00
25	Cricketers Series 1			1999	30p	£7.50
25	Cricketers Series 2			1999	—	£7.50
20	Famous Footballers Series 1			1999	—	£6.00
20	Famous Footballers Series 2			1999	30p	£6.00
20	Famous Footballers Series 3			1999	50p	£10.00
20	Famous Footballers Series 4 (Managers)			1999	30p	£6.00
20	Famous Footballers Series 5			1999	—	£10.00
L10	Famous Footballers Series 6 (Teams)			2000	—	£4.00
L10	Famous Footballers Series 7 (Teams)			2000	—	£4.00
L20	Liverpool F.C. 2002-03			2004	—	£12.00
L20	Manchester City F.C. 2002-03			2004	—	£12.00
L20	Manchester United F.C. 2002-03			2004	—	£12.00
L20	Wolverhampton Wanderers F.C. 2002-03			2004	—	£12.00

ROWNTREE & CO.

Qty				Date	Odds	Sets
25	Celebrities of 1900 Period			1900	£28.00	—
M20	Merry Monarchs			1977	20p	£4.00
	The Old and the New:					
25	A	i	Rowntree's Elect Chocolate (with coupon)	c1920	£9.00	—
25	A	ii	Rowntree's Elect Chocolate (without coupon)	c1920	£5.00	—
48	B	i	Rowntree's Elect Chocolate Delicious (with coupon)	c1920	£9.00	—
48	B	ii	Rowntree's Elect Chocolate Delicious (without coupon)	c1920	£5.00	—
M18	Prehistoric Animals			1978	30p	£5.00
M10	Texan Tall Tales of The West			1977	—	£20.00
120	Treasure Trove Pictures			c1930	£2.00	—
24	York Views:					
	A	Unicoloured		c1920	£14.00	—
	B	Coloured		c1920	£14.00	—

ROYAL ARMY MEDICAL CORPS HISTORICAL MUSEUM

Qty				Date	Odds	Sets
M16	Centenary Year Royal Army Medical Corps Victoria Crosses 1898-1998			1998	—	£6.00

ROYAL LEAMINGTON SPA

Qty				Date	Odds	Sets
25	Royal Leamington Spa			1971	20p	£2.50
	Album				—	£4.00

ROYAL NATIONAL LIFEBOAT INSTITUTION

Qty				Date	Odds	Sets
M16	Lifeboats			1979	30p	£5.00

ROYAL NAVY SUBMARINE MUSEUM

Qty				Date	Odds	Sets
M25	History of R.N. Submarines (including album)			1996	—	£10.00

Qty		Date	Odds	Sets

ROYAL SOCIETY FOR THE PREVENTION OF ACCIDENTS (RoSPA)

Qty		Date	Odds	Sets
24	Modern British Cars...	1953	£2.00	£50.00
22	Modern British Motor Cycles	1953	£3.60	—
25	New Traffic Signs	1966	24p	£6.00
24	Veteran Cars 1st Series	1955	£1.50	£36.00
24	Veteran Cars 2nd Series	1957	£2.00	£50.00

ROY ROGERS BUBBLE GUM

M24	Roy Rogers — In Old Amarillo (plain back)	1955	25p	£6.00
M24	Roy Rogers — South of Caliente (plain back)	1955	25p	£6.00

RUBY

L10	Famous Beauties of the Day...	1923	£10.00	—
L6	Famous Film Stars	1923	£10.00	—

RUBY CARDS

10	A Tribute to Dad's Army	2009	—	£5.00

RUGBY FOOTBALL UNION

50	English Internations 1980-1991	1991	—	£12.50

RUGLYS

L12	England Rugby Stars (Series Ref 1003)	2000	—	£6.00
L8	England Soccer Stars (Series Ref 1006)	2000	—	£4.00
L20	Manchester United Soccer Stars (Series Ref 1004)	2000	—	£10.00
L4	Shearer (Alan) Soccer Star (Series Ref 1005)	2000	—	£2.50
L8	Snooker Stars (Series Ref 1007)	2000	—	£4.00
L12	Wales Rugby Classics (Series Ref 1002)	2000	—	£6.00
L20	Wales Rugby Stars (Series Ref 1001)	2000	—	£10.00

S. & B. PRODUCTS

?69	Torry Gillicks's Internationals...	c1950	£10.00	—

S.C.M.C.C.

15	Stoke's Finest Hour (1972 Football Cup Final)... ...	2002	—	£5.50

S.P.C.K.

L12	Bible Promises Illustrated, Series VIII...	c1940	£2.00	—
L12	Cathedrals of Northern England, Series VII...	c1940	£2.00	—
L12	Palestine, Series II	c1940	£2.00	—
L12	Scenes from English Church History, Series V ...	c1940	60p	£7.50
L12	Scenes from Genesis, Series XI	c1940	£2.00	—
L12	Scenes from Lives of the Saints, Series VI	c1940	£1.00	£12.00
L12	Southern Cathedrals, Series XVI	c1940	£2.00	—
L12	Stories of Joseph and David, Series I...	c1940	£2.00	—

SSPC (USA)

LT45	200 Years of Freedom 1776-1976	1976	—	£7.50

SAINSBURY LTD

M12	British Birds	1924	£8.00	—
M12	Foreign Birds	1924	£8.00	—

Qty		Date	Odds	Sets
	SANDERS BROTHERS			
25	Birds, Poultry, etc	1924	£7.00	—
20	Dogs	1924	£4.00	£80.00
25	Recipes	1924	£4.40	—
	SANDERSON			
24	World's Most Beautiful Birds	c1925	£10.00	—

SANITARIUM HEALTH FOOD CO. LTD (New Zealand)

Qty		Date	Odds	Sets
EL12	Airliners of the 90's	1991	—	£6.00
EL12	Alpine Flora of New Zealand.....................	1975	40p	£5.00
EL12	Alpine Sports	1986	35p	£4.00
EL12	Amazing Animals of the World	1985	60p	—
LT8	Amazing Facts	1998	—	£4.00
M30	Another Look at New Zealand	1971	20p	£4.50
M30	Antarctic Adventure	1972	30p	—
M20	The Aviation Card Series	1995	—	£3.50
LT16	Babe & Friends — The Film	1999	—	£4.00
EL12	Ball Sports	1989	50p	£6.00
M4	Bee — 3D Motion Cards	1998	—	£2.50
EL12	Big Cats...	1992	—	£4.50
M20	Big Rigs...	1983	20p	£3.50
M20	Big Rigs at Work	1986	20p	£3.50
M20	Big Rigs 3	1992	—	£3.00
EL12	Big Sea Creatures	1994	35p	£4.00
L12	Boarding Pass (Landmarks Around the World) ...	1998	—	£5.00
EL12	Bush Birds of New Zealand	1981	50p	—
M20	Cars of the Seventies	1976	30p	£6.00
LT20	Centenaryville.....................................	1999	—	£4.00
EL12	Clocks Through the Ages	1990	40p	£5.00
M20	Conservation Caring for Our Land	1974	25p	£5.00
EL12	Curious Conveyances	1984	40p	£5.00
EL12	Did You Know.....................................	1994	35p	£4.00
M4	Discount Destination Passport	1991	—	£4.00
M20	Discover Indonesia	1977	20p	£3.00
M20	Discover Science With the DSIR	1989	20p	£3.00
EL12	Discovering New Zealand Reptile World	1983	35p	£4.00
M20	Exotic Cars	1987	25p	£5.00
M20	Exploring Our Solar System	1982	25p	—
M24	Famous New Zealanders	1971	25p	£6.00
M20	Farewell to Steam	1981	30p	£6.00
M30	Fascinating Orient	1966	20p	£4.00
EL12	Focus on New Zealand 1st Series	1982	35p	£4.00
EL12	Focus on New Zealand 2nd Series	1982	35p	£4.00
LT12	Have You Had Your Weet-Bix (Sports)	1997	—	£4.00
EL12	High Action Sports	1994	35p	£4.00
EL12	Historic Buildings 1st Series	1982	50p	£6.00
EL12	Historic Buildings 2nd Series	1984	35p	£4.00
M30	The History of New Zealand Railways	1968	50p	—
M20	History of Road Transport in New Zealand	1979	25p	£5.00
EL12	Horse Breeds	1990	40p	£5.00
LT15	Hunchback of Notre Dame (Disney)	1996	—	£5.00
EL10	Hunchback of Notre Dame (Disney)	1996	—	£4.50
LT8	It's Showtime (Disney)	1997	—	£4.00
EL12	Jet Aircraft	1974	60p	—
M20	Kiwi Heroes	1994	20p	£3.00

SANITARIUM HEALTH FOOD CO. LTD (New Zealand) (continued)

Qty		Date	Odds	Sets
LT9	Kiwi Kids Tryathlon	1999	—	£4.00
M20	Kiwis Going for Gold	1992	—	£3.00
EL12	The Lion King (Disney)	1995	—	£4.00
M20	Living in Space	1992	—	£3.00
M20	Looking at Canada	1978	20p	£3.00
M20	Mammals of the Seas	1985	20p	£3.00
EL12	Man Made Wonders of the World	1987	35p	£4.00
M20	The Many Stranded Web of Nature	1983	25p	£6.00
M30	Marineland Wonders	1967	50p	£15.00
M20	Motor Bike Card Series	1995	—	£5.00
EL12	Mountaineering	1987	35p	£4.00
LT10	Mr Men	1997	40p	£4.00
M25	National Costumes of the Old World	1968	50p	£12.50
M20	New Zealand's Booming Industries	1975	20p	£3.00
EL12	New Zealand Custom Vans	1994	—	£4.00
EL12	New Zealand Disasters	1991	35p	£4.00
M20	N.Z. Energy Resources	1976	20p	£3.50
EL12	New Zealand Inventions and Discoveries	1991	35p	£4.00
EL12	New Zealand Lakes 1st Series	1977	60p	—
EL12	New Zealand Lakes 2nd Series	1978	35p	£4.00
M30	New Zealand National Parks	1973	33p	£10.00
M20	New Zealand Reef Fish	1984	20p	£3.00
M20	New Zealand Rod & Custom Cars	1979	25p	£5.00
M20	New Zealand Summer Sports	1984	20p	£3.50
M30	New Zealand Today	1966	25p	£7.50
EL12	New Zealand Waterfalls	1981	50p	—
M20	New Zealanders in Antarctica	1987	25p	£5.00
M20	New Zealanders on Top of the World	1991	20p	£3.00
EL12	N.Z.R. Steam Engines	1976	—	£12.00
M20	The 1990 Commonwealth Games	1989	20p	£4.00
M20	1990 Look How We've Grown	1990	20p	£3.00
EL12	Ocean Racers	1986	35p	£4.00
M20	100 Years of New Zealand National Parks	1987	20p	£3.00
EL12	Our Fascinating Fungi	1980	50p	—
M20	Our Golden Fleece	1981	20p	£3.00
M20	Our South Pacific Island Neighbours	1974	25p	£5.00
M20	Our Weather	1980	20p	£3.00
EL12	Party Tricks	1993	—	£4.00
M20	Peanuts (Cartoon Characters)	1993	50p	—
M20	The Phonecard Collection	1994	—	£3.00
EL12	Power Boats in New Zealand	1990	35p	£4.00
EL12	Robin Hood (Disney)	1996	—	£4.00
M20	Saving the World's Endangered Wildlife	1991	20p	£3.00
EL12	Shipping in Our Coastal Waters	1988	50p	£6.00
EL12	Silly Dinosaurs	1997	—	£4.00
M8	Snow White & the Seven Dwarfs (3-D)	1997	—	£4.00
EL12	Spanning New Zealand	1992	—	£4.00
M20	Spectacular Sports	1974	25p	£5.00
LT12	Speed	1998	—	£4.00
M20	The Story of New Zealand Aviation	1977	25p	£5.00
M20	The Story of New Zealand in Stamps	1977	25p	£5.00
M20	Super Cars	1972	50p	£10.00
EL12	Surf Life Saving	1986	35p	£4.00
LT12	Then & Now	1998	—	£4.00
M20	Timeless Japan	1975	25p	£5.00

SANITARIUM HEALTH FOOD CO. LTD (New Zealand) (continued)

Qty		Date	Odds	Sets
M20	Treasury of Maori Life	1980	20p	£3.00
EL12	Veteran Cars	1971	50p	—
M20	Vintage Cars	1973	40p	£8.00
M20	Weet-bix Stamp Album (Stamp Collecting)	1994	30p	—
M30	What Makes New Zealand Different	1967	60p	£18.00
EL12	Wild Flowers of New Zealand	1979	50p	£6.00
EL12	Wildlife Wonders — Endangered Animals of NZ ...	1993	—	£4.00
M20	The Wild South	1986	20p	£3.00
EL12	Windsports...	1989	35p	£4.00
M20	Wonderful Ways of Nature	1978	20p	£3.00
EL12	Wonderful Wool	1988	50p	—
M20	The Wonderful World of Disney...	1993	30p	£6.00
LT17	World Ball (Basketball)...	1997	—	£4.00
M20	World's Greatest Fun Parks	1990	20p	£4.00
M20	Your Journey Through Disneyland	1988	35p	£7.00

SAVOY PRODUCTS

Qty		Date	Odds	Sets
M56	Aerial Navigation...	c1925	£2.50	—
M56	Aerial Navigation Series B	c1925	£2.25	—
M56	Aerial Navigation, Series C	c1925	£2.25	—
M56	Famous British Boats	1928	£2.00	—

SCANLEN (Australia)

Qty		Date	Odds	Sets
M208	Cricket Series No. 3	1984	—	£30.00
L84	Cricketers 1989/90	1989	—	£20.00
L84	Cricketers 1990/91	1990	—	£20.00
L90	World Series Cricket	1981	—	£20.00

SCHOOL & SPORT

Qty		Date	Odds	Sets
M4	British Railway Engines	1922	£7.00	—
M4	British Regiments	1922	£7.00	—
M4	County Cricket Captains	1922	£15.00	—
M4	Wild Animals	1922	£7.00	—

THE SCHOOL FRIEND

Qty		Date	Odds	Sets
LP6	Famous Film Stars	1927	£10.00	—
EL10	Popular Girls of Cliff House School	1922	£10.00	—
L6	Popular Pictures	1923	£4.00	—

THE SCHOOL GIRL

Qty		Date	Odds	Sets
M12	Zoological Studies	1923	£3.00	—
M4	Zoological Studies (anonymous)	1923	£3.00	—

THE SCHOOLGIRLS OWN PAPER

Qty		Date	Odds	Sets
L3	Royal Family Portraits (anonymous)	c1925	£4.00	—

THE SCHOOLGIRLS' WEEKLY

Qty		Date	Odds	Sets
L1	HRH The Duke of York...	1922	—	£6.00
L4	Popular Pictures	1922	£4.00	—

SCORE (USA)

Qty		Date	Odds	Sets
LT704	Baseball...	1990	—	£30.00
LT47	Dallas Cowboys Cheerleaders	1993	—	£12.00
LT110	1991 NHL Rookie and Traded (Ice Hockey)	1991	—	£6.00

Qty		Date	Odds	Sets
	SCORE CARD COLLECTABLES			
10	Score (Footballers of the 1970s) 1st Series............	2011	—	£5.00
10	Score (Footballers of the 1970s) 2nd Series	2011	—	£5.00
	SCOTTISH DAILY EXPRESS			
EL24	Scotcard — Scottish Footballers	1973	£7.00	—
	SCOTTISH TOURIST BOARD			
L40	Places of Interest	1992	20p	£4.00
	THE SCOUT			
M9	Birds Eggs..	1925	£7.00	—
M12	Railway Engines...................................	1924	£7.00	—
	SCRAPBOOK MINICARDS			
27	Pendon Museum (model railway and village)	1978	20p	£2.50
	SCREEN ICONS			
10	Gregory Peck.....................................	2013	—	£5.00
10	Paul Newman......................................	2013	—	£5.00
10	Steve McQueen	2013	—	£5.00
	SEAGRAM			
25	Grand National Winners	1995	—	£20.00
	SECRETS			
K52	Film Stars Miniature Playing Cards	c1930	£1.70	—
	SELF SERVICE LAUNDERETTES			
50	150 Years of Locomotives	1955	£5.00	—
	SELLOTAPE PRODUCTS LTD			
35	Great Homes and Castles	1974	50p	£17.50
	SEMIC			
LT275	Equestrianism....................................	1997	—	£18.00
	SEW & SEW			
25	Bandsmen of the British Army	1960	£2.20	—
	A.J. SEWARD & CO. LTD			
40	Stars of the Screen..............................	1935	£11.00	—
	SEYMOUR MEAD & CO. LTD (Tea)			
24	The Island of Ceylon	1961	20p	£2.50
	SHARMAN NEWSPAPERS			
L24	Golden Age of Flying	1979	40p	£10.00
L24	Golden Age of Motoring	1979	40p	£10.00
L24	Golden Age of Steam	1979	40p	£10.00
	Albums for the three sets		—	£4.50
	EDWARD SHARP & SONS			
20	Captain Scarlet	c1970	£8.00	—
25	Hey Presto!	1968	20p	£2.50
100	Prize Dogs.......................................	c1925	£6.00	—

T. SHELDON COLLECTIBLES

L18	Central Lancashire Cricket League Clubs and Pavilions...	1997	—	£7.00
20	The Don (Reproductions of Don Bradman Cricket Cards) 2nd Series	2010	—	£10.00
10	Famous Old Standians...	2002	—	£4.00
20	Fryer's Roses	1999	—	£10.00
20	Kenyan Cricket I.C.C. World Cup	1999	—	£8.00
L6	Mailey Master of His Art (Cricketers)	2003	—	£4.00
L10	Match of The Day Aldershot Town v Accrington Stanley (10.8.03)	2004	—	£4.00
L10	Match of The Day Cwmbran Town v Maccabi Haifa (14.8.03)...	2004	—	£4.00
L10	Match of The Day Rochdale v Yeovil Town (9.8.03)	2003	—	£4.00
20	Olden Goldies (Cricketers)	1998	—	£10.00
L18	Out of the Blue into the Red (Labour Politicians) ...	1997	—	£7.00
18	Prominent Cricketers 1924 (reprint, G. Goode, Australia)	1999	—	£9.50
20	Stalybridge Celtic Football Club...	1996	—	£4.50
L18	We're Back Halifax Town A.F.C. 1998/99	1999	—	£7.00

SHELL (Oil)

14	Bateman Series	1930	£8.00	—
EL20	Great Britons	1972	£1.50	£30.00
16	History of Flight (metal coins)	1970	£1.50	—
M12	Olympic Greats including album	1992	—	£7.00
M16	3-D Animals	1971	£1.25	—
M16	Wonders of the World	c1975	£1.00	—

SHELL (Oil) (Australia)

M60	Beetle Series (Nd 301-360)	1962	60p	£36.00
M60	Birds (Nd 121-180)	1960	60p	—
M60	Butterflies & Moths (Nd 181-240)	1960	70p	—
M60	Citizenship (Nd 1-60)	1964	40p	£24.00
M60	Discover Australia with Shell (Nd 1-60)	1959	60p	—
M60	Meteorology (Nd 361-420)	1963	40p	£24.00
M60	Pets (Nd 481-540)	1965	50p	£30.00
M60	Shells, Fish and Coral (Nd 61-120)	1959	50p	—
M60	Transportation (Nd 241-300)	1961	40p	£24.00

SHELL (Oil) (New Zealand)

M48	Aircraft of the World...	1963	—	£20.00
M60	Cars of the World	1964	50p	£30.00
M40	Cars of the World	1992	—	£7.00
M20	The Flintstones (Film)	1994	40p	£8.00
M48	Racing Cars of the World	1964	—	£30.00
M37	Rugby Greats (The All Blacks)	1992	—	£12.00
M40	World of Cricket	1992	30p	£12.00

SHELLEY'S ICE CREAM

25	Essex — County Champions (cricket)	1984	—	£9.00

SHEPHERDS DAIRIES

100	Shepherds War Series	1915	£9.00	—

SHERIDAN COLLECTIBLES

LT12	Bobby Jones at St Andrews (Golf)	1995	—	£6.50
LT12	The Bobby Jones Story (Golfer)	1993	—	£6.50
L6	Golf Adventures of Par Bear	1994	—	£3.00
LT25	Players of the Ryder Cup '93 (Golf)	1994	—	£10.00
L7	Railway Posters — Golf	1996	—	£2.50
LT12	The Tom Morris Story (Golfer)	1994	—	£6.50
L7	Underground Art — Football & Wembley	1996	—	£2.50
L7	Underground Art — Rugby	1996	—	£2.50
L7	Underground Art — Wimbledon (Tennis)...	1996	—	£2.50
L7	Underground Art — Windsor	1996	—	£2.50
L12	Winners of the Ryder Cup 95	1996	—	£6.50

SHERMAN'S POOLS LTD

EL8	Famous Film Stars	1940	75p	£6.00
EL38	Searchlight on Famous Players...	1937	£5.50	—
EL37	Searchlight on Famous Teams (Football):			
	A 35 different	1938	£5.00	—
	B Aston Villa and Blackpool	1938	75p	£1.50

W. SHIPTON LTD

Trojan Gen-Cards Series 1:

5	Group 1 Famous Buildings	1959	£1.00	—
5	Group 2 Characters of Fiction	1959	£1.00	—
5	Group 3 Stars of Entertainment...	1959	£1.00	—
5	Group 4 Fight Against Crime...	1959	£1.00	—
5	Group 5 Prehistoric Monsters	1959	£1.00	—
5	Group 6 Railways	1959	£1.00	—
5	Group 7 Racing Cars	1959	£1.00	—
5	Group 8 Insect World	1959	£1.00	—
5	Group 9 Stars of Sport...	1959	£1.00	—
5	Group 10 Animal World	1959	£1.00	—
5	Group 11 Nursing	1959	£1.00	—
5	Group 12 Under the Sea	1959	£1.00	—
5	Group 13 Ballet	1959	£1.00	—
5	Group 14 Wild West	1959	£1.00	—
5	Group 15 Motor Cars	1959	£1.00	—

SIDELINES

| M23 | 19th Century Cricket Teams ... ... | 1987 | 20p | £4.00 |

SILVER KING & CO

| 1 | Advertisement Card... ... ... | 1905 | — | £15.00 |

SILVER SHRED

| 6 | British Medals... ... ... | c1920 | £20.00 | — |

SKETCHLEY CLEANERS

25	Communications	1960	30p	£7.50
25	Nature Series	1960	36p	£9.00
25	Tropical Birds	1960	50p	£12.50

SKYBOX (USA)

LT90	The Adventures of Batman & Robin (Cartoon)	1995	—	£9.50
LT60	Babylon 5	1996	—	£10.00
LT100	Babylon 5 Profiles	1999	—	£9.50

Qty		Date	Odds	Sets
	SKYBOX (USA) (continued)			
LT81	Babylon 5 Season Four	1998	—	£9.50
LT81	Babylon 5 Season Five	1998	—	£9.50
EL10	Babylon 5 Posters	1996	—	£6.00
LT72	Babylon 5 Special Edition...	1997	—	£9.50
EL72	Batman & Robin the Film	1997	—	£12.00
EL24	Batman & Robin Storyboards	1997	—	£12.00
LT90	Batman Master Series (Cartoon)	1995	—	£9.50
LT100	Batman Saga of The Dark Knight	1994	—	£12.00
LT94	Bill Nye The Science Guy...	1995	—	£8.50
LT90	Blue Chips (Basketball Film)	1994	—	£8.00
LT90	Cinderella — Walt Disney Film	1996	—	£9.50
LT45	D.C. Comics Stars	1994	—	£7.50
EL90	D.C. Comics Vertigo	1994	—	£9.50
LT100	D.C. Milestone (Comic Book Story)	1993	—	£8,00
LT100	Demolition Man — The Film	1993	—	£9.50
LT90	Disney's Aladdin	1993	—	£9.50
LT90	Free Willy 2 — The Film	1995	—	£8.00
LT75	Gargoyles Series 2	1996	—	£9.50
LT90	Harley Davidson Motor Cycles	1994	—	£9.50
LT101	Hunchback of Notre Dame — Disney Film	1996	—	£9.50
LT90	Jumanji — The Film...	1995	—	£9.50
LT90	The Lion King 1st Series — Walt Disney Film	1995	—	£9.50
LT80	The Lion King 2nd Series — Walt Disney Film ...	1995	—	£9.50
LT90	Lois & Clark — New Adventures of Superman... ...	1995	—	£9.50
LT100	The Making of Star Trek The Next Generation... ...	1994	—	£12.00
LT90	Mortal Kombat The Film	1995	—	£9.50
LT101	101 Dalmations — The Movie	1996	—	£9.50
LT90	The Pagemaster (Film)	1994	—	£12.50
LT102	Pocahontas (Disney film)	1997	—	£9.50
LT100	The Return of Superman	1993	—	£8.50
LT100	Sea Quest DSV	1993	—	£12.00
LT90	Snow White and the Seven Dwarfs	1994	—	£12.50
LT100	Star Trek Cinema 2000	2000	—	£12.00
LT48	Star Trek Deep Space Nine	1993	—	£9.50
LT100	Star Trek Deep Space Nine	1993	—	£15.00
LT100	Star Trek Deep Space Nine Memories From the			
	Future	1999	—	£9.50
LT82	Star Trek Deep Space Nine Profiles	1997	—	£9.50
EL60	Star Trek — First Contact	1996	—	£10.00
EL72	Star Trek — Generations	1994	—	£15.00
EL72	Star Trek — Insurrection	1998	—	£13.00
LT90	Star Trek Master Series 1st Series	1993	—	£13.50
LT100	Star Trek Master Series 2nd Series	1994	—	£12.00
LT39	Star Trek The Next Generation Behind the Scenes	1993	—	£9.50
LT82	Star Trek The Next Generation Profiles	2000	—	£12.00
LT96	Star Trek The Next Generation Season Two	1995	—	£9.50
LT108	Star Trek The Next Generation Season Three... ...	1995	—	£9.50
LT108	Star Trek The Next Generation Season Four	1996	—	£9.50
LT108	Star Trek The Next Generation Season Five	1996	—	£9.50
LT6	Star Trek The Next Generation Season Five foil			
	embossed	1996	—	£24.00
LT108	Star Trek The Next Generation Season Six...	1997	—	£9.50
LT103	Star Trek The Next Generation Season Seven ...	1999	—	£12.00
LT90	Star Trek The Original Series, Series One	1997	—	£9.50
LT81	Star Trek The Original Series, Series Two	1998	—	£9.50

Qty		Date	Odds	Sets
	SKYBOX (USA) (continued)			
LT75	Star Trek The Original Series, Series Three	1999	—	£15.00
LT12/13	Star Trek The Original Series, Series Three			
	Challenge Game (minus Letter C)	1999	—	£5.00
LT58	Star Trek The Original Series Character Log,			
	1st Series	1997	—	£9.50
LT52	Star Trek The Original Series Character Log,			
	2nd Series	1998	—	£9.50
LT48	Star Trek The Original Series Character Log,			
	3rd Series	1999	—	£12.00
LT100	Star Trek 30 Years Phase One	1995	—	£12.00
LT100	Star Trek 30 Years Phase Two	1996	—	£15.00
LT100	Star Trek 30 Years Phase Three	1996	—	£12.00
LT100	Star Trek Voyager — Closer to Home	1999	—	£13.00
LT90	Star Trek Voyager Profiles	1998	—	£14.00
LT98	Star Trek Voyager Season One, Series 1	1995	—	£9.50
LT90	Star Trek Voyager Season One, Series 2	1995	—	£9.50
LT100	Star Trek Voyager Season Two	1996	—	£9.50
LT3	Star Trek Voyager Season Two Xenobio.........	1997	—	£9.00
EL90	Superman Platinum Series	1994	—	£12.00
LT90	The Three Musketeers — The Movie	1997	—	£9.50
LT98	Toy Story — The Film	1996	—	£9.50
LT74	Toy Story 2 — The Film	1996	—	£9.50
LT100	Ultraverse	1993	—	£9.50
LT81	Wild Wild West — The Movie	1999	—	£9.50

SKYFOTOS LTD

Qty		Date	Odds	Sets
?38	Merchant Ships	c1965	£2.50	—

SLADE & BULLOCK LTD

Qty		Date	Odds	Sets
25	Cricket Series...	c1925	£60.00	—
25	Football Terms	c1925	£30.00	—
	Modern Inventions:			
25	A Front light and dark blue	c1925	£12.00	—
25	B Front yellow and purple	c1925	£15.00	—
20	Now and Then Series	c1925	£15.00	—
25	Nursery Rhymes	c1925	£15.00	—
25	Science and Skill Series	c1925	£15.00	—
25	Simple Toys and How to Make Them	c1925	£15.00	—
24	World's Most Beautiful Butterflies	c1925	£10.00	—

SLOAN & GRAHAM

Qty		Date	Odds	Sets
L20	Magnificent Magpies 92/93 squad (Newcastle FC)	1993	—	£5.00
L5	Magnificent Magpies 92-93 2nd Series			
	(Newcastle F.C.)	1993	—	£3.00
25	Newcastle All Time Greats (Football)	1993	—	£5.00
L2	Newcastle Footballers (Keegan/Beardsley)			
	Plain back	1993	—	£1.50
L12	Sunderland All Time Greats (Football)	1993	—	£5.00
L14	Sunderland Legends of '73 (Football)............	1993	—	£5.00

P. SLUIS

Qty		Date	Odds	Sets
EL30	Tropical Birds	1962	£1.00	—

SMART NOVELS

Qty		Date	Odds	Sets
MP12	Stage Artistes and Entertainers	c1925	£5.00	—

Qty		Date	Odds	Sets

SNAP CARDS PRODUCTS LTD

Qty		Date	Odds	Sets
L50	ATV Stars 1st Series	1958	£2.80	—
L48	ATV Stars 2nd Series	1960	£2.20	£110.00
L50	Associated Rediffusion Stars	1960	£2.80	£140.00
L25	Dotto (Celebrities) (photo)	1959	£1.80	—
L25	Dotto (Celebrities) (sketches)	1959	£1.80	—

H.A. SNOW

Qty		Date	Odds	Sets
12	Hunting Big Game in Africa	c1920	£7.00	

SOCCER BUBBLE GUM

Qty		Date	Odds	Sets
L48	Soccer Teams, No. 1 Series	1957	£2.50	—
L48	Soccer Teams, No. 2 Series	1958	£3.50	—

SOCCER STAR CARDS

Qty		Date	Odds	Sets
20	Soccer Star 1st Series	2010	—	£7.50
20	Soccer Star 2nd Series	2010	—	£7.50
20	Soccer Star 3rd Series	2010	—	£7.50
20	Soccer Star 4th Series	2010	—	£7.50

SODASTREAM

Qty		Date	Odds	Sets
25	Historical Buildings	1957	20p	£5.00

SOLDIER MAGAZINE

Qty		Date	Odds	Sets
M24	The British Army	1993	—	£5.00

SOMPORTEX LTD

Qty		Date	Odds	Sets
L50	The Exciting World of James Bond 007	1965	£7.00	—
L60	Famous TV Wrestlers	1964	£3.50	—
L60	Film Scene Series James Bond 007	1964	£6.50	—
L72	John Drake — Danger Man	1966	£6.00	—
L72	The Saint	1967	£7.00	—
L78	Sean Connery as James Bond (You Only Live Twice) (real colour film, issued in strips of 3) ...	1967	£11.00	—
L72	Thunderball James Bond 007:			
	A Complete set...........................	1966	—	£325.00
	B 71 different (minus No. 24)	1966	£3.75	£275.00
L73	Thunderbirds (coloured)	1966	£7.00	—
L72	Thunderbirds (black and white):			
	A Size 90 × 64mm..........................	1966	£3.00	—
	B Size 77 × 57mm..........................	1966	£5.50	—
L36	Weirdies	1968	£1.25	—

SONNY BOY

Qty		Date	Odds	Sets
50	Railway Engines:			
	A White back	c1960	20p	£8.00
	B Cream back	c1960	20p	£8.00

SOUTH WALES CONSTABULARY

Qty		Date	Odds	Sets
EL36	British Stamps	1983	—	£12.00
EL36	Castles and Historic Places in Wales	1988	33p	£12.00
EL36	City of Cardiff	1989	60p	—
EL35	The '82 Squad (rugby union).....................	1982	£1.25	—
EL36	Merthyr Tydfil Borough Council	1987	—	£12.00
EL37	Payphones Past and Present	1987	70p	£25.00
EL36	Rhymney Valley District Council	1986	—	£12.00

Qty		Date	Odds	Sets
	SOUTH WALES CONSTABULARY (continued)			
EL20	South Wales Constabulary	1990	—	£10.00
M32	Sport-a-Card	1991	—	£16.00
	SOUTH WALES ECHO			
L36	Cardiff City Legends (Footballers)	2003	—	£7.50
50	Great Welsh Rugby Players	1992	—	£7.50
	SPACE VENTURES (USA)			
LT37	Moon Mars Space Shots (embossed)......	1991	—	£10.00
LT110	Space Shots 1st Series	1990	—	£16.00
LT110	Space Shots 2nd Series	1991	—	£9.50
LT110	Space Shots 3rd Series	1992	—	£12.00
	SPAR GROCERS			
EL30	Walt Disney	1972	£2.00	£60.00
	SPILLERS NEPHEWS			
25	Conundrum Series	c1910	£20.00	—
40	Views of South Wales and District	c1910	£20.00	—
	SPOOKTASTIC CARDS			
10	Karloff (Boris Karloff Tribute to the Horror Legend)	2010	—	£5.00
	SPORT AND ADVENTURE			
M46	Famous Footballers......	1922	£4.50	—
	SPORT IN PRINT			
M64	Nottinghamshire Cricketers	1989	—	£35.00
	SPORT IN VIEW			
25	Pro's and Poetry 1920s Football and Cricket	2012	—	£7.00
	The Sporting Art of Amos Ramsbottom from 1900s:			
L16	Set 1 Football and Rugby......	2012	—	£6.00
EL10	Set 2 Football......	2012	—	£6.00
EL10	Set 3 Cricket	2012	—	£6.00
EL6	Set 4 Lancashire League Cricket	2012	—	£5.00
EL7	Set 5 Rugby Union	2012	—	£5.00
EL6	Set 6 Rugby League	2012	—	£5.00
EL5	Set 7 General Sport	2012	—	£4.50
	P. J. SPORTING			
L10	International Cricketers	2001	—	£8.00
	SPORTING PROFILES			
L8	Arsenal F.C. F.A. Cup Winners 1930 Programme			
	Covers	2006	—	£5.00
L9	Arsenal F.C. F.A. Cup Winners 1971 Programme			
	Covers	2006	—	£5.00
L13	Ashes Set Match Action — Cricketers	2005	—	£6.50
L5	Ashes Set Match Action — Cricket Bonus Set			
	Programme Covers..	2005	—	£3.50
L10	Aston Villa F.C. European Cup Winners 1982			
	Programme Covers...	2006	—	£6.00
L15	Ayrton Senna 1960-1994	2005	—	£6.50

		Date	Odds	Sets

SPORTING PROFILES (continued)

Qty		Date	Odds	Sets
L12	The Beatles Magazine Covers	2006	–	£6.00
L20	Bob Dylan Concert Posters	2009	–	£7.50
15	Boxing Greats	2003	–	£5.00
L15	Bruce Lee Film Posters	2005	–	£6.50
L15	Bruce Springsteen Concert Posters	2009	–	£6.50
L20	Cardiff City F.C. European Adventure 1964-70 Programme Covers	2005	–	£7.50
L20	Carry On Up The Card Set (Carry On Film Stars)	2005	–	£9.00
L16	Cassius Clay The Early Years	2002	–	£9.00
L10	Celtic F.C. 1967 European Cup Winners Programme Covers	2004	–	£6.50
L20	Charles Buchan's Football Monthly Magazine Covers	2004	–	£9.50
L10	Chelsea F.C. European Cup Winners 1971 Programme Covers	2006	–	£6.00
L10	Chelsea F.C. F.A Cup Winners 1970 Programme Covers	2006	–	£5.00
L8	Circus Posters From Around 1900	2005	–	£5.00
L15	Classic Le Mans Posters	2007	–	£6.50
L15	Classic Monaco Posters (Grand Prix)	2007	–	£6.50
EL8	Classic Teams Arsenal F.C.	2006	–	£4.00
EL8	Classic Teams Chelsea F.C.	2006	–	£4.00
EL8	Classic Teams Liverpool F.C.	2006	–	£4.00
EL8	Classic Teams Manchester United F.C.	2006	–	£4.00
EL8	Classic Teams Tottenham Hotspur F.C.	2006	–	£4.00
EL8	Classic Teams West Ham United F.C.	2006	–	£4.00
L15	The Cliff Richard Collection	2004	–	£7.50
L10	Dads Army	2006	–	£5.00
L15	David Bowie Concert Posters	2010	–	£6.50
L12	England Players World Cup 1966	2007	–	£6.00
L6	England World Cup 1966 (Programme Covers, Posters & Ticket)	2006	–	£4.50
L9	Everton F.C. F.A. Cup Winners 1966 Programme Covers	2007	–	£5.00
L17	F.A. Cup Final Programme Covers 1923-1939	2001	–	£8.00
L20	F.A. Cup Final Programme Covers 1946-1965	2003	–	£8.00
L20	F.A. Cup Final Programme Covers 1966-1982	2004	–	£8.00
L21	F.A. Cup Final Programme Covers 1983-2000	2006	–	£8.00
L12	Fawlty Towers	2005	–	£6.50
L20	Frank Bruno Programme Covers	2005	–	£7.50
L9	The Golden Age of Middleweights 1980-1989	2006	–	£5.00
L15	Great British Cars of the 1950s	2004	–	£7.50
L12	The Greatest Cassius Clay Bonus Card Set Programme Covers 1958-1962	2010	–	£6.00
L50	The Greatest Muhammad Ali	1993	–	£12.00
L4	Heavyweight Champions of the Naughty 1890s (Boxing)	2000	–	£2.50
L40	Henry Cooper (Boxer)	1997	–	£10.50
L20	Heroes of the Prize Ring	1994	–	£6.00
L14	Houdini Show Posters	2007	–	£6.50
L8	Ipswich Town F.C. F.A. Cup Winners 1978 Programme Covers	2007	–	£5.00
L15	Iron Maiden Concert Posters	2010	–	£6.50
L30	'Iron' Mike Tyson (Boxer)	2004	–	£10.00
L5	'Iron' Mike Tyson (Boxer) Bonus Series	2004	–	£2.50
L20	Jack Nicklaus – Sports Illustrated	2005	–	£7.50

140

SPORTING PROFILES (continued)

Qty		Date	Odds	Sets
L25	Joe Louis A Career History (Boxer)	2000	—	£12.50
L20	Johnny Cash Concert Posters	2009	—	£7.50
L20	The Krays	2009	—	£7.50
L36	Larry Holmes (Boxer) Programme Covers............	2006	—	£10.00
L10	Led Zeppelin Album Covers	2006	—	£5.00
L8	Leeds United F.C. F.A. Cup Winners 1972			
	Programme Covers	2007	—	£5.00
L30	Lennox Lewis Programme Covers	2006	—	£10.00
L15	Liverpool F.C. Champions League Winners 2005			
	Programme Covers	2005	—	£6.50
L6	Liverpool F.C. European Cup Finals 1977-2005			
	Programme Covers	2006	—	£4.00
L9	Liverpool F.C. F.A. Cup Winners 1974			
	Programme Covers	2008	—	£5.00
L7	Manchester City F.C. F.A. Cup Winners 1969			
	Programme Covers	2007	—	£5.00
L10	Manchester United 1968 European Cup Winners ...	2004	—	£6.50
L15	Marilyn Monroe	2006	—	£6.50
L20	Marvin Hagler (Boxer) Programme Covers...........	2006	—	£8.00
L30	Movie Idols — Alfred Hitchcock	2005	—	£10.00
L15	Movie Idols — Basil Rathbone is Sherlock Holmes	2004	—	£7.50
L30	Movie Idols — Errol Flynn	2004	—	£10.00
L10	Movie Idols — Fred Astaire & Ginger Rogers	2005	—	£5.50
L10	Movie Idols — Greta Garbo	2007	—	£5.00
L30	Movie Idols — Humphrey Bogart Film Posters......	2003	—	£10.00
L15	Movie Idols — James Cagney	2008	—	£6.50
L20	Movie Idols — John Wayne Series 1 (Cowboy			
	Films)..	2007	—	£7.50
L30	Movie Idols — John Wayne Series 2 (Cowboy			
	Films)	2006	—	£10.00
L15	Movie Idols — John Wayne Series 3 (War Films)...	2010	—	£6.50
L30	Movie Idols — Marlon Brando	2004	—	£10.00
L12	Movie Idols — The Marx Brothers	2006	—	£6.00
L15	Movie Idols — Modern Gangster Classics	2008	—	£6.50
L15	Movie Idols — Paul Newman Classics	2010	—	£6.50
L15	Movie Idols — Steve McQueen Film Posters	2006	—	£6.50
L30	Muhammad Ali — Sports Illustrated	2002	—	£12.00
L10	The Muhammad Ali Story	2010	—	£6.00
L12	Newcastle United 1968/69 Fairs Cup Winners			
	Programme Covers	2005	—	£7.00
L10	Nottingham Forest European Cup Winners 1980			
	Programme Covers	2006	—	£6.00
L25	Olympic Posters — Summer Games	2003	—	£8.50
L20	Olympic Posters — Winter Games.................	2003	—	£8.00
L15	Only Fools & Horses (Caricatures)...............	2002	—	£9.00
L15	Only Fools & Horses Volume 1 (Scenes)	2003	—	£9.00
L20	Only Fools & Horses Volume II (Scenes)	2005	—	£7.50
L4	Only Fools & Horses Bonus Set A	2003	—	£2.50
L15	Pele (Footballer)	2005	—	£6.50
L12	Pink Floyd — Album Covers and Concert Posters	2008	—	£6.00
L20	Princess Diana Magazine Covers	2006	—	£7.50
L15	Queen Concert Posters	2010	—	£6.50
L8	Rocky Marciano (Boxer)	2001	—	£5.00
L20	Rod Stewart Concert Posters	2013	—	£7.50
L13	The Rolling Stones Concert Posters	2006	—	£6.00

Qty		Date	Odds	Sets

SPORTING PROFILES (continued)

Qty		Date	Odds	Sets
L20	Smokin' Joe Frazier — A Career History...............	2005	—	£9.00
L20	Steptoe & Son	2003	—	£9.00
L12	Stoke City F.C. 1972 League Cup Winners			
	Programme Covers	2005	—	£6.00
LT11	John L. Sullivan (Boxer) Cradle to Grave	1997	—	£6.00
L9	Sunderland F.C. F.A. Cup Winners 1973			
	Programme Covers	2007	—	£5.00
L20	Team GB 19 Golds Beijing 2008 Olympics	2008	—	£7.50
L9	Tony Hancock...	2002	—	£6.50
L8	Tottenham Hotspur F.A. Cup Winners 1961			
	Programme Covers	2008	—	£5.00
L9	Tottenham Hotspur F.A. Cup Winners 1967			
	Programme Covers	2008	—	£5.00
L9	Tottenham Hotspur F.A. Cup Winners 1981			
	Programme Covers	2008	—	£5.00
L6	Tottenham Hotspur League Cup Winners 2008			
	Programme Covers	2008	—	£4.50
L10	West Bromwich Albion F.A. Cup Winners 1968			
	Programme Covers	2007	—	£6.00
L7	West Ham United F.A. Cup Winners 1964			
	Programme Covers	2005	—	£5.00
L8	West Ham United F.A. Cup Winners 1975			
	Programme Covers	2007	—	£5.00
L8	West Ham United F.A. Cup Winners 1980			
	Programme Covers	2005	—	£5.00
L20	When Ali Met Pele	2007	—	£7.50
L20	The Who Concert Posters	2009	—	£7.50
L7	Wolverhampton Wanderers F.A. Cup Winners 1960			
	Programme Covers	2007	—	£5.00
L15	World Cup 1966 England	2002	—	£9.00
L17	World Cup Posters 1930-2002 (Football)	2002	—	£8.00
L4	The Young Ones (TV Comedy Show)	2006	—	£3.00

SPORTS TIME (USA)

Qty		Date	Odds	Sets
LT100	The Beatles	1996	—	£16.00
LT100	Marilyn Monroe 1st Series	1993	20p	£16.00
LT100	Marilyn Monroe 2nd Series	1995	—	£16.00

SPRATTS PATENT LTD

Qty		Date	Odds	Sets
K100	British Birds (numbered)	c1925	£6.50	—
K50	British Birds (unnumbered)	c1925	£4.50	—
42	British Birds	c1925	£6.50	—
25	Bonzo Series	1924	£6.00	—
36	Champion Dogs	c1930	£14.00	—
K20	Fish	c1925	£14.00	—
K100	Poultry	c1925	£14.00	—
12	Prize Dogs (multi-backed)	c1910	£45.00	—
12	Prize Poultry (multi-backed)	c1910	£45.00	—

STAMP KING

Qty		Date	Odds	Sets
L7	Robin Hood	2002	—	£3.00

STAMP PUBLICITY

Qty		Date	Odds	Sets
M40	1990 Cricket Tours	1990	—	£9.00
	Album		—	£8.00

Qty		Date	Odds	Sets
	STAR CARDS			
LT99	Riders of the World (Equestrian)	1995	20p	£9.50
	STAR DISC ENTERPRISE (Canada)			
K58	Star Trek The Next Generation (circular)...	1994	—	£9.50
	STAR INTERNATIONAL (USA)			
LT100	Venus Swimwear International Model Search	1994	20p	£9.50
	STAR JUNIOR CLUB			
10	Do You Know About Animals...	1960	£1.50	—
10	Do You Know About Sports and Games	1960	£2.50	—
5	Do You Know About Sports and Games	1960	£2.50	—
	STAR PICS (USA)			
LT80	Alien 3 — The Movie	1992	—	£9.50
LT72	All My Children	1991	—	£8.00
LT6	All My Children Insert Set...	1991	—	£3.00
LT80	Dinamation (Dinosaurs)	1992	—	£8.50
LT72	Playboy (Magazine)...	1992	—	£12.00
LT150	Saturday Night Live	1992	—	£12.00
LT76	Twin Peaks (TV Series)	1991	—	£8.00
	STARLINE (USA)			
LT250	Americana (USA History)	1992	—	£18.00
LT125	Hollywood Walk of Fame Nos 1-125	1991	—	£9.50
LT125	Hollywood Walk of Fame Nos 126-250	1991	—	£9.50
	STATE OF THE ARTS			
L6	Sex, Drugs & Rock 'n Roll	1994	—	£7.50
	STAVELEY'S LUDGATE HILL			
24	World's Most Beautiful Birds	c1920	£10.00	—
24	World's Most Beautiful Butterflies	c1920	£10.00	—
	STERLING CARDS (USA)			
LT100	Country Gold (Country & Western Singers)	1992	—	£9.50
LT150	Country Gold (Country & Western Singers)	1993	—	£12.00
	STOKES & DALTON LTD			
M20	Dick Dalton in The Mystery of the Crimson Cobra	1950	£3.25	—
28	Dominoes (without the dot)	1939	20p	£5.00
	STOLL			
25	The Mystery of Dr. Fu-Manchu	c1930	£12.00	—
25	Stars of Today	c1930	£8.00	—
	STOLLWERCK			
L216	Animal World	c1910	£1.50	—
?92	Views of the World	c1910	£6.00	—
	STRICTLY INK			
LT100	The Avengers Series 1...	2003	20p	£10.00
LT100	The Avengers Series 2 Season 4 and 5 1965-1967	2005	—	£12.00

Qty		Date	Odds	Sets
	STRICTLY INK (continued)			
LT54	The Avengers 3rd Series Additions The Archive Collection	2010	—	£5.00
LT100	CSI — Crime Scene Investigation Series 1	2003	—	£9.50
LT100	CSI — Crime Scene Investigation Series 2	2004	—	£9.50
LT72	CSI — Crime Scene Investigation Series 3	2006	—	£8.50
LT100	CSI Miami Series 1	2004	—	£9.50
LT72	CSI Miami Series 2	2007	—	£8.00
LT72	CSI NY Series 1	2008	—	£8.50
LT10	Doctor Who Promotional Series	2000	—	£10.00
LT120	Doctor Who 1st Series	2000	20p	£12.00
LT120	Doctor Who 2nd Series	2001	20p	£12.00
LT120	Doctor Who 3rd Series	2002	20p	£12.00
LT200	Doctor Who	2006	—	£20.00
LT100	Doctor Who Big Screen	2003	20p	£12.00
	Doctor Who Big Screen Additions Collection:			
LT72	A Coloured	2008	—	£9.50
LT72	B Black and white	2008	—	£9.50
LT100	Doctor Who 40th Anniversary	2003	20p	£12.00
LT54	Hammer Horror Series 2	2010	—	£6.00
LT72	The New Avengers Season 1	2006	—	£12.00

SUMMER COUNTY SOFT MARGARINE

Countryside Cards:

Qty		Date	Odds	Sets
5	Birds	c1975	£2.00	—
5	Birds of Prey	c1975	£2.00	—
5	Butterflies	c1975	£2.00	—
5	Corn Crops	c1975	£2.00	—
5	Herbs & Berries	c1975	£2.00	—
5	The Hedgerow	c1975	£2.00	—
5	Horses & Ponies	c1975	£2.00	—
5	Mills	c1975	£2.00	—
5	Nocturnal Animals	c1975	£2.00	—
5	Trees	c1975	£2.00	—
5	Water Fowl	c1975	£2.00	—
5	Water Life	c1975	£2.00	—
5	Wild Animals	c1975	£2.00	—
5	Wild Flowers	c1975	£2.00	—

THE SUN

Qty		Date	Odds	Sets
M134	Football	1970	60p	—
M52	Gallery of Football Action	1972	£3.00	—
	6 different numbers		—	£6.00
M6	How To Play Football	1972	£4.00	—
M54	Page 3 Playing Cards (Pin-Up Girls)	1979	—	£8.00
50	Soccercards — Nos 1 to 50	1979	25p	£12.50
50	Soccercards — Nos 51 to 100	1979	20p	£10.00
50	Soccercards — Nos 101 to 150...	1979	20p	£10.00
50	Soccercards — Nos 151 to 200...	1979	20p	£10.00
50	Soccercards — Nos 201 to 250...	1979	20p	£10.00
50	Soccercards — Nos 251 to 300...	1979	20p	£10.00
50	Soccercards — Nos 301 to 350...	1979	20p	£10.00
50	Soccercards — Nos 351 to 400...	1979	20p	£10.00
50	Soccercards — Nos 401 to 450...	1979	20p	£10.00
50	Soccercards — Nos 451 to 500...	1979	20p	£10.00
50	Soccercards — Nos 501 to 550...	1979	20p	£10.00

Qty		Date	Odds	Sets
	THE SUN (continued)			
50	Soccercards — Nos 551 to 600...	1979	20p	£10.00
50	Soccercards — Nos 601 to 650...	1979	20p	£10.00
50	Soccercards — Nos 651 to 700...	1979	20p	£10.00
50	Soccercards — Nos 701 to 750...	1979	20p	£10.00
50	Soccercards — Nos 751 to 800...	1979	20p	£10.00
50	Soccercards — Nos 801 to 850...	1979	20p	£10.00
50	Soccercards — Nos 851 to 900...	1979	20p	£10.00
50	Soccercards — Nos 901 to 950...	1979	20p	£10.00
50	Soccercards — Nos 951 to 1000	1979	20p	£10.00
EL50	3-D Gallery of Football Stars...	1972	£5.00	—
	SUNBLEST TEA			
25	Inventions and Discoveries 1st Series	1962	50p	£12.50
25	Inventions and Discoveries 2nd Series	1962	60p	£15.00
25	Prehistoric Animals 1st Series	1966	30p	£7.50
25	Prehistoric Animals 2nd Series	1966	30p	£7.50
	SUNBLEST (Australia)			
M25	Great Explorers	c1975	40p	£10.00
M24	Sports Action Card Series	c1975	—	£10.00
	SUNDAY STORIES			
M5	Flags (silk)	1915	£15.00	—
M6	The King and His Soldiers (silk)	1916	£15.00	—
	SUNNY BOY			
50	British Naval Series	c1960	£2.00	—
	SWEETULE PRODUCTS LTD			
25	Animals of the Countryside	1959	20p	£2.50
25	Archie Andrews' Illustrated Jokes	1957	£8.00	—
25	Birds and Their Eggs ('Junior Service')	1955	20p	£2.50
25	Birds and Their Eggs:			
	A Black back	1959	20p	£5.00
	B Blue back	1959	20p	£5.00
25	Birds and Their Haunts	1958	£5.00	—
25	Birds of the British Commonwealth (Canada):			
	A Black back	1958	20p	£5.00
	B Blue back	1958	20p	£5.00
25	Do You Know?	1963	20p	£5.00
25	Family Crests	1961	20p	£3.00
25	Famous Sports Records:			
	A Blue back	1956	70p	£17.50
	B Black back	1956	£1.20	—
25	Football Club Nicknames	1959	40p	£10.00
K18	Historical Cars and Cycles	1957	50p	£9.00
25	Junior Service Quiz	1958	20p	£3.00
50	Modern Aircraft	1954	20p	£6.00
25	Modern Transport	1955	30p	£7.50
50	Motor Cycles Old and New	1963	£1.60	—
30	National Flags and Costumes	1957	70p	£20.00
52	Natural History Playing Card inset	1961	40p	£20.00
25	Nature Series	1959	20p	£3.00
25	Naval Battles	1959	20p	£3.00

Qty		Date	Odds	Sets
	SWEETULE PRODUCTS LTD (continued)			
25	Products of the World	1960	20p	£2.50
25	Sports Quiz	1958	20p	£5.00
25	Stamp Cards	1960	24p	£6.00
EL30	Trains of the World	1960	£1.50	—
25	Treasure Island	1958	30p	£7.50
25	Tropical Birds	1954	20p	£3.00
25	Vintage Cars	1964	50p	£12.50
25	Weapons of Defence	1959	20p	£2.50
25	Wild Animals	1958	20p	£3.00
25	Wild Flowers	1960	20p	£3.00
25	The Wild West:			
	A Black back	1960	50p	£12.50
	B Blue back	1960	20p	£4.00
25	Wonders of the World	1956	20p	£3.50
	Package Issues:			
18	Aircraft	c1954	£6.00	—
M12	Coronation Series	1953	£7.00	—
M18	Home Pets	c1955	£7.00	—
25	International Footballers	c1962	£9.00	—
18	Landmarks of Flying	c1960	£7.00	—
M18	Railway Engines	c1955	£7.00	—
M18	Railway Engines Past & Present	c1960	£7.00	—
	SWETTENHAM TEA			
25	Aircraft of the World...	1959	60p	£15.00
25	Animals of the Countryside	1958	20p	£2.50
25	Birds and Their Eggs	1958	20p	£2.50
25	Butterflies and Moths	1960	20p	£2.50
25	Evolution of the Royal Navy	1957	20p	£3.50
25	Into Space	1959	24p	£6.00
25	Wild Animals	1958	30p	£7.50
	W. SWORD & CO.			
25	British Empire at Work	c1930	£15.00	—
20	Dogs	c1930	£17.00	—
20	Inventors and Their Inventions	c1930	£17.00	—
25	Safety First...	c1930	£13.00	—
25	Sports and Pastimes Series	c1930	£17.00	—
25	Vehicles of All Ages	c1930	£15.00	—
25	Zoo Series (brown gravures)...	c1930	£10.00	£250.00
25	Zoo Series (coloured)	c1930	£12.00	—
	T C M ASSOCIATES (USA)			
LT100	Earthmovers 2nd Series (Tractors etc)	1994	—	£12.00
LT72	Santa Around the World (Premier Edition)	1994	—	£9.50
LT72	Santa Around The World 2nd Series (with snow			
	flake border)	1994	—	£9.50
LT100	Winnebago (Mobile Homes etc.)	1994	—	£9.50
	T & M ENTERPRISES (USA)			
LT45	The Bikini Open	1992	—	£8.00
	TAMWORTH POLICE			
L18	Keepers of the Peace	1990	25p	£4.50
	Album		—	£5.00

Qty		Date	Odds	Sets
	DES TAYLOR			
L20	My Favourite Fish	2000	—	£7.50
	TEA TIME ASSORTED BISCUITS (NABISCO)			
12	British Soldiers Through the Ages	1974	20p	£2.50
	Album		—	£4.00
	TEACHERS WHISKY			
L12	Scottish Clans and Castles (circular)	1971	£3.00	£36.00
	TEASDALE & CO.			
25	Great War Series	c1920	£24.00	—
	TELLY CLASSICS			
10	Telly Classics Nearest & Dearest 1960/70s Comedy with Jimmy Jewell & Hilda Baker	2009	—	£5.00
	TENNYSON ENTERPRISES (USA)			
LT100	Super Country Music	1992	—	£9.50
	TESCO			
EL6	Nature Trail	1988	—	£3.00
	TETLEY TEA			
48	British Birds	c1975	£5.00	—
	TEXACO (Petrol)			
12	Cricket	1984	40p	£5.00
K24	England Squad 2006 (Football)	2006	—	£7.50
K5	England Squad 2006 Additions (Carson, Downing, Hargreaves, Lennon, Walcott) (Football)	2006	—	£5.00
K24	F.A. Cup Winners Hall of Fame	2007	—	£10.00
	Album and DVD	2007	—	£7.00
	D.C. THOMSON			
	Adventure Pictures:			
L10	Set 1 White borders, glazed	1922	£3.00	—
L10	Set 2 White borders, matt	1922	£3.00	—
L10	Set 3 Brown borders, glazed	1922	£3.00	—
M16	Badges of the Fighting Fliers	1937	£4.50	—
	Battles for the Flag:			
EL13	Inscribed 'Rover'	c1935	£5.50	—
EL13	Inscribed 'Wizard' (different)	c1935	£5.50	—
K80	Boys of All Nations	1936	£1.30	—
LP11	British Team of Footballers	1922	£3.25	—
L20	Canvas Masterpieces (silk)	1925	£10.00	—
16	Catch-My-Pal Cards	1938	£2.00	—
M12	Coloured Photos of Star Footballers	c1930	£7.50	—
16	County Cricketers (Adventure)	1957	£2.50	—
16	County Cricketers (Hotspur)	1957	£2.50	—
16	County Cricketers (Rover)	1957	£2.50	—
16	County Cricketers (Wizard)	1957	£2.50	—
	Cricketers:			
EL12	Inscribed 'Rover'	1924	£8.00	—
EL12	Inscribed 'Vanguard'...	1924	£8.00	—

Qty		Date	Odds	Sets
	D.C. THOMSON (continued)			
KP8	Cricketers	c1925	£3.00	—
EL16	Cup Tie Stars of All Nations (Victor)	1962	£4.00	—
K28	Dominoes — School Caricatures	c1935	£2.25	—
MP35	Famous British Footballers:			
	A 18 Different English Players...	c1925	£3.25	—
	B 17 Different Scottish Players	c1925	£9.00	—
K80	Famous Feats	1937	£1.30	—
24	Famous Fights	c1935	£3.00	—
24	Famous Footballers (Wizard)	1955	£2.20	—
25	Famous Footballers (Wizard)	c1955	£2.20	—
L32	Famous Ships	1931	£4.00	—
EL12	Famous Teams in Football History	1961	£5.00	—
EL16	Famous Teams in Football History 2nd Series			
	(New Hotspur)...	1962	£5.00	—
K80	Flags of the Sea	1937	£1.30	—
P40	Football Photos	c1925	£6.00	—
48	Football Stars (Adventure and Hotspur)	1957	£2.50	—
44	Football Stars of 1959 (Wizard)...	1959	£3.00	—
K64	Football Team Cards	1933	£1.25	—
64	Football Tips and Tricks	1959	£1.00	—
L32	Football Towns and Their Crests	1931	£6.00	—
KP137	Footballers	c1925	£1.40	—
L8	Footballers	c1930	£7.50	—
MP18	Footballers	1922	£3.00	—
K52	Footballers — Hunt the Cup Cards	c1935	£3.00	—
24	Footballers — Motor Cars (Double Sided)	c1930	£8.00	—
MP35	Footballers — Signed Real Photos:			
	A 22 Different English Players...	c1930	£2.50	—
	B 13 Different Scottish Players	c1930	£9.00	—
L12	Great Captains (Wizard)	c1970	£6.00	—
12	Guns in Action	1940	£2.25	—
M8	Hidden Treasure Clue Cards...	1926	£13.00	—
EL16	International Cup Teams (Hornet)	1963	£5.00	—
6	Ju-Jitsu Cards	1929	£5.00	—
24	Motor Bike Cards	1929	£6.00	—
K100	Motor Cars	1934	£1.50	—
11	Mystic Menagerie	c1930	£6.00	—
36	1930 Speedway Stars	1930	£8.00	—
K80	Punishment Cards	1936	£1.30	—
	Puzzle Prize Cards:			
12	Dandy Dogs	1928	£5.00	—
12	Queer Animals	1928	£3.25	—
12	Speedsters of the Wilds	1928	£3.25	—
	Q Prize Cards:			
16	Cricket Crests	1929	£9.00	—
16	Flags of All Nations	1929	£2.75	—
16	Queer Birds	1929	£3.00	—
K80	Secrets of Cricket	1936	£2.25	—
36	Spadger's Monster Collection of Spoofs	c1935	£3.25	—
48	Speed	1932	£1.20	—
EL22	Star Teams of 1961	1961	£4.00	—
24	Stars of Sport and Entertainment (Hotspur)...	1958	£2.00	—
24	Stars of Sport and Entertainment (Rover)	1958	£2.00	—
L24	Superstars of '72 (Footballers) 'Victor'	1972	£2.50	—
24	This Year's Top Form Footballers	1924	£3.50	—

Qty		Date	Odds	Sets
	D.C. THOMSON (continued)			
EL12	Top Cup Teams	1964	£6.00	—
10	Vanguard Photos Gallery	1923	£13.00	—
32	V.P. Flips (Adventure)	1932	£1.50	—
32	V.P. Flips (Rover)	1932	£1.50	—
32	V.P. Flips (Skipper)	1932	£1.50	—
24	Warrior Cards	1929	£2.50	—
K28	Warrior Cards (back with Dominoes)	1935	£2.00	—
K80	Warrior Cards	1937	£1.30	—
K28	Wild West Dominoes	c1935	£2.00	—
	Wizard Series:			
20	British Birds and Eggs	1923	£3.00	—
20	Easy Scientific Experiments	1923	£2.75	—
20	Famous Liners	1923	£4.00	—
20	Motor Cycles	1923	£7.00	—
20	Why?	1923	£2.75	—
20	The Wireless Telephone	1923	£2.75	—
20	Wonders of the Rail	1923	£4.50	—
20	Wonders of the World	1923	£2.50	—
16	World Cup Footballers (Adventure)	1958	£3.00	—
16	World Cup Footballers (Hotspur)	1958	£3.00	—
16	World Cup Footballers (Rover)	1958	£3.00	—
16	World Cup Footballers (Wizard)...	1958	£3.00	—
M72	World Cup Stars (Hornet/Hotspur)	1970	£3.00	—
32	The World's Best Cricketers (back in black)	1932	£3.00	—
	The World's Best Cricketers:			
12	Inscribed 'Adventure' (back in mauve)	1930	£6.00	—
12	Inscribed 'Rover' (back in mauve)	1930	£6.00	—
12	Inscribed 'Wizard' (back in mauve)	1930	£6.00	—
18	The World's Best Cricketers (Adventure)	1956	£3.25	—
18	The World's Best Cricketers (Hotspur)	1956	£3.25	—
18	The World's Best Cricketers (Rover)	1956	£3.25	—
18	The World's Best Cricketers (Wizard)...	1956	£3.25	—

HY. THORNE & CO.

?16	Royalty	c1905	£30.00	—

THUNDER PRODUCTIONS (USA)

LT100	Custom Motorcycles	1993	—	£9.50

TIMARU MILLING CO. (New Zealand)

M36	Focus on Fame	1948	75p	£27.00
M37	Peace and Progress	1947	75p	£28.00
M36	Victory Album Cards	1946	£1.00	—

TIMES CONFECTIONERY CO. LTD

M24	Roy Rogers — In Old Amarillo	1955	50p	£12.00
M24	Roy Rogers — South of Caliente	1955	50p	£12.00

TITBITS

K54	Pin-Up Girls (playing cards)	1976	24p	£12.50
M20	Star Cover Girls	1953	£5.00	—

Qty		Date	Odds	Sets
	CHOCOLAT TOBLER LTD			
12	Famaza Pedagogi (Famous People) Series 17 ...	c1960	—	£2.50
50	Famous Footballers with 'Tobler' on front	c1937	£12.00	—
50	Famous Footballers without 'Tobler' on front	c1939	£12.00	—
12	Infanto En Arto (Children in Art) Series 21	c1960	—	£2.50
12	Planets and Fixed Stars, Series 45	c1960	—	£6.00
12	Infanto — Ludi (Children's Games) Series 52	c1960	—	£3.00
12	Tobler Posters 2nd Series, Series 58	c1960	—	£2.50
12	Different Ways of Travelling, Series 62	c1960	—	£4.00
	TOBY			
24	Dogs 1st Series	c1920	£4.50	—
24	Dogs 2nd Series	c1920	£4.50	—
24	Sights of London	c1920	£4.00	—
24	Toby's Bird Series	c1920	£4.00	—
24	Toby's Ship Series	c1920	£4.00	—
24	Toby's Travel Series	c1920	£4.00	—
	TODAY NEWSPAPER			
LT14	Around Britain	1991	—	£3.00
	TOM THUMB (New Zealand)			
M24	Supercars	1980	—	£12.00
	TOMMY GUN			
50	Medals	1971	20p	£4.00
	TONIBELL (Ice Cream)			
M20	Banknotes of the World	1974	25p	£5.00
M12	Beautiful Butterflies	1977	35p	£4.00
M20	County Badge Collection	1976	20p	£4.00
L12	Did You Know	1976	£1.50	—
25	Did You Know?	1963	20p	£3.00
EL12	England's Soccer Stars	1970	£3.75	£45.00
L19	Famous Sports Trophies	c1970	50p	£10.00
M12	Farmyard Stencils	1977	38p	£4.50
M24	1st Division Football League Club Badges	1972	£2.50	—
EL12	Horses in the Service of Man	1977	—	£10.00
25	Inventions that Changed the World	1963	20p	£3.00
EL10	Junior Champs	1979	—	£6.00
M24	Kings of the Road (car radiator badges)	1977	£1.00	—
M24	Pop Star Cameos (circular cards)	c1970	40p	£10.00
M10	Pop Stars (Star Shaped)	c1975	—	£15.00
K36	Team of All Time	1971	£2.25	£80.00
25	This Changing World:			
	A Black line under Tonibell	1963	30p	£7.50
	B Without black line under Tonibell	1963	40p	£10.00
25	Wonders of the Heavens	1963	60p	£15.00
25	World's Passenger Liners	1963	20p	£3.00
	TONIBELL & CADBURY			
12	Action Soldiers	1976	30p	£3.50
	TOP SELLERS LTD			
M54	Crazy Stickers	1975	—	£5.00

Qty		Date	Odds	Sets
	TOP TRUMPS			
L30	Football South Africa 2010 World Cup Goalscorers	2010	—	£4.00
L30	Football South Africa 2010 World Cup Keepers &			
	Defenders	2010	—	£4.00
L30	Football South Africa 2010 World Cup Legends ...	2010	—	£4.00
L30	Football South Africa 2010 World Cup Managers...	2010	—	£4.00
L30	Football South Africa 2010 World Cup Moments ...	2010	—	£4.00
L30	Football South Africa 2010 World Cup Stadiums ...	2010	—	£4.00
L35	Prehistoric Monsters	1979	—	£4.00
L33	Rockets	1980	—	£4.00
	TOPICAL TIMES			
M24	Footballers — English (Head and Shoulders)	1939	£3.50	£85.00
M24	Footballers — Scottish (Head and Shoulders)	1939	£12.00	—
L48	Footballers — English, Size 125 × 46mm:			
	A First 24 Subjects	1937	£3.50	£85.00
	B Second — 24 Subjects	1938	£3.50	£85.00
L46	Footballers — Scottish, Size 125 × 46mm	1937	£12.00	—
EL120	Footballers, Size 250 × 95mm (black and white) ...	1935	£4.50	—
EL16	Footballers, Size 250 × 95mm (coloured)	1936	£6.00	—
MP10	Footballers (2 players per card)	c1930	£5.00	—
EL8	Footballers (3 players per card)...	1937	£6.00	—
EL8	Footballers, Size 253 × 190mm (coloured)	1936	£6.00	—
MP6	Football Teams (card)	c1930	£6.00	—
M6	Football Teams (metal)...	c1925	£14.00	—
	TOPPS (Australia)			
LT63	Australian Cricket	2000	—	£25.00
	TOPPS (Germany)			
LT99	Jurassic Park (including Sticker Set)	1993	—	£10.00
	TOPPS (UK)			
M80	Alf His Life and Times	1988	20p	£12.00
M88	American Baseball	1988	20p	£18.00
M88	American Baseball	1989	20p	£18.00
M88	American NFL Football	1987	22p	£20.00
LT99	Autos of 1977	1977	£1.50	—
M132	Batman (size 77 x 55mm)...	1989	20p	£7.50
M22	Batman stickers	1989	20p	£2.50
LT88	Batman Returns	1992	20p	£8.50
M10	Batman Returns stickers	1992	25p	£2.50
LT66	Battlestar Galactica (Nos 1-66)	1979	20p	£12.00
LT66	Battlestar Galactica (Nos 67-132)	1979	20p	£12.00
LT66	Bay City Rollers	1976	40p	—
LT132	Beavis and Butt-Head (No 6934 unissued, 7769			
	not on check list)	1994	20p	£11.00
LT88	Beverly Hills 90210	1991	20p	£8.50
M11	Beverly Hills 90210 stickers	1991	25p	£2.50
LT88	The Black Hole	1980	25p	£22.00
LT49	Comic Book Heroes...	1977	£2.00	—
LT88	Desert Storm	1991	20p	£16.00
M22	Desert Storm Stickers	1991	20p	£2.50
LT60	England 2002 (Football)	2002	—	£14.00

Qty		Date	Odds	Sets
	TOPPS (UK) (continued)			
LT10	England 2002 (Football) Electric Foil Series			
	Nd. E1 to E10	2002	–	£7.00
EL30	English League Football Internationals	1980	60p	£18.00
LT88	The Flintstones (The Movie)	1994	20p	£5.00
M11	The Flintstones (The Movie) stickers	1994	25p	£2.50
LT124	Football Premier Gold	2001	–	£20.00
LT125	Football Premier Gold	2002	–	£20.00
LT125	Football Premier Gold	2003	–	£20.00
LT125	Football Premier Gold	2004	–	£20.00
	Football Saint and Greavsie:			
M175	A Complete set	1988	20p	£20.00
M264	B Complete set plus varieties	1988	–	£25.00
LT132	Footballers, Nd 1-132 (red back)	1975	£1.75	–
LT88	Footballers, Nd 133-220 (red back)	1975	£1.75	–
LT88	Footballers, Scottish (blue back)	1975	£2.50	–
LT110	Footballers, Nd 1-110 (blue back)	1976	£1.20	–
LT110	Footballers, Nd 111-220 (blue back)	1976	£1.20	–
LT110	Footballers, Nd 221-330 (blue back)	1976	£1.20	–
LT132	Footballers, Scottish (red back)	1976	£2.20	–
LT110	Footballers, Nd 1-110 (red back)	1977	£1.25	–
LT110	Footballers, Nd 111-220 (red back)	1977	£1.25	–
LT110	Footballers, Nd 221-330 (red back)	1977	£1.25	–
LT132	Footballers, Scottish (yellow back)	1977	£1.50	–
LT132	Footballers, Nd 1-132 (orange back)	1978	35p	£45.00
LT132	Footballers, Nd 133-264 (orange back)	1978	35p	£45.00
LT132	Footballers, Nd 265-396 (orange back)	1978	35p	£45.00
LT132	Footballers, Scottish (green back)	1978	£1.50	–
LT132	Footballers, Nos 1-132 (light blue back)	1979	£1.50	–
LT132	Footballers, Nos 133-264 (light blue back)	1979	£1.50	–
LT132	Footballers, Nos 265-396 (light blue back)	1979	£1.50	–
LT132	Footballers, Scottish (red back)	1979	£1.75	–
LT66	Footballers (pink back)	1980	£1.25	£90.00
EL18	Footballers Posters	1980	80p	£14.00
LT65	Footballers (blue back)	1981	£1.00	£65.00
	Album		–	£8.00
LT100	Footballers Stadium Club nos 1-100	1992	20p	£16.00
LT100	Footballers Stadium Club nos 101-200	1992	20p	£16.00
LT10/14	Footballers Stadium Club Promotional Series	1992	25p	£2.50
LT21	Funny Puzzles	1978	£1.50	–
M39	The Garbage Gang nd 1a-39a	1990	40p	–
M39	The Garbage Gang nd 1b-39b (except for subjects			
	15b & 39b, incorrectly numbered 15a & 39a) ...	1990	40p	£16.00
M42	The Garbage Gang Nos 418A-459A	1991	40p	–
M41	The Garbage Gang Nos 460A-500A	1991	40p	–
M41	Garbage Pail Kids 1st Series A	1986	40p	–
M41	Garbage Pail Kids 1st Series B	1986	40p	–
M42	Garbage Pail Kids 2nd Series A	1986	40p	–
M42	Garbage Pail Kids 2nd Series B	1986	40p	–
M44	Garbage Pail Kids 3rd Series A	1987	40p	–
M37	Garbage Pail Kids 3rd Series B	1987	40p	–
M42	Garbage Pail Kids 4th Series A	1987	40p	–
M42	Garbage Pail Kids 4th Series B	1987	40p	–
M39	Garbage Pail Kids 5th Series A	1987	40p	–
M39	Garbage Pail Kids 5th Series B	1987	40p	–
M44	Garbage Pail Kids 6th Series A	1988	40p	–

Qty		Date	Odds	Sets
	TOPPS (UK) (continued)			
M44	Garbage Pail Kids 6th Series B	1988	40p	£17.50
M86	The Goonies	1986	30p	—
M15	The Goonies stickers	1986	30p	—
LT88	Gremlins 2 The Movie (white card)	1990	20p	£9.00
LT66	Home Alone 2 The Movie	1993	20p	£4.50
M11	Home Alone 2 The Movie stickers	1993	25p	£2.50
LT44	Home & Away...	1990	20p	£5.00
LT99	Hook — The Film	1992	20p	£8.50
M11	Hook — The Film stickers	1992	25p	£2.50
LT88	Jurassic Park	1993	20p	£9.00
M11	Jurassic Park stickers	1993	25p	£2.50
LT66	Kings of Rap (including stickers)	1991	20p	£8.00
M111	Mad Cap Alphabet (including All Varieties)	1994	20p	£12.00
LT49	Marvel Super Heroes	1980	£1.50	£75.00
LT83	Match Attax Extra 2007/08 (red backs)	2007	—	£9.50
LT20	Match Attax Extra 2007/08 Club Captains (foil fronts)	2007	—	£6.00
LT92	Match Attax Extra 2008/09 (blue backs)	2008	—	£9.50
LT20	Match Attax Extra 2008/09 Club Captains	2008	—	£5.00
LT20	Match Attax Extra 2008/09 Fans Favourite (foil fronts)	2008	—	£6.00
LT112	Match Attax Extra 2009/10 (orange backs)	2010	—	£9.50
LT20	Match Attax Extra 2009/10 I-Card Chromium	2010	—	£10.00
LT20	Match Attax Extra 2009/10 Man of The Match	2010	—	£15.00
LT224	Match Attax World Cup 2010 (red backs)	2010	—	£12.00
LT32	Match Attax World Cup 2010 International Legends	2010	—	£5.00
LT8	Match Attax World Cup 2010 International Masters (foil fronts)	2010	—	£4.00
LT16	Match Attax World Cup 2010 Managers	2010	—	£5.00
LT6	Match Attax World Cup 2010 Star Legends (foil fronts)	2010	—	£5.00
LT25	Match Attax World Cup 2010 Star Players (foil fronts)	2010	—	£5.00
LT66	Michael Jackson	1984	50p	—
LT49	Monster in My Pocket	1991	20p	£5.00
LT66	Neighbours...	1988	20p	£5.00
LT66	Neighbours 2nd Series...	1988	20p	£5.00
LT88	New Kids on the Block	1990	20p	£6.00
M11	New Kids on the Block stickers, red borders	1990	25p	£2.50
M11	New Kids on the Block stickers, yellow borders ...	1990	25p	£2.50
LT66	Planet of the Apes (TV Series)	1974	£1.50	£100.00
LT90	Pokemon 1st Series	2000	25p	£16.00
LT72	Pokemon 2nd Series	2000	25p	£16.00
LT72	Pokemon 3rd Series	2000	—	£16.00
LT72	Pokemon The Movie	2000	25p	£16.00
LT72	Pokemon 2000 The Movie	2000	—	£16.00
M75	Pro-Cycling	1988	20p	£10.00
M66	Put On Stickers (including varieties)	1992	20p	£7.00
LT50	Shocking Laffs (No.17 not issued, but two Nos 47):			
	A Grey card	1977	£2.20	—
	B White card	1977	£2.40	—
LT88	The Simpsons	1991	20p	£18.00
M22	The Simpsons Stickers	1991	40p	—
LT66	Spitting Image	1990	20p	£10.00
LT88	Star Trek, The Motion Picture	1980	£1.50	£130.00

Qty		Date	Odds	Sets
	TOPPS (UK) (continued)			
LT66	Star Wars, Nd 1-66	1978	£1.75	£115.00
LT66	Star Wars, Nd 1A-66A	1978	£3.00	—
LT80	Star Wars Attack of The Clones (white Star Wars			
	on front)	2002	—	£15.00
LT10	Star Wars Attack of The Clones — Characters ...	2002	—	£10.00
LT5	Star Wars Attack of The Clones — Planets	2002	—	£5.00
LT10	Star Wars Attack of The Clones — Vehicles	2002	—	£10.00
LT66	Stingray — Thunderbirds — Captain Scarlet	1993	20p	£8.00
M44	Stupid Smiles	1990	30p	—
M64	Super Mario Bros — Nintendo	1992	20p	£6.00
LT66	Superman The Movie 1st Series	1979	27p	£18.00
LT66	Superman The Movie 2nd Series	1979	24p	£16.00
LT66	Take That (Pop Group)...	1994	20p	£5.00
M11	Take That (Pop Group) stickers	1994	25p	£2.50
LT66	Teenage Mutant Hero Turtles	1990	20p	£5.00
M11	Teenage Mutant Hero Turtles Stickers	1990	25p	£2.50
LT132	Teenage Mutant Ninja Turtles Movie	1990	20p	£6.50
M11	Teenage Mutant Ninja Turtles Movie Stickers	1990	25p	£2.50
M44	Terminator 2 (size 77 × 55mm)	1991	20p	£5.00
LT77	Toxic Crusaders	1993	20p	£9.00
M11	Toxic Crusaders stickers	1993	25p	£2.50
M54	Toxic High School	1991	30p	—
M23	Toxic High School Senior stickers	1991	20p	£4.00
M44	Trash Can Trolls nos 1A-44A	1993	40p	£17.50
M44	Trash Can Trolls nos 1B-44B	1993	50p	—
LT66	Trolls	1992	20p	£7.50
M11	Trolls stickers	1992	25p	£2.50
LT38	Wacky Packages 1st Series	c1978	£1.50	—
LT38	Wacky Packages 2nd Series...	c1978	£1.50	—
M30	Wacky Packages...	1982	60p	—
LT42	Wanted Posters	1978	70p	—
LT66	World Championship Wrestling	1992	20p	£6.00
EL18	World Cup Supersquad England (Football)	1990	60p	£11.00
EL18	World Cup Supersquad Scotland (Football)...	1990	70p	£12.00
	TOPPS (USA)			
LT66	The 'A' Team	1984	—	£8.00
LT84	Alien — The Movie	1979	—	£15.00
LT66	Baby	1985	—	£8.00
LT88	Back to the Future Part II — The Film	1989	—	£8.00
LT72	Barb Wire (Pamela Anderson Film)	1996	—	£9.50
LT12	Barb Wire Embossed Series (Pamela Anderson			
	Film)	1996	—	£5.00
LT132	Batman (size 89 x 64mm)...	1989	20p	£7.50
LT90	Batman Begins — The Film	2005	—	£12.00
LT100	Batman Returns (Stadium Club)	1992	—	£9.50
LT72	The Blair Witch Project — The Movie...	1999	—	£9.50
LT88	Buck Rogers in the 25th Century	1979	—	£18.00
LT66	Charlie's Angels 3rd Series	1977	—	£25.00
LT66	Close Encounters of The Third Kind — The Movie	1978	—	£12.00
LT72	Daredevil — The Movie	2003	20p	£12.00
LT72	Dark Angel 1st Series	2002	—	£9.50
LT88	Desert Storm 2nd Series	1991	—	£9.50
LT88	Desert Storm 3rd Series	1991	—	£8.00

Qty		Date	Odds	Sets
	TOPPS (USA) (continued)			
LT88	Dick Tracy — The Movie	1990	—	£8.00
LT55	Dinosaurs Attack (including Set LT11 Stickers) ...	1988	—	£9.50
EL72	Dragon Heart The Film — Widevision	1996	—	£9.50
LT87	ET — The Extra Terrestrial	1982	—	£9.00
LT54	Goosebumps	1996	—	£8.00
LT99	Greatest Olympians...	1983	—	£12.00
LT88	Gremlins 2 — The Movie (grey card)	1990	—	£9.00
LT66	Growing Pains (TV Series)	1988	—	£9.50
LT77	Harry and The Hendersons	1987	—	£9.50
LT90	Heroes Series 1	2008	—	£9.50
LT90	Heroes Volume 2	2008	—	£8.50
LT77	Howard The Duck	1986	—	£8.00
LT88	In Living Colour — Fox TV Series	1992	—	£9.50
LT72	The Incredible Hulk	2003	—	£9.50
EL72	Independence Day — The Film Widevision...	1996	—	£9.50
LT90	Indiana Jones and The Kingdom of The Crystal Skull	2008	—	£8.00
LT90	Indiana Jones Masterpieces	2008	—	£8.00
LT59	Jaws 2	1978	—	£15.00
LT44	Jaws 3-D The Film	1983	—	£8.00
LT80	Kong The 8th Wonder of The World	2005	—	£9.50
LT88	Last Action Hero — The Film	1993	—	£9.50
LT44	Little Shop of Horrors	1986	—	£7.50
LT72	Lord of The Rings Evolution...	2006	—	£9.50
LT90	Lord of The Rings Fellowship of the Ring Series 1	2001	—	£30.00
LT72	Lord of The Rings Fellowship of the Ring Series 2	2002	—	£12.00
LT90	Lord of The Rings Masterpieces Series 1	2006	—	£9.50
LT72	Lord of The Rings Masterpieces Series 2	2008	—	£8.50
LT90	Lord of The Rings The Return of the King Series 1	2003	—	£9.50
LT72	Lord of The Rings The Return of the King Series 2	2004	—	£12.00
LT90	Lord of The Rings The Two Towers Series 1	2002	—	£12.00
LT72	Lord of The Rings The Two Towers Series 2	2003	—	£12.00
LT72	The Lost World of Jurassic Park + Set L11 Stickers	1997	—	£9.50
LT56	Mars Attacks	1962	—	—
EL72	Mars Attacks — Widevision	1996	—	£9.50
LT66	Menudo (Pop Group)	1983	—	£9.50
LT33	Michael Jackson 1st Series	1984	—	£10.00
LT33	Michael Jackson 2nd Series	1984	—	£10.00
LT99	Moonraker James Bond 007	1979	—	£18.00
LT99	Mork and Mindy	1978	—	£18.00
LT88	Nicktoons	1993	—	£9.50
LT50	NSYNC (Pop Group)	2000	—	£9.50
LT50	Outer Limits	1964	—	—
LT33	Pee Wee's Playhouse	1989	—	£7.50
LT90	Planet of the Apes — The Movie	2001	—	£9.50
LT55	Prelorian Cats...	1982	—	£7.50
LT44	Return to Oz	1985	—	£12.00
LT55	Robin Hood Prince of Thieves — The Film	1991	—	£8.00
LT88	Robocop 2 — The Film	1990	—	£8.00
LT99	The Rocketeer — The Film	1991	—	£8.00
LT99	Rocky II	1979	—	£10.00
LT90	The Shadow — The Movie	1994	—	£8.00
LT100	Star Wars Attack of The Clones (silver Star Wars on front)	2002	—	£16.00

Qty		Date	Odds	Sets
	TOPPS (USA) (continued)			
EL80	Star Wars Attack of The Clones — Widevision ...	2002	—	£18.00
LT90	Star Wars Clone Wars	2004	—	£12.00
LT90	Star Wars The Clone Wars — The Film	2008	—	£9.50
EL80	Star Wars The Clone Wars (Widevision)	2009	—	£9.50
LT90	Star Wars Clone Wars Rise of The Bounty Hunters	2010	—	£8.00
LT132	Star Wars The Empire Strikes Back 1st Series	1980	—	£20.00
LT132	Star Wars The Empire Strikes Back 2nd Series ...	1980	—	£20.00
EL48	Star Wars The Empire Strikes Back 30th Anniversary (3-D) Widevision	2010	—	£15.00
EL80	Star Wars Episode 1 Series 1 — Widevision (red)	1999	—	£15.00
EL80	Star Wars Episode 1 Series 2 — Widevision (blue)	1999	—	£15.00
LT93	Star Wars Evolution	2001	—	£15.00
LT120	Star Wars Galaxy Series 4	2009	—	£9.50
LT120	Star Wars Galaxy Series 5	2010	—	£9.50
LT120	Star Wars Galaxy Series 6	2011	—	£9.50
LT110	Star Wars Galaxy Series 7	2012	—	£9.50
LT12	Star Wars Galaxy Lucas Art	1995	—	£15.00
LT120	Star Wars Heritage	2004	—	£12.00
LT90	Star Wars Jedi Legacy	2013	—	£9.50
LT132	Star Wars Return of The Jedi 1st Series	1983	—	£20.00
LT88	Star Wars Return of The Jedi 2nd Series	1983	—	£20.00
LT90	Star Wars Revenge of The Sith	2005	—	£9.50
EL80	Star Wars Revenge of The Sith — Widevision	2005	—	£14.00
LT120	Star Wars The 30th Anniversary	2007	—	£9.50
EL72	Star Wars Trilogy — Widevision	1997	—	£16.00
LT72	Star Wars Vehicles	1997	—	£15.00
LT44	Supergirl — The Film	1994	—	£6.00
LT88	Superman II — The Film	1980	—	£9.50
LT99	Superman III — The Film	1983	—	£9.50
LT90	Superman Returns — The Film	2007	—	£9.50
LT44	T.2 — Terminator 2 — The Movie (size 89 × 64mm)	1991	—	£5.00
LT90	Terminator Salvation Movie	2009	—	£8.50
LT16	Three's Company (Puzzle Picture)	1978	—	£5.00
LT72	WCW Nitro (Wrestling)	1999	—	£8.00
LT132	Who Framed Roger Rabbit — The Movie	1987	—	£9.50
LT100	Wild C.A.T.S Covert Action Teams by Jim Lee (2 different No. 66, No.68 not issued)	1983	—	£8.00
LT72	World Championship Wrestling Embossed	1999	—	£10.00
LT72	The X Files Fight for the Future	1998	—	£12.00
LT72	The X Files Season 1	1996	—	£9.50
LT72	The X Files Season 2	1996	—	£9.50
LT72	The X Files Season 3	1997	—	£9.50
EL72	The X Files Showcase — Widevision	1997	—	£12.00
LT72	X-Men — The Movie	2000	—	£9.50
LT72	X-Men 2 United — The Movie	2003	—	£8.00
LT72	Xena Warrior Princess Season 1	1998	—	£9.50
LT72	Xena Warrior Princess Season 2	2000	—	£12.00

JOHN TORDOFF & SON

K25	The Growth and Manufacture of Tea	c1930	£11.00	—
25	Safety First	c1930	£11.00	—

TOTAL UK

L25	Return to Oz	1985	20p	£3.50
	Album		—	£5.00

Qty		Date	Odds	Sets
	TOURISM RESOURCES			
L24	Historic Irish Houses	1993	—	£15.00
	TOURIST BOARD			
L40	Places to Visit Cumbria	1992	—	£4.00
L40	Places to Visit Cumbria	1993	—	£4.00
L40	Places to Visit Cumbria	1995	—	£4.00
L40	Places to Visit North West	1991	—	£5.00
L40	Places to Visit North West	1992	—	£5.00
L40	Places to Visit North West	1993	—	£4.00
L40	Places to Visit North West	1994	—	£4.00
L40	Places to Visit North West	1995	—	£4.00
L40	Places to Visit North West	1996	—	£4.00
L40	Places to Visit North West	1999	—	£4.00
L40	Places to Visit Stockport	1992	—	£4.00
L40	Places to Visit Stockport	1993	—	£4.00
L40	Places to Visit Stockport	1994	—	£4.00
L40	Places to Visit Trafford	1990	—	£4.00
L40	Places to Visit Trafford	1991	—	£4.00
L40	Places to Visit Wigan & District	1991	—	£4.00
L40	Places to Visit Wigan & District	1992	—	£4.00
	TOWER TEA			
24	Illustrated Sayings	c1910	£25.00	—
	TRADE CARDS (EUROPE) LTD			
	(SEE ALSO FUTERA)			
LT90	Arsenal F.C. — Fans Selection	1998	—	£16.00
LT18	Arsenal F.C. — Fans Selection (embossed)	1998	—	£5.00
LT99	Arsenal F.C. plus Set LT9 embossed	1999	20p	£15.00
LT9	Arsenal F.C. Hot Shots (foil fronts)	1999	£2.00	£18.00
LT9	Arsenal F.C. Vortex (foil fronts)	1999	£2.00	£18.00
LT50	Arsenal F.C. Greatest	1999	—	£25.00
LT50	Arsenal F.C. — Main Series	2000	20p	£7.50
LT6	Arsenal F.C. — Electric Series	2000	£3.00	£18.00
LT90	Aston Villa F.C. — Fans Selection	1998	—	£17.50
LT18	Aston Villa F.C. — Fans Selection (embossed) ...	1998	—	£5.00
LT99	Aston Villa F.C. plus Set LT9 embossed	1999	20p	£15.00
LT9	Aston Villa F.C. Hot Shots (foil fronts)	1999	£2.00	£18.00
LT9	Aston Villa F.C. Vortex (foil fronts)	1999	£2.00	£18.00
LT90	Celtic F.C. — Fans Selection	1998	—	£17.50
LT18	Celtic F.C. — Fans Selection (embossed)	1998	—	£5.50
LT99	Celtic F.C. plus Set LT9 embossed	1999	20p	£15.00
LT9	Celtic F.C. Hot Shots (foil fronts)	1999	£2.00	£18.00
LT9	Celtic F.C. Vortex (foil fronts)	1999	£2.00	£18.00
LT50	Celtic F.C. — Main Series	2000	20p	£7.50
LT4	Celtic F.C. — Electric Series	2000	£3.00	£12.00
LT90	Chelsea F.C. — Fans Selection	1998	—	£17.50
LT18	Chelsea F.C. — Fans Selection (embossed)	1998	—	£6.00
LT99	Chelsea F.C. plus Set LT9 embossed	1999	20p	£15.00
LT9	Chelsea F.C. Hot Shots (foil fronts)	1999	£2.00	£18.00
LT9	Chelsea F.C. Vortex (foil fronts)	1999	£2.00	£18.00
LT50	Chelsea F.C. Greatest	1999	—	£25.00
LT90	Leeds United F.C. — Fans Selection	1998	—	£17.50
LT18	Leeds United F.C. — Fans Selection (embossed)	1998	—	£6.00

Qty		Date	Odds	Sets
	TRADE CARDS (EUROPE) LTD (continued)			
LT99	Leeds United F.C. plus Set LT9 embossed	1999	20p	£15.00
LT9	Leeds United F.C. Hot Shots (foil fronts)...	1999	£2.00	£18.00
LT9	Leeds United F.C. Vortex (foil fronts)	1999	£2.00	£18.00
LT50	Leeds United F.C. Greatest	1999	–	£25.00
LT50	Leeds United F.C. – Main Series	2000	20p	£7.50
LT4	Leeds United F.C. – Electric Series	2000	£3.00	£12.00
LT99	Liverpool F.C. – Main Series	1998	–	£16.00
LT99	Liverpool F.C. plus Set LT9 embossed	1999	20p	£15.00
LT9	Liverpool F.C. Hot Shots (foil fronts)	1999	£2.00	£18.00
LT9	Liverpool F.C. Vortex (foil fronts)	1999	£2.00	£18.00
LT50	Liverpool F.C. – Main Series	2000	20p	£7.50
LT6	Liverpool F.C. – Electric Series	2000	£3.00	£18.00
LT100	Manchester United F.C.	1997	–	£17.50
LT90	Manchester United F.C. – Fans Selection	1998	–	£16.00
LT18	Manchester United F.C. – Fans Selection			
	(embossed)...	1998	–	£5.00
LT99	Manchester United F.C. – Main Series	1998	–	£17.50
LT99	Manchester United F.C. plus Set LT9 embossed ...	1999	20p	£15.00
LT9	Manchester United F.C. Hot Shots (foil fronts)	1999	£2.00	£18.00
LT9	Manchester United F.C. Vortex (foil fronts)	1999	£2.00	£18.00
LT99	Manchester United F.C. – Main Series	2000	20p	£15.00
LT9	Manchester United F.C. – Electric Series	2000	£3.00	–
LT99	Newcastle United F.C. plus Set LT9 embossed ...	1999	20p	£15.00
LT9	Newcastle United F.C. Hot Shots (foil fronts)	1999	£2.00	£18.00
LT9	Newcastle United F.C. Vortex (foil fronts)	1999	£2.00	£18.00
LT50	Newcastle United F.C. Greatest...	1999	–	£25.00

TRADING CARDS INTERNATIONAL (USA)

LT50	Princess Diana 1961-1997	1997	–	£9.50

TREASURE

L18	Zoo Time plus album	1966	–	£9.00

TREBOR LTD

M42	Space Series (Waxed Paper issue):			
	A Top 'Victory Bubble Gum'	1964	£5.00	–
	B Top 'Trebor Zip Bubble Gum'	1964	£5.00	–
M48	V.C. Heroes (Waxed Paper issue):			
	A Inscribed 'Zip'	1967	£5.00	–
	B Inscribed 'Zoom Bubble Gum'	1967	£5.00	–

TREBOR BASSETT LTD (SEE GEO. BASSETT)

TREBOR/SHARP

24	Famous Pets	1972	20p	£2.50
	Album		–	£5.00

TRIBUTE COLLECTABLES

10	Abbott and Costello	2010	–	£5.00
10	Astair Legend of Dance (Fred Astaire)	2010	–	£5.50
10	Cyd Charisse	2010	–	£5.50
10	Ella Fitzgerald	2010	–	£5.50
10	Ginger Rogers	2010	–	£5.50
10	Humphrey Bogart	2010	–	£5.50

Qty		Date	Odds	Sets
	TRIBUTE COLLECTABLES (continued)			
10	John Wayne A Tribute To The Duke	2010	—	£5.00
10	Josephine Baker (Dancer & Actress)...	2010	—	£5.50
10	Marty (Marty Feldman Commemorating the British			
	Comedy Star)	2010	—	£5.00
10	A Tribute to Danny Kaye	2010	—	£5.50
10	A Tribute to Dean Martin...	2010	—	£5.00
10	A Tribute to Diana Dors	2010	—	£5.00
20	A Tribute to Gene Kelly	2010	—	£9.00
10	A Tribute to Judy Garland...	2010	—	£5.50
10	Victor Mature	2010	—	£5.50
	TRUCARDS			
M30	Animals	1970	20p	£2.50
M30	Battle of Britain	1970	20p	£4.00
M30	Flowers	1970	20p	£2.50
M30	History of Aircraft...	1970	20p	£3.00
M30	Sport	1970	20p	£2.50
M30	Veteran and Vintage Cars	1970	20p	£3.00
M30	World War I	1970	20p	£3.00
M30	World War II	1970	20p	£3.00
	TUCKETTS			
25	Cricketers	1926	£32.00	—
50	Film Stars	1935	£6.00	—
25	Football Stars	1928	£25.00	—
	TUCKFIELD (Australia)			
M32	Australiana Animals	c1970	£1.60	—
M48	Australiana Birds Nos 1-48	c1970	70p	—
M48	Australiana Birds Nos 49-96	c1970	70p	—
M48	Australiana Birds Nos 97-144	c1970	70p	—
M48	Australiana Birds Nos 145-192	c1970	70p	—
M48	Australiana Birds Nos 193-240	c1970	70p	—
M48	Australiana Birds Nos 241-288	c1970	70p	—
M48	Australiana Birds Nos 289-336	c1970	70p	—
M48	Australiana Birds Nos 337-384	c1970	70p	—
	TUFF STUFF (USA)			
LT33	Peanuts by Schulz	1992	—	£6.00
LT50	Remember Pearl Harbor	1991	—	£15.00
LT15	World War II Propaganda Diamond Edition	1991	—	£6.50
	W.E. TURNER			
20	War Pictures	1915	£17.00	—
	21st CENTURY ARCHIVES (USA)			
LT50	The Comic Art Tribute To Joe Simon and Jack Kirby	1994	—	£8.00
LT100	National Lampoon	1993	—	£9.50
	TWININGS TEA			
30	Rare Stamps 1st Series	1958	80p	£24.00
30	Rare Stamps 2nd Series			
	A No overprint	1960	20p	£4.00
	B Red overprint...	1960	20p	£2.50

Qty		Date	Odds	Sets
	TYPHOO TEA			
	(36 page Illustrated Reference Book — £4.50)			
25	Aesop's Fables	1924	£3.20	£80.00
M12	The Amazing World of Doctor Who	1976	£2.25	£27.00
25	Ancient and Annual Customs	1924	£2.40	£60.00
L25	Animal Friends of Man	1927	£5.00	—
L25	Animal Offence and Defence	1928	£1.60	£40.00
24	British Birds and Their Eggs	1914	£12.00	—
L25	British Birds and Their Eggs	1936	£1.80	£45.00
	British Empire at Work:			
30	1 Normal set with pictures	1925	£1.70	£50.00
30	2 Wording only 'This is a Continuation Card' ...	1925	£7.00	—
1	3 The Last Chance Card	1925	—	£10.00
22	Calendar 1934 (Dogs)	1933	£30.00	—
25	Calendar	1936	£15.00	—
L1	Calendar	1937	—	£9.00
L25	Characters from Shakespeare	1937	£1.40	£35.00
25	Common Objects Highly Magnified	1925	£1.40	£35.00
25	Conundrums	1915	£18.00	—
24	Do You Know?	1962	20p	£3.00
L25	Famous Voyages	1933	£1.60	£40.00
M20	Flags and Arms of Countries	1916	£15.00	—
24	Great Achievements	1967	£1.20	£30.00
L25	Historical Buildings	1939	£2.00	£50.00
L25	Homes of Famous Men	1934	£1.40	£35.00
L25	Horses	1934	£1.80	£45.00
L25	Important Industries of the British Empire	1938	50p	£12.50
L25	Interesting Events in British History	1938	50p	£12.50
10	Nursery Rhymes	c1910	£25.00	—
24	Our Empire's Defenders	c1915	£30.00	—
48	Puzzle Pictures	c1915	£30.00	—
L30	Robin Hood and His Merry Men:			
	A Back with Oval Imprint	1926	£8.00	—
	B Back without Oval Imprint	1926	£8.00	—
L25	Scenes from John Halifax, Gentleman	1931	£2.40	£60.00
L25	Scenes from Lorna Doone:			
	A Lemon borders to picture side	1930	£3.60	—
	B Orange borders to picture side	1930	£3.60	—
L25	Scenes from a Tale of Two Cities by Charles Dickens:			
	A Back inscribed '897.1/31'	1931	£3.60	£90.00
	B Back inscribed '897.10/31'	1931	£4.50	
L30	The Story of David Copperfield:			
	A Coupon inscribed 'until 30th September' ...	1930	£2.80	£80.00
	B Coupon inscribed 'until end of October'	1930	£5.00	—
	C With coupon cut off	1930	£2.20	£65.00
L25	The Swiss Family Robinson	1935	£2.00	£50.00
24	Travel Through the Ages	1961	20p	£3.50
L25	Trees of the Countryside	1937	80p	£20.00
L25	Whilst We Sleep Series:			
	A Back with inscription '79610/10/28'	1928	£3.40	—
	B Back without inscription '79610/10/28'	1928	£3.00	£75.00
24	Wild Flowers	1963	20p	£4.00
L25	Wild Flowers in Their Families 1st Series	1935	£1.00	£25.00
L25	Wild Flowers in Their Families 2nd Series	1936	£1.00	£25.00
L25	Wonder Cities of the World	1933	£1.80	£45.00

TYPHOO TEA (continued)

Qty		Date	Odds	Sets
M24	Wonderful World of Disney	1975	£3.50	—
L25	Work on the Farm	1932	£3.60	£90.00
25	Zoo Series	1932	£1.20	£30.00

Package issues:
Children's series of:

Qty		Date	Odds	Sets
L20	By Pond and Stream	1960	50p	£10.00
L20	Common British Birds	1954	50p	£10.00
L20	Costumes of the World	1961	70p	—
L20	Famous Bridges	1958	50p	—
L20	Famous Buildings	1953	50p	£10.00
L20	Pets	1959	50p	—
L20	Some Countryside Animals	1957	50p	—
L20	Some Popular Breeds of Dogs	1955	80p	£16.00
L20	Some World Wonders	1959	50p	£10.00
L20	Types of Ships	1956	50p	£10.00
L20	Wild Animals	1952	50p	£10.00
L24	Do You Know?	1962	50p	£12.00
L24	Famous Football Clubs	1964	£2.00	—
	Famous Football Clubs 2nd Series:			
L24	A With 'Second Series' in red above picture ...	1965	£2.50	—
L24	B Without 'Second Series' in red above picture	1965	£2.50	—
L26	Football Club Plaques	1973	£7.00	—
L24	Football Stars, New Series	1973	£2.80	—
L24	Great Voyages of Discovery	1966	50p	£12.00
L24	International Football Stars	1967	£2.80	—
L24	International Football Stars 2nd Series	1969	£2.80	—
L24	100 Years of Great British Achievements	1972	75p	—
L24	Travel Through the Ages	1961	50p	—
L24	Wild Flowers	1963	60p	£15.00

Premium issues:

Qty		Date	Odds	Sets
EL24	Famous Football Clubs 1st Series	1964	£12.00	—
EL24	Famous Football Clubs 2nd Series	1965	£10.00	—
EL24	Football Stars	1973	£9.00	—
EL24	International Football Stars 1st Series	1967	£9.00	—
EL24	International Football Stars 2nd Series	1969	£9.00	—
EL24	100 Years of Great British Achievements:			
	A Plain back	1972	£1.25	—
	B Printed back	1972	£5.00	—

TYSON & CO. LTD

Qty		Date	Odds	Sets
28	Semaphore Signals	c1912	£18.00	—

'UNION JACK'

Qty		Date	Odds	Sets
MP6	Monarchs of the Ring	1923	£10.00	—
M8	Police of All Nations	1922	£7.50	—

UNITED AUTOMOBILE SERVICES

Kodak Views Series:

Qty		Date	Odds	Sets
25	Castles, Series No. 1	1925	£7.00	—
25	Churches, Series No. 2	1925	£7.00	—
25	United, Series No. 3	1925	£7.00	—
25	Places of Interest, Series No. 4	1925	£7.00	—

Qty		Date	Odds	Sets

THE UNITED CONFECTIONERY CO. LTD

Qty		Date	Odds	Sets
50	Wild Animals of the World...	1905	£12.00	—

UNITED DAIRIES (Tea)

25	Aquarium Fish	1964	24p	£6.00
25	Birds and Their Eggs	1961	70p	£17.50
25	British Uniforms of the 19th Century	1962	70p	£17.50
25	The Story of Milk...	1966	30p	£7.50
25	The West	1963	80p	£20.00

UNIVERSAL AUTOMATICS LTD

L30	Trains of the World	1958	£1.20	—

UNIVERSAL CCC

15	Australia Cricket Team 1905	1986	—	£3.00
15	English Cricketers 1902	1987	—	£3.00

UNSTOPABLE CARDS

LT72	The Avengers 50 (TV Series of the 1960s)	2012	—	£8.00

UPPER DECK (Germany)

LT45	Werder Bremen F.C.	1997	—	£6.00

UPPER DECK (Italy)

LT45	Italian Footballers World Cup	1998	—	£6.00
LT90	Juventus F.C. 1994/95	1994	—	£7.50
LT45	Juventus F.C. Centenary 1897-1997	1997	—	£7.50

UPPER DECK (Spain)

LT45	Spanish Footballers World Cup	1998	—	£6.00

UPPER DECK (Sweden)

LT224/225	Swedish Hockey League (minus No. 36) 1997/98	1997	20p	£15.00
LT30	Swedish Hockey League Crash Cards 1997/98 ...	1997	—	£10.00
LT15	Swedish Hockey League Stickers 1997/98	1997	—	£5.00
LT15	Swedish Hockey League Update Series 1997/98...	1997	—	£10.00

UPPER DECK (UK)

LT34	Digimon Digital Monsters	2000	—	£7.00
LT45	England's Qualifying Campaign (Football World Cup) 1st Series Nos 1 to 45	1997	—	£10.00
LT37	England's Qualifying Campaign (Football World Cup) 2nd Series Nos 46 to 82	1998	—	£10.00
LT135	Manchester United F.C. 2001	2001	20p	£17.50
LT14	Manchester United F.C. 2001 Legends of Old Trafford	2001	—	£14.00
LT7	Manchester United F.C. 2001 Magnificent 7's	2001	—	£7.00
LT7	Manchester United F.C. 2001 Strike Force	2001	—	£7.00
LT14	Manchester United F.C. 2001 We Are United	2001	—	£14.00
LT90	Manchester United F.C.	2002	—	£17.50
LT100	Manchester United F.C. Play Makers	2003	—	£17.50
LT100	Manchester United F.C. Strike Force	2003	—	£17.50
LT90	Manchester United Legends	2002	—	£17.50
LT45	Manchester United World Premiere	2001	—	£20.00
LT45	The Mini (Car) Collection	1996	—	£15.00

UPPER DECK (UK) (continued)

		Date	Odds	Sets
LT250	World Cup Football	1994	—	£25.00
LT17	World Cup Football nos 251-267 Unissued	1994	—	£10.00
LT30	World Cup Football All Stars	1994	—	£5.00

UPPER DECK (USA)

LT90	Adventures in Toon World...	1993	—	£9.50
LT99	Anastasia — The Movie	1998	—	£8.50
LT90	Battlefield Earth — The Film	2000	—	£8.00
LT198	Beauty and the Beast	1992	—	£12.00
LT90	Congo The Film	1995	—	£9.50
LT89	Disney Treasures 1st Series	2003	—	£15.00
LT45	Disney Treasures 1st Series — Mickey Mouse	2003	—	£18.00
LT10	Disney Treasures 1st Series — Walt Disney Retrospective	2003	—	£3.50
LT90	Disney Treasures 2nd Series	2003	—	£12.00
LT45	Disney Treasures 2nd Series — Donald Duck	2003	—	£15.00
LT10	Disney Treasures 2nd Series The Lion King Special Edition	2003	—	£3.50
LT89	Disney Treasures 3rd Series...	2004	—	£12.00
LT10	Disney Treasures 3rd Series Aladdin Special Edition	2004	—	£3.50
LT45	Disney Treasures 3rd Series — Winnie The Pooh ..	2004	—	£18.00
LT75	Disney Treasures Celebrate Mickey 75 Years of Fun	2004	—	£12.00
LT75	Iron Man 2 — The Film	2010	—	£8.00
LT55	Looney Tunes Olympics 1996	1996	—	£8.00
LT210	N.H.L. Hockey Players 1st Series 1997/98	1997	20p	£15.00
LT55	Princess Gwenevere and The Jewell Riders	1996	—	£8.00
LT60	Space Jam — The Film	1996	—	£7.50
LT120	The Valiant Era	1993	—	£12.00
LT120	World Cup Toons	1994	—	£9.50

UPPER DECK/HOOLA HOOPS (UK)

L40	Basketball Players (NBA) (No. HH1 to HH40)	1997	—	£8.00

VAN DEN BERGHS LTD

EL8	Birds	1974	45p	£3.50
LT24	Pirates	1968	£3.00	—
LT24	This Modern World	1968	£2.00	£50.00

VAUXHALL MOTORS

L25	Vauxhall's 90th Anniversary Series	1993	—	£10.00

VENORLANDUS LTD

M48	Our Heroes, World of Sport	1979	50p	£24.00
	Album		—	£5.00

VERKADE (Holland)

L120	Cactussen (Cacti)	1931	25p	—
L140	De Bloemen en Haar Vrienden (Flowers and Their Friends)	1933	20p	£20.00
L140	De Boerderil (The Farm)	c1930	30p	—
L138	Hans de Torenkraai (Hans the Crow)	c1930	20p	£20.00
L132	Kamerplanten (House Plants)	1928	25p	—
L126	Mijn Aquarium (My Aquarium)	1925	30p	—
L132	Texel District	1927	30p	—
L126	Vetplanten (Succulents)	1932	20p	£25.00

VICTORIA GALLERY

Qty		Date	Odds	Sets
L6	A Gathering of Spirits (Red Indians)	1994	—	£3.00
L20	American Civil War Leaders	1992	—	£7.00
L25	Ashes Winning Captains (cricket)	1993	—	£8.50
L20	Boxing Champions 1st Series	1991	—	£10.00
L21	Boxing Champions 2nd Series	1992	—	£7.00
L6	British Birds of Prey by D. Digby	1994	—	£3.00
L6	British Birds of Prey 2nd Series	1996	—	£3.00
L20	Caricatures of the British Army 1st Series	1994	—	£7.00
L20	Caricatures of the British Army 2nd Series	1994	30p	£7.00
L6	Classic Motor Cycles (Harley Davidson)	1993	—	£3.00
50	Deep Sea Diving	1997	20p	£10.50
L20	Embassy Snooker Celebrities	1988	—	£7.00
L20	Endangered Wild Animals	1992	—	£7.00
L10	Formula One 91 (Cars)	1991	—	—
L25	Hollywood Moviemen	1993	—	£8.50
L20	Legends of Hollywood	1991	—	£7.00
L25	Olympic Greats	1992	—	£8.50
L20	Partners (Film Stars)	1992	—	£7.00
L15	The Ryder Cup (Golf)	1987	—	£15.00
L25	The Ryder Cup 1991 (Golf)	1991	—	£15.00
L12	Samurai Warriors	1996	—	£10.00
L10	Spirit of a Nation (Red Indians)	1991	—	£5.00
L12	Twelve Days of Christmas	1992	—	£6.00
L20	Uniforms of the American Civil War	1992	—	£7.00
L24	Uniforms of the American War of Independence	1993	—	£8.50
L12	Wild West — Frontiersmen	1993	—	£4.00
L12	Wild West — Indians	1993	—	£4.00
L12	Wild West — Lawmen	1993	—	£4.00
L12	Wild West — Outlaws	1993	—	£4.00

VICTORIAN CRICKET ASSOCIATION (Australia)

Qty		Date	Odds	Sets
L20	Bushrangers Cricketers	1998	—	£6.00
L20	Bushrangers Cricketers	1999	—	£6.00

VINCENT GRAPHICS

Qty		Date	Odds	Sets
M48	The Life and Times of Nelson	1991	—	£20.00

VISION (USA)

Qty		Date	Odds	Sets
LT150	Generation Extreme (Extreme Sports)	1994	—	£15.00

VOMO AUTOMATICS

Qty		Date	Odds	Sets
LT50	Flags of the World	c1960	£1.00	—

WAKEFORD

Qty		Date	Odds	Sets
30	Army Pictures, Cartoons, etc	1916	£90.00	—

JONATHAN WALES LTD

Qty		Date	Odds	Sets
25	The History of Flight 1st Series	1963	£6.00	—
25	The History of Flight 2nd Series	1963	£6.00	—

WALES ON SUNDAY

Qty		Date	Odds	Sets
L40	British Lions on Tour Australia (Rugby Union)	2001	20p	£8.00
L36	World Cup Heroes (Rugby Union Players)	1995	33p	£12.00
L24	World Cup Rugby Greats (including album)	1999	—	£10.00

Qty		Date	Odds	Sets

WALES ON SUNDAY/WESTERN MAIL

Qty		Date	Odds	Sets
EL13	Welsh Rugby Union — Graham Henry's Wales ...	2001	—	£4.00

WALKER HARRISON AND GARTHWAITE LTD

M15	Dogs	1902	£24.00	—

WALKERS SNACK FOODS

K50	Looney Tunes — Tazos Nos 1-50 (circular)	1996	20p	£10.00
K10	Monster Munch Tazos (circular)	1996	—	£3.00
K35	Pokemon Tazos (circular)	2001	40p	—
K50	Star Wars Trilogy — Tazos (circular)	1997	25p	£12.50
K20	World Tazos Nos 51-70 (circular)	1996	25p	£5.00

T. WALL & SONS

24	Do You Know?	1965	20p	£4.00
36	Dr. Who Adventure	1967	£3.00	£110.00
20	Incredible Hulk	1979	£1.00	£20.00
M6	Magicards — Prehistoric Animals	1971	40p	£2.50
48	Moon Fleet	1966	20p	£10.00
EL6	Sea Creatures	1971	40p	£2.50
20	Skateboard Surfer	1978	25p	£5.00
20	Time Travel with Starship 4	1984	£3.50	—

WALLIS CHOCOLATES

24	British Birds	c1920	£10.00	—

WALTERS' 'PALM' TOFFEE

50	Some Cap Badges of Territorial Regiments	1938	50p	£25.00

WAND CONFECTIONERY LTD

EL10	Chubby Checker — How To Do the Twist	1964	£8.00	—
25	Commemoration Stamp Series	1962	£3.00	£75.00
EL35	Pop DJs	1967	£3.50	—
25	They Gave Their Names	1963	50p	£12.50

WARUS (UK)

10	The Beatles — Abbey Road	1998	—	£5.00
10	The Beatles — Beatles for Sale	1998	—	£5.00
10	The Beatles — Beatles for Sale No. 2 EP Series .	2005	—	£5.00
10	The Beatles — Beatles Second Album	2005	—	£5.00
10	The Beatles — Beatles 65	2005	—	£5.00
10	The Beatles — EP Series	2005	—	£5.00
10	The Beatles — Hard Day's Night	1998	—	£5.00
10	The Beatles — Help	1998	—	£5.00
10	The Beatles — Hits EP Series	2005	—	£5.00
10	The Beatles — Let It Be	1998	—	£5.00
10	The Beatles — Long Tall Sally EP Series	2005	—	£5.00
10	The Beatles — Magical Mystery Tour	1998	—	£5.00
10	The Beatles — Meet The Beatles	2005	—	£5.00
10	The Beatles — Million Sellers EP Series	2005	—	£5.00
10	The Beatles — Nowhere Man EP Series	2005	—	£5.00
10	The Beatles — Please Please Me	1998	—	£5.00
10	The Beatles — Revolver	1998	—	£5.00
10	The Beatles — Rubber Soul	1998	—	£5.00
10	The Beatles — Sgt. Pepper	1998	—	£5.00

WARUS (UK) (continued)

Qty		Date	Odds	Sets
10	The Beatles — Something New	2005	—	£5.00
10	The Beatles — Twist and Shout EP Series...	2005	—	£5.00
10	The Beatles — White Album	1998	—	£5.00
10	The Beatles — With the Beatles	1998	—	£5.00
10	The Beatles — Yellow Submarine	1998	—	£5.00
10	The Beatles — Yesterday and Today...	2005	—	£5.00
10	The Beatles — Yesterday EP Series	2005	—	£5.00
10	The Rolling Stones Urban Jungle Tour	1998	—	£5.00

WARWICK DISTRICT COUNCIL

Qty		Date	Odds	Sets
30	England's Historic Heartland	1980	20p	£3.00

WATFORD BISCUITS

Qty		Date	Odds	Sets
KP48	Cinema Stars	1955	£3.00	—

JOHN WATSON

Qty		Date	Odds	Sets
M56	Norfolk Churches	2012	—	£9.50
M52	Taverns of East Anglia Series 1	2004	—	£9.50
M56	Taverns of Norfolk Series 2	2008	—	£9.50

WEBCOSA & CO. LTD

Qty		Date	Odds	Sets
L20	Trail Town	1964	£2.50	£50.00
M48	Victoria Cross Heroes (waxed paper issue)...	c1963	£4.00	—

WEEKLY WELCOME

Qty		Date	Odds	Sets
12	'Lest We Forget' cards	1916	£9.00	—

WEETABIX LTD

Qty		Date	Odds	Sets
L25	Animal Cards	1960	70p	£17.50
L28	Asterix — His Friends and Foes	1976	£2.50	—
L18	Batman and Wonderwoman	1979	£3.00	—
L25	British Birds	1962	£2.40	—
L25	British Cars	1963	£3.60	—
L25	Conquest of Space, Series A	1958	£2.40	£60.00
L25	Conquest of Space, Series B	1959	£2.40	£60.00
L24	Dr. Who — Coloured background	1977	£6.00	—
L24	Dr. Who — White background	1975	£6.00	—
L18	Flash Gordon	1981	£2.50	—
L18	Huckleberry Hound	1977	£2.50	—
L25	Our Pets	1961	80p	£20.00
L18	Robin Hood Characters from Walt Disney	1974	£3.00	—
L18	Star Trek	1979	£4.00	£70.00
L18	Superman	1978	£2.50	—
L25	Thrill Cards	1961	£2.20	—
L18	Walt Disney Cartoon Characters	1978	£2.50	—
L25	The Western Story	1959	£1.60	£40.00
L25	Working Dogs...	1960	30p	£7.50
L18	World of Sport	1986	£4.00	—

WELSH RUGBY UNION

Qty		Date	Odds	Sets
50	Great Welsh Rugby Players	1980	20p	£6.00

Qty		Date	Odds	Sets

WEST BROMWICH ALBION FOOTBALL CLUB

Qty		Date	Odds	Sets
M25	West Bromwich Albion Footballers...	1993	—	£12.50
L12	West Bromwich Albion Footballers Plus Folder			
	(VE/VJ Day Issue)	1995	—	£6.00

J. WEST FOODS LTD

Qty		Date	Odds	Sets
M8	Famous Sea Adventurers (inscribed series of 14,			
	only 8 cards issued)	1972	30p	£2.50

WEST LONDON HOSPITAL

Qty		Date	Odds	Sets
EL1	Calendar 1947 (size 125 × 75mm)	1947	—	£1.50

WEST LONDON SYNAGOGUE

Qty		Date	Odds	Sets
25	Hebrew Texts Illustrated	1960	£2.00	—

WEST MIDLANDS COLLECTORS

Qty		Date	Odds	Sets
24	Busby Babes (Football)	1990	—	£12.00
12	Busby Babes Nos 25-36 (Football)	1991	—	£3.00
36	Busby Babes (revised combined 1990/91 issues)	1994	—	£12.00
2	Busby Babes Additional Cards Nos 24 & 25 Error			
	Marked Series of 25	1991	—	£1.50
30	England Captains (Football)	1997	—	£5.00
24	Golden Wolves (Football)	1989	25p	£6.00
24	Vintage Spurs (Football)	1993	—	£15.00

WEST MIDLANDS POLICE

Qty		Date	Odds	Sets
EL24	The Old Bill Collection	1990	20p	£5.00
	Album		—	£5.00
EL36	Pictorial History of Walsall and District	1986	50p	£18.00
EL8	Play Safe — Stay Safe (including Album)	1992	—	£4.00

WEST RIDING COUNTY COUNCIL

Qty		Date	Odds	Sets
20	Health Cards	c1920	£6.00	—

WEST YORKSHIRE FIRE SERVICE

Qty		Date	Odds	Sets
M29	Huddersfield Giants R.L.F.C.	1999	—	£10.00

WEST YORKSHIRE POLICE

Qty		Date	Odds	Sets
EL20	Great Britain Rugby League Stars	2003	—	£6.00

WESTERN MAIL

Qty		Date	Odds	Sets
L24	Wales Soccer Stars	2003	—	£6.00
L36	Welsh Grand Slam (Rugby Union)	2005	—	£6.00

WESTON BISCUITS CO. LTD (Australia)

Qty		Date	Odds	Sets
50	Dogs	c1965	£3.00	—
M24	Veteran and Vintage Cars 1st Series	1961	£1.80	£45.00
	Album		—	£5.00
M24	Veteran and Vintage Cars 2nd Series	1962	30p	£7.50

WHAT CAMERA

Qty		Date	Odds	Sets
EL12	Photocards...	1988	—	£3.00

R. WHEATLEY

Qty		Date	Odds	Sets
36	Animal Pictures	c1920	£6.00	—

Qty		Date	Odds	Sets

WHITBREAD & CO. LTD

Qty		Date	Odds	Sets
M1	The Britannia Inn Sign:			
	A Printed Back	1958	—	£50.00
	B Plain Back...	1958	—	£35.00
M1	Duke Without a Head Inn Sign	1958	—	£9.00
M50	Inn Signs 1st Series (metal)	1951	£3.50	£175.00
M50	Inn Signs 2nd Series (metal)...	1951	£3.50	£175.00
M50	Inn Signs 3rd Series:			
	A Metal	1951	£4.50	£225.00
	B Card...	1952	£3.50	£175.00
M50	Inn Signs 4th Series (card)	1952	£3.50	£175.00
M50	Inn Signs 5th Series (card)	1953	£3.50	£175.00
M4	Inn Signs (special issue)	1951	£6.00	—
M25	Inn Signs, Bournemouth	1973	£7.00	—
M25	Inn Signs, Devon and Somerset	1973	£1.80	£45.00
M25	Inn Signs, Isle of Wight	1974	£7.00	—
M25	Inn Signs, Kent	1973	£7.00	—
M15	Inn Signs, London:			
	A Complete set...	1973	—	£85.00
	B 12 different (minus Nos 3, 10 & 13)	1973	£3.00	£35.00
M10	Inn Signs, London	1974	£5.00	—
	Album		—	£8.00
M25	Inn Signs, Maritime	1974	30p	£7.50
M25	Inn Signs, Marlow	1973	£7.00	—
M25	Inn Signs, Portsmouth	1973	£9.00	—
M25	Inn Signs, Stratford-upon-Avon	1974	£6.00	—
M25	Inn Signs, West Pennine	1973	£7.00	—
M1	The Railway Inn Sign	1958	—	£12.00
M1	The Startled Saint Inn Sign:			
	A With Printed in Great Britain	1958	—	£60.00
	B Without Printed in Great Britain	1958	—	£40.00

THE WHITE FISH AUTHORITY

Qty		Date	Odds	Sets
25	Fish We Eat	1954	20p	£2.50

WHITEHAVEN MUSEUM

Qty		Date	Odds	Sets
M6	The Port of Whitehaven	1978	85p	£5.00

WHITEHEAD (NOTTINGHAM) LTD

Qty		Date	Odds	Sets
L25	Kings and Queens	1980	20p	£3.25

WIKO (Germany)

Qty		Date	Odds	Sets
50	Soldaten Der Welt	1969	30p	£15.00

WILCOCKS & WILCOCKS LTD

Qty		Date	Odds	Sets
25	Birds	1965	£2.40	—
25	British Cavalry Uniforms of the 19th Century	1964	60p	£15.00
25	Garden Flowers	1964	20p	£5.00
24	The Island of Ceylon	1964	£5.00	—
25	Passenger Liners	1967	80p	£20.00
25	People and Places	1967	20p	£4.00
25	Tropical Birds	1965	40p	£10.00
25	Wonders of the Deep	1965	20p	£3.50
25	Wonders of the World	1971	20p	£5.00

Qty		Date	Odds	Sets
	A.S. WILKIN LTD			
25	Into Space	1960	30p	£7.50
	W.R. WILKINSON & CO. LTD			
M25	Popular Footballers	c1955	£40.00	—
	WILKINSON SWORD LTD			
K4	Garden Tools (Firm's name in black on white background)	1961	£2.50	£10.00
K2/4	Garden Tools (Firm's name in white on black background)	1961	—	£2.00
K16	Regimental Swords	1995	£4.00	—
	WILLARDS CHOCOLATE LTD (Canada)			
50	Indian Series c1925...		£8.00	—
	R.J. WILSON			
L5	B.R. Preserved Diesel-Electric Locomotives	2005	—	£5.00
LT6	British Birds	2005	—	£3.00
L10	British Steam Locomotives	2000	—	£5.50
L6	Eggs of British Birds	2004	—	£4.00
L6	Glamour Girls (Pin Up Girls)	2004	—	£4.00
L10	Hunting With the South Wold	2000	—	£6.25
LT6	Lincolnshire Village Churches 1st Series	2006	—	£5.00
LT6	Lincolnshire Village Churches 2nd Series	2007	—	£5.00
LT6	Nests and Eggs of British Birds 1st Series	2005	—	£4.00
LT6	Nests and Eggs of British Birds 2nd Series	2005	—	£4.00
LT6	Nests and Eggs of British Birds 3rd Series	2006	—	£4.00
LT6	Nests and Eggs of British Birds 4th Series	2007	—	£4.00
L6	Railway Engines	2004	—	£3.00
10	Railway Locomotives	2000	—	£5.00
L4	The South Wold (Lincolnshire) Foxhounds	2004	—	£2.50
L10	Traditional Lincolnshire Country Life	2001	—	£6.25
L6	Vintage Agricultural Traction	2003	—	£6.50
L6	Vintage Motive Power	2004	—	£5.00
L10	Vintage Tractors	2002	—	£4.50
LT6	Wilford Bowls Club	2007	—	£4.00
LT6	Young of British Birds	2007	—	£4.00
	WILTSHIRE LIBRARY			
EL13	Wiltshire Railcards 1st Series	1978	—	£3.50
EL8	Wiltshire Railcards 2nd Series	1979	—	£3.00
	WIMPY			
M20	Super Heroes Super Villains	1979	£1.25	£25.00
	WINGS			
M5	Back to the Egg — Paul McCartney	c1980	£3.00	—
	WINTERLAND (USA)			
LT10	Backstreet Boys Awards	2000	—	£4.00
LT4	Backstreet Boys Black & Blue	2000	—	£3.00
LT15	Backstreet Boys Hot Shots	2000	—	£4.00
LT25	Backstreet Boys Millennium	2000	—	£5.00

Qty		Date	Odds	Sets
	WIZARDS			
EL81	Harry Potter & The Sorcerer's Stone	2001	—	£20.00
	A Nos 1 to 40		30p	—
	B Nos 41 to 81		20p	£8.00
EL40	Harry Potter & The Sorcerer's Stone			
	Parallel Series	2001	£2.00	—
	WOMAN'S OWN			
8	Film Stars	c1955	£6.00	—
	WONDERBREAD (USA)			
LT24	Close Encounters of The Third Kind	1977	—	£10.00
	WONDERBREAD/TOPPS (USA)			
LT24	American Football Stars	1976	—	£6.00
	E. WOODHEAD & SONS			
25	Types of British Soldiers	1914	£30.00	—
	WOOLWORTHS			
M24	Guinness Book of Records	1989	—	£6.00
	WOOLWORTHS-TOPPS (USA)			
LT33	Baseball Highlights	1988	—	£8.00
	WORLD CRICKET INC (New Zealand)			
LT18	New Zealand Cricketers 2007	2007	75p	—
LT27	New Zealand Cricketers 2008	2008	—	£9.50
LT25	New Zealand Cricketers 2009	2009	50p	—
	WRIGHTS BISCUITS LTD			
24	Marvels of the World	1968	20p	£2.50
24	Mischief Goes to Mars:			
	A 'Join the Mischief Club' at base	1954	20p	£5.00
	B 'Issued by Wright's Biscuits Ltd' at base ...	1954	40p	£10.00
	C Name at side, but not at base	1954	20p	£3.50
	YORKSHIRE FRAMING CO			
25	England World Cup 2006 (Football)	2006	—	£6.00
14	The 36th Ryder Cup	2006	—	£4.50
	YOUNG BRITAIN			
MP15	Favourite Cricketers Series	1922	£7.00	—
	ZELLERS (Canada)			
L24	Batman Returns	1992	—	£8.00

Qty		Date	Odds	Sets
	ANONYMOUS			
50	Animals of the World	1954	20p	£4.00
4	Birds, Nests and Eggs	c1960	60p	£2.50
25	Bridges of the World	1958	20p	£2.50
25	British Coins and Costumes	1958	20p	£2.50
25	British Uniforms of the 19th Century:			
	A Black back	c1965	32p	£8.00
	B Blue back	c1965	20p	£3.50
20	Budgerigars	1957	60p	£12.00
25	Cacti	c1965	20p	£2.50
25	Castles of Britain.................................	c1960	50p	—
25	Children of All Nations	1958	20p	£2.50
25	The Circus	1964	50p	—
25	Family Pets	1964	24p	6.00
? K300	Film & Entertainment Stars	c1960	40p	—
	A 10 Different Male Stars size 44 x 28mm			
	(our selection)	c1960	—	£3.00
	B 10 Different Female Stars size 50 x 25mm			
	(our selection)	c1960	—	£3.00
25	Flags and Emblems...............................	c1965	24p	£6.00
25	Flowers	c1970	20p	£3.00
25	Football Clubs and Badges	c1960	20p	£4.00
110	General Interest Series	c1970	—	£12.00
40	Greats from the States (Golf)	1994	—	£20.00
50	Jewish Life in Many Lands	c1960	£1.20	£60.00
	Jewish Symbols & Ceremonies:			
50	A Complete set...............................	1961	£2.00	£50.00
25	B Numbers 1 to 25 only	1961	20p	£2.50
25	Modern Aircraft	1958	20p	£4.00
L12	Motor Cycles 1907-1950	1987	20p	£2.50
25	Musical Instruments..............................	1967	20p	£2.50
25	Pigeons	1971	20p	£5.00
25	Pond Life	c1970	20p	£2.50
1	Soldier — Bugler...................................	c1970	—	£2.50
25	Sports of the Countries	c1970	80p	—
25	Tropical Birds	c1960	20p	£4.00
1	Venice in London	c1970	—	£1.00

FILM AND ENTERTAINMENT
⭑ ⭑ ⭑ STARS ⭑ ⭑ ⭑

These miniature glossy photographs
were issued anonymously around
1960 and we can supply the
following at 40p each

Size approx 44 x 28mm

Pier Angelli	Susan Hayward	Terry Moore
Brigitte Bardot	Audrey Hepburn	Kenneth More
* Warren Beatty	Robert Horton	George Nader
Ann Blyth	* Jeffrey Hunter	Sheree North
Dirk Bogarde	Glynis Johns	Kim Novak
Marlon Brando	Shirley Jones	Debra Paget
Rossano Brazzi	Kay Kendall	Laya Raki
Tony Britton	Deborah Kerr	Johnnie Ray
Max Bygraves	Frankie Laine	Debbie Reynolds (swimsuit)
* Eddie Byrnes	Mario Lanza (light suit)	Debbie Reynolds (head)
Rory Calhoun	Piper Laurie	* Cliff Richard
Jeff Chandler	June Laverick	Jane Russell
Rosemary Clooney	Belinda Lee	Janette Scott
Perry Como	Janet Leigh	Jean Simmons
Michael Craig	Liberace	* Roger Smith
Doris Day	Gina Lollobrigida	* Tommy Steele
Yvonne De Carlo	Sophia Loren	Maureen Swanson
Diana Dors	Dennis Lotis	Elizabeth Taylor
* Duanne Eddy	Virginia McKenna	Dickie Valentine
Anita Ekberg	Gordon Macrae	Mamie Van Doren
Vera-Ellen	Jayne Mansfield	* Frankie Vaughan (h&s)
Ava Gardner	Dean Martin	Frankie Vaughan (singing)
* James Garner	Victor Mature	Esther Williams
Mitzi Gaynor	Virginia Mayo	Shelley Winters
Richard Greene	* Sal Mineo	Natalie Wood
	Guy Mitchell	

Size approx 50 x 25mm

Lucille Ball	Yvonne De Carlo	* Hedy Lamarr
* Cyd Charisse	* Dale Evans (sitting)	Ann Miller
Jeanne Crain	* Dale Evans (standing)	* Gale Robbins
* Linda Darnell (black top)	Ava Gardner (black top)	* Jane Russell
Linda Darnell (swimsuit)	* Ava Gardner (skirt)	* Beryl Wallace
Doris Day	* Gloria Grahame	Esther Williams
	Susan Hayward	

SPECIAL OFFER:
The 10 male stars marked with an asterisk * for £3.00
The 10 female stars marked with an asterisk * for £3.00

172

REPRINT SERIES

During the past twenty years or so, around 350 classic cigarette and trade card series have been reprinted. Many of the originals are extremely rare and do not often turn up in collections, so reprints provide an opportunity to enjoy cards rarely seen. At such low prices, reprints have established a following in their own right, and have also become popular for framing to make an interesting decorative feature. The quality of reproduction is very good, and they are clearly marked as reprints to avoid confusion.

NOTE: C.C.S. = Card Collectors Society

Qty		Sets
	ADKIN & SONS	
EL4	Games by Tom Browne (135 x 83mm) c1900 (reprinted 2001)	£4.00
	A. W. ALLEN LTD (Australia)	
18	Bradman's Records (Cricketer) 1932 (reprinted 2002)	£7.00
	ALLEN & GINTER/GOODWIN/KIMBALL (USA)	
28	Baseball Greats of 1890 (reprinted 1991)	£6.00
	ALLEN & GINTER (USA)	
50	Celebrated American Indian Chiefs 1888 (reprinted 1989)...	£8.50
50	Fans of The Period 1890 (reprinted 2005)	£8.50
50	Fruits (Children) 1891 (reprinted 1989)	£8.50
50	Pirates of the Spanish Main 1888 (reprinted 1996)	
50	Prize and Game Chickens c1890 (reprinted 2000)	£10.00
9	Women Baseball Players c1888 (reprinted 2001)...	£3.00
EL50	The World's Champions 2nd Series (82 x 73mm) c1890 (reprinted 2001)	£17.50
	AMERICAN TOBACCO CO. (USA)	
L50	Lighthouse Series 1912 (reprinted 2000)	£12.00
25	Military Uniforms, numbered (green net design back) 1900 (reprinted 2003)	£6.25
	ARDATH TOBACCO CO. LTD	
35	Hand Shadows c1930 (reprinted 2001)	£7.50
	A. BAKER & CO. LTD	
25	Star Girls c1898 (reprinted 2001)	£6.00
	BARBERS TEA LTD	
24	Cinema & Television Stars 1955 (reprinted 1993)...	£6.25
	BENSDORP COCOA (Holland)	
EL3	Deep Sea Divers c1900 (reprinted c1995)	£2.50
	FELIX BERLYN	
25	Golfing Series Humorous 1910 (reprinted 1989)	£6.00
	ALEXANDER BOGUSLAVSKY LTD	
EL12	Big Events on the Turf (133 x 70mm) 1924 (reprinted 1995)	—
25	Conan Doyle Characters 1923 (reprinted 1996)	£6.25
25	Winners on the Turf 1925 (reprinted 1995)	£6.25

BOWMAN GUM INC. (USA)

M108   Jets-Rockets-Spacemen 1951 (reprinted 1985) £9.00

WM. BRADFORD

20   Boer War Cartoons c1901 (reprinted 2001) £5.00

BRIGHAM & CO.

L16   Down The Thames From Henley to Windsor c1912 (reprinted 2001) £6.50

BRITISH AMERICAN TOBACCO CO LTD

50	Aeroplanes 1926 (reprinted 2001)	£8.50
25	Beauties — Blossom Girls c1904 (reprinted 2001)	£6.00
32	Drum Horses 1910 (reprinted 2001)	£6.25
50	Indian Regiments 1912 (reprinted 2001)	£8.50
50	Lighthouses 1926 (reprinted 2000)	£8.50
45	Melbourne Cup Winners 1906 (reprinted 1992)	£8.50
50	Motorcycles 1927 (reprinted 1991)	£8.50
33	Regimental Pets 1911 (reprinted 1998)	£6.25

CADBURY BROS. LTD

EL6   Sport Series (109 x 35mm) c1905 (reprinted 2001) £3.00

CARRERAS LTD

50	Famous Airmen & Airwomen 1936 (reprinted 1996)	£8.50
75	Footballers 1934 (reprinted 1997)	£13.50

H. CHAPPEL & CO.

10   British Celebrities 1905 (reprinted 2001) £3.00

W.A. & A.C. CHURCHMAN

50	Boxing Personalities 1938 (reprinted 1990)	£8.50
50	Cricketers 1936 (C.C.S. reprinted 1999)	£10.00
52	Frisky 1935 (reprinted 1994)	£8.50
50	In Town To-Night 1938 (C.C.S. reprinted 1999)	£10.00
50	Landmarks in Railway Progress 1931 (reprinted 1994)	£8.50
50	Pioneers 1956 (reprinted 2000)	£9.50
25	Pipes of The World 1927 (C.C.S. reprinted 2000)	£6.50
50	Prominent Golfers 1931 (reprinted 1989)	£8.50
L12	Prominent Golfers 1931 (reprinted 1989)	£6.00
50	Racing Greyhounds 1934 (reprinted 1989)	£8.50
M48	The RAF at Work (68 x 53mm) 1938 (reprinted 1995)	£14.00
50	The Story of Navigation 1936 (C.C.S. reprinted 1999)	£10.00

WM. CLARKE & SON

30   Cricketer Series 1901 (reprinted 2001) £7.50

COHEN WEENEN & CO. LTD

60	Football Club Captains 1907-8 (reprinted 1998)	£10.00
40	Home & Colonial Regiments 1901 (reprinted 1998)	£8.50
50	Star Artists 1905 (reprinted 1998)	£8.50
50	V.C. Heroes (of World War I) 1915 (reprinted 1998)	£8.50

CO-OPERATIVE WHOLESALE SOCIETY LTD (C.W.S.)

25	Parrot Series 1910 (reprinted 1996)	£6.00
48	Poultry 1927 (reprinted 1996)	£8.50

COPE BROS. & CO. LTD

Qty		Sets
50	British Warriors 1912 (reprinted 1996)	£8.50
50	Cope's Golfers 1900 (reprinted 1983)	£8.50
50	Dickens' Gallery 1900 (reprinted 1989)	—
EL7	The Seven Ages of Man (114 x 78mm) c1885 (reprinted 2001)	£6.00
50	Shakespeare Gallery 1900 (reprinted 1989)	—
25	Uniforms of Soldiers and Sailors 1898 (reprinted 1996)	£6.25
25	The World's Police 1935 (reprinted 2005)	£6.00

DAH TUNG NAN (China)

Qty		Sets
M18	Golf Girls Series c1920 (reprinted 1997)	£6.00

W. DUKE SONS & CO (USA)

Qty		Sets
25	Fishers c1890 (reprinted 2002)	£6.00
30	Generals of American Civil War (Histories of Generals) 1888 (reprinted 1995)	£6.25

J. DUNCAN & CO. LTD

Qty		Sets
50	Evolution of The Steamship 1925 (reprinted 2002)	£8.50

H. ELLIS & CO. (USA)

Qty		Sets
25	Generals of the Late Civil War 1890 (reprinted 1991)	£6.00

EMPIRE TOBACCO CO.

Qty		Sets
6	Franco-British Exhibition 1907 (reprinted 2001)	£2.00

W. & F. FAULKNER

Qty		Sets
25	Beauties (coloured) c1898 (reprinted 2001)	£6.00
12	Cricket Terms 1899 (reprinted 1999)	£2.50
12	Football Terms 1st Series 1900 (reprinted 1999)	£2.50
12	Football Terms 2nd Series 1900 (reprinted 1999)	£2.50
12	Golf Terms (with 'Faulkners' on front) 1901 (reprinted 1999)	£2.50
12	Golf Terms (without 'Faulkners' titled Golf Humour) 1901 (reprinted 1998)	£2.50
12	Grenadier Guards 1899 (reprinted 1999)	£2.50
12	Military Terms 1st Series 1899 (reprinted 1999)	£2.50
12	Military Terms 2nd Series 1899 (reprinted 1999)	£2.50
12	Nautical Terms 1st Series 1900 (reprinted 1999)	£2.50
12	Nautical Terms 2nd Series 1900 (reprinted 1999)	£2.50
12	Policemen of the World 1899 (reprinted 1999)	£2.50
12	Police Terms (with 'Faulkners' on front) 1899 (reprinted 1999)	£2.50
12	Police Terms (without 'Faulkners' titled Police Humour) 1899 (reprinted 1998)	£2.50
25	Prominent Racehorses of the Present Day 1923 (reprinted 1993)	£6.00
12	Puzzle Series 1897 (reprinted 1999)	£2.50
12	Sporting Terms 1900 (reprinted 1999)	£2.50
12	Street Cries 1902 (reprinted 1999)	£2.50

FRANKLYN, DAVEY & CO.

Qty		Sets
25	Boxing 1924 (reprinted 2002)	£6.00

J. S. FRY & SONS LTD

Qty		Sets
25	Days of Nelson 1906 (reprinted 2003)	£6.25
25	Days of Wellington 1906 (reprinted 2003)	£6.25

Qty		Sets

J. GABRIEL
20   Cricketers Series 1901 (reprinted 1992) £5.00

GALLAHER LTD
48	Army Badges 1939 (reprinted 2001)	£8.50
50	The Great War Nos. 1-50 1915 (reprinted 2001)	£8.50
50	The Great War Nos 51-100 1915 (reprinted 2003)	£8.50
25	The Great War Victoria Cross Heroes 1st Series 1915 (reprinted 2001) ...	£6.25
25	The Great War Victoria Cross Heroes 2nd Series 1915 (reprinted 2001) ...	£6.25
25	The Great War Victoria Cross Heroes 3rd Series 1915 (reprinted 2001) ...	£6.25
25	The Great War Victoria Cross Heroes 4th Series 1915 (reprinted 2001) ...	£6.25
25	The Great War Victoria Cross Heroes 5th Series 1915 (reprinted 2003) ...	£6.25
25	The Great War Victoria Cross Heroes 6th Series 1915 (not issued)	—
25	The Great War Victoria Cross Heroes 7th Series 1915 (reprinted 2003) ...	£6.25
25	The Great War Victoria Cross Heroes 8th Series 1915 (reprinted 2003) ...	£6.25
50	Lawn Tennis Celebrities 1928 (reprinted 1997)	£8.50
25	Motor Cars 1934 (reprinted 1995)	£6.25
50	Regimental Colours and Standards 1899 (reprinted 1995)...	£8.50
48	Signed Portraits of Famous Stars 1935 (reprinted 1997)	£8.50
50	South African Series Nd 101-150 (Boer War Uniforms) 1901 (reprinted 2000)	£8.50
50	South African Series Nd 151-200 (Boer War Uniforms) 1901 (reprinted 2000)	£8.50
50	Types of the British Army Nd. 1-50 1900 (reprinted 1995)	£8.50
50	Types of the British Army Nd. 51-100 1900 (reprinted 1996)	£8.50

GLOBE CIGARETTE CO.
25   Actresses — French c1900 (reprinted 2001) £6.00

GLOBE INSURANCE
M11   Famous Golfers 1929 (reprinted 1996) £6.00

G.G. GOODE LTD (Australia)
17   Prominent Cricketer Series 1924 (reprinted 2001) £5.00

THOS. H. HALL (USA)
M8   Presidential Candidates & Actresses 1880 (reprinted 2001) £2.00

HIGNETT BROS. & CO.
25	Greetings of The World 1907 (C.C.S. reprinted 2000)	£6.50
50	Prominent Racehorses of 1933 (C.C.S. reprinted 2000)	£10.00

R. & J. HILL LTD
25	Battleships and Crests 1901 (reprinted 1995)	£6.25
20	Types of the British Army 1914 (reprinted 2001)	£6.25

HUDDEN & CO. LTD
25   Famous Boxers 1927 (reprinted 1992) £6.25

HUNTLEY & PALMER (France)
EL12   Aviation (114 x 85mm) c1908 (reprinted 2001)... ... ...   £7.50

IMPERIAL TOBACCO COMPANY OF CANADA LTD
45	Hockey Players 1912 (reprinted 1987)	—
36	Hockey Series 1911 (reprinted 1987)	—

Qty   *Sets*

INTERNATIONAL CHEWING GUM (USA)
M24   Don't Let It Happen Over Here 1938 (reprinted 1984) £10.0

JAMES & CO.
M20   Arms of Countries (70 x 52mm) c1915 (reprinted 2001) £7.50

JONES BROS., Tottenham
18   Spurs Footballers 1912 (reprinted 1986) £2.50

WM. S. KIMBALL & CO. (USA)
50   Champions of Games & Sports c1890 (reprinted 2001) £10.00

KINNEAR LTD
15   Australian Cricketers 1897 (reprinted 2001) £4.00

KINNEY BROS. (USA)
25   Famous English Running Horses 1889 (reprinted 1996) £6.25
25   Leaders 1889 (reprinted 1990) £6.00

J. KNIGHT (HUSTLER SOAP)
30   Regimental Nicknames 1925 (reprinted 1996) £6.25

B. KRIEGSFELD & CO.
50   Phrases and Advertisements c1900 (reprinted 2001) £10.00

A. KUIT LTD
25   Principal Streets of British Cities and Towns 1916 (reprinted 2001) £6.00

LACEY'S CHEWING GUM
50   Footballers c1925 (reprinted 2001) £10.00

LAMBERT & BUTLER
25   Aviation 1915 (reprinted 1997) £6.00
25   Dance Band Leaders 1936 (reprinted 1992) £6.00
50   Empire Air Routes 1936 (C.C.S. reprinted 2000) £10.00
25   Hints and Tips for Motorists 1929 (reprinted 1994) £6.00
50   Horsemanship 1938 (reprinted 1994) £8.50
50   Interesting Sidelights On The Work of The GPO 1939 (C.C.S. reprinted
        1999) £10.00
20   International Yachts 1902 (reprinted 2001) £5.00
25   London Characters 1934 (reprinted 1992) £6.00
25   Motor Cars 1st Series 1922 (reprinted 1988) £6.25
25   Motor Cars 2nd Series 1923 (reprinted 1988) £6.25
25   Motor Cars 1934 (reprinted 1992) £6.25
50   Motor Cycles 1923 (reprinted 1990) £8.50
25   Motors 1908 (reprinted 1992) £6.00
25   Winter Sports 1914 (reprinted 1998) £6.00
50   World's Locomotives 1912 (reprinted 1988) £8.50

R. J. LEA LTD
50   Flowers to Grow 1913 (reprinted 1997) £8.50

LEAF GUM CO. (USA)
L72   Star Trek 1967 (reprinted 1981) £12.50

177

J. LEES
20   Northampton Town Football Club c1912 (reprinted 2001) £5.00

LIEBIG (France)
EL6   Famous Explorers (F1088) 1914 (reprinted 2001) £5.00

LUSBY LTD
25   Scenes From Circus Life c1900 (reprinted 2001) £6.00

MARBURG BROS. (USA)
15   Beauties 'PAC' c1890 (reprinted 2001) £4.00

P. H. MAYO & BROTHER (USA)
35   Prizefighters c1890 (reprinted 2001) £7.50

STEPHEN MITCHELL & SON
25	Angling 1925 (reprinted 1993)	£6.00
50	Famous Scots 1933 (C.C.S. reprinted 1999)	£10.00
50	A Gallery of 1935 (C.C.S. reprinted 1999)	£10.00
50	Humorous Drawings 1924 (C.C.S. reprinted 1999)	£10.00
25	Money 1913 (C.C.S. reprinted 2000)	£6.50
25	Regimental Crests, Nicknames and Collar Badges 1900 (reprinted 1993)	£6.50
50	Scotland's Story (C.C.S. reprinted 2000)	£10.00

MURRAY, SONS & CO LTD
20	Cricketers 1912 (reprinted 1991)	£7.50
20	War Series K — Uniforms 1915 (reprinted 2000)	£6.25
15	War Series K — World War 1 Leaders & Generals 1915 (reprinted 2000)	—

NATIONAL CIGARETTE CO. (Australia)
13   English Cricket Team 1897-8 (reprinted 2001) £4.00

NATIONAL EXCHANGE BANK (USA)
EL9   Seven Ages of Golf c1885 (reprinted 1995) £4.50

OGDENS LTD
50	A.F.C. Nicknames 1933 (reprinted 1996)	£8.50
50	Air Raid Precautions 1938 (C.C.S. reprinted 1999)	£10.00
50	British Birds 1905 (C.C.S. reprinted 2000)	£10.00
50	By The Roadside 1932 (C.C.S. reprinted 2000)	£10.00
50	Champions of 1936 (C.C.S. reprinted 2000)	£10.00
50	Cricketers and Sportsmen c1898 (reprinted 2001)	£10.00
50	Flags and Funnels of Leading Steamship Lines 1906 (reprinted 1997) ...	£8.50
50	Jockeys 1930 (reprinted 1990)	—
50	Modern Railways 1936 (reprinted 1996)	£8.50
50	Motor Races 1931 (reprinted 1993)	£8.50
25	Poultry 1st Series 1915 (reprinted 1998)	£6.00
25	Poultry 2nd Series 1916 (reprinted 2000)	£6.00
50	Shakespeare Series 1903 (C.C.S. reprinted 2000)	£10.00
50	Smugglers & Smuggling 1931 (C.C.S. reprinted 1999)	£10.00
50	Soldiers of the King 1909 (reprinted 1993)	£8.50
50	The Story of the Life Boat 1940 (reprinted 1989)	—
50	The Story of The Lifeboat 1940 (without 'Ogdens') (reprinted 2001)	£8.50
50	Swimming, Diving and Life-Saving 1931 (C.C.S. reprinted 2000)	£10.00

OLD CALABAR BISCUIT CO. LTD
EL16   Sports and Games c1900 (reprinted 2001) £7.50

THE ORLANDO CIGARETTE & CIGAR CO.
40   Home & Colonial Regiments c1901 (reprinted 2001) £8.50

PALMER MANN & CO (SIFTA SAM)
25   Famous Cricketers (Set 24 + 1 Variety) 1950 (reprinted 2001) £6.00

J.A. PATTREIOUEX
75   Cricketers Series 1926 (reprinted 1997) £13.50

GODFREY PHILLIPS LTD
30   Beauties 'Nymphs' c1896 (reprinted 2001) £7.50
25   Railway Engines 1924 (reprinted 1997) ... ...   —
20   Russo-Japanese War Series 1904 (reprinted 2001) £5.00
25   Territorial Series 1908 (reprinted 2001) £6.25
25   Types of British Soldiers 1900 (reprinted 1997) £6.25

JOHN PLAYER & SONS
50   Aeroplanes (Civil) 1935 (reprinted 1990)... ... ...   £8.50
50   Aircraft of The Royal Air Force 1938 (reprinted 1990) £8.50
50   Animals of The Countryside 1939 (C.C.S. reprinted 1999)... ... ...   £10.00
50   Aviary & Cage Birds 1933 (reprinted 1989) £8.50
L25   Aviary and Cage Birds 1935 (reprinted 1987) £8.50
50   British Empire Series 1904 (C.C.S. reprinted 1999) £10.00
50   Butterflies & Moths 1904 (C.C.S. reprinted 2000) £10.00
L24   Cats 1936 (reprinted 1986) £8.50
25   Characters from Dickens 1912 (reprinted 1990) £6.00
25   Characters from Dickens 2nd Series 1914 (reprinted 1990) £6.00
50   Cities of The World 1900 (C.C.S. reprinted 1999)... ... ...   £10.00
L25   Country Sports 1930 (reprinted 2000)... ... ...   £8.50
50   Cricketers 1930 (reprinted 2000) £8.50
50   Cricketers 1934 (reprinted 1990) £8.50
50   Cricketers 1938 (C.C.S. reprinted 2000) £10.00
50   Cricketers Caricatures by 'Rip' 1926 (reprinted 1993) £8.50
50   Derby and Grand National Winners 1933 (reprinted 1988) £8.50
50   Dogs' Heads (silver-grey backgrounds) 1940 (reprinted 1994) £8.50
25   England's Naval Heroes 1898 descriptive (reprinted 1987) ... ...   —
50   Film Stars 1st Series 1934 (C.C.S. reprinted 2000) £10.00
50   Film Stars 3rd Series 1938 (reprinted 1989) £8.50
50   Fire-Fighting Appliances 1930 (reprinted 1991) £8.50
50   Game Birds and Wild Fowl 1927 (C.C.S. reprinted 1999) £10.00
L25   Game Birds and Wild Fowl 1928 (reprinted 1987) £8.50
50   Gilbert & Sullivan 2nd Series 1927 (reprinted 1990) £8.50
L25   Golf 1939 (reprinted 1986) £8.50
25   Highland Clans 1908 (reprinted 1997) £6.00
50   Kings & Queens 1935 (reprinted 1990) £8.50
50   Military Head-Dress 1931 (C.C.S. reprinted 1999) £10.00
50   Military Series 1900 (reprinted 1983) £8.50
50   Motor Cars 1st Series 1936 (reprinted 1990) £8.50
50   Motor Cars 2nd Series 1937 (C.C.S. reprinted 2000) £10.00
25   Napoleon 1916 (reprinted 1989) £6.00
50   Nature Series 1909 (C.C.S. reprinted 2000) £10.00
50   Old England's Defenders 1898 (reprinted 1987) ... ...   —

JOHN PLAYER & SONS (continued)

Qty		Sets
L25	Old Hunting Prints 1938 (reprinted 1989)	£8.50
L25	Old Naval Prints 1936 (reprinted 1989)	£8.50
L25	Picturesque London 1931 (reprinted 1997)	£8.50
50	Poultry 1931 (reprinted 1993)	£8.50
50	Products of The World 1928 (C.C.S. reprinted 1999)	£10.00
L25	Racing Yachts 1938 (reprinted 1987)	£8.50
50	Regimental Standards & Cap Badges 1930 (reprinted 1993)	£8.50
50	Regimental Uniforms Nd. 51-100 1914 (reprinted 1995)	£8.50
50	Speedway Riders 1937 (C.C.S. reprinted 2000)	£10.00
50	Tennis 1936 (C.C.S. reprinted 1999)	£10.00
L24	Treasures of Britain 1931 (reprinted 1996)	£8.50
L25	Types of Horses 1939 (reprinted 1998)	£8.50
50	Uniforms of the Territorial Army 1939 (reprinted 1990)	£8.50
L25	Wild Birds 1934 (reprinted 1997)	£8.50

JOHN PLAYER & SONS (Overseas)

Qty		Sets
50	Ships Flags and Cap Badges 1930 (reprinted 1997)	—

REEVES LTD

Qty		Sets
25	Cricketers 1912 (reprinted 1993)	£8.00

RICHMOND CAVENDISH CO. LTD

Qty		Sets
20	Yachts c1900 (reprinted 2001)	£5.00

E. ROBINSON & SONS LTD

Qty		Sets
6	Medals & Decorations of Great Britain c190 (reprinted 2001)	£2.00
25	Regimental Mascots 1916 (reprinted 2001)	£6.00

S.D.V. TOBACCO CO. LTD

Qty		Sets
16	British Royal Family c1901 (reprinted 2001)	£4.00

SALMON & GLUCKSTEIN LTD

Qty		Sets
15	Billiard Terms 1905 (reprinted 1997)	£5.00
25	Coronation Series 1911 (C.C.S. reprinted 2000)	£6.50
30	Music Hall Celebrities c1902 (reprinted 2001)	£7.50

JOHN SINCLAIR LTD

Qty		Sets
50	British Sea Dogs 1926 (reprinted 1997)	£8.50

SINGLETON & COLE LTD

Qty		Sets
35	Famous Boxers 1930 (reprinted 1992)	£6.25
50	Footballers c1905 (reprinted 2001)	£10.00

F. & J. SMITH

Qty		Sets
25	Advertisement Cards 1899 (reprinted 2001)	£6.00
50	Champions of Sport (unnumbered) 1902 (reprinted 2001)	£10.00
25	Cinema Stars 1920 (reprinted 1987)	£6.50
50	Fowls, Pigeons and Dogs 1908 (C.C.S. reprinted 2000)	£10.00
25	Holiday Resorts 1925 (C.C.S. reprinted 2000)	£6.50
25	Prominent Rugby Players 1924 (reprinted 1992)	£8.00

SPIRO VALLERI & CO.

Qty		Sets
10	Noted Footballers c1905 (reprinted 2001)	£3.00

SPRATTS PATENT LTD

12	Prize Dogs c1910 (reprinted 2001)	£3.50

TADDY & CO.

20	Clowns & Circus Artists 1920 (reprinted 1991)	£6.00
238	County Cricketers 1907 (reprinted 1987)	£40.00
	Individual Counties of the above set:	
15	Derbyshire	£2.50
15	Essex	£2.50
16	Gloucestershire	£2.50
15	Hampshire	£2.50
15	Kent	£2.50
15	Lancashire	£2.50
14	Leicestershire	£2.50
15	Middlesex	£2.50
15	Northamptonshire	£2.50
14	Nottinghamshire	£2.50
15	Somersetshire	£2.50
15	Surrey	£2.50
15	Sussex	£2.50
15	Warwickshire	£2.50
14	Worcestershire	£2.50
15	Yorkshire	£2.50
5	English Royalty c1898 (reprinted 2001)	£2.00
25	Famous Jockeys 1910 (reprinted 1996)	£6.25
25	Natives of the World c1900 (reprinted 1999)	£6.00
15	Prominent Footballers Aston Villa 1907 (reprinted 1992)	£2.50
15	Prominent Footballers Chelsea 1907 (reprinted 1998)	£2.50
15	Prominent Footballers Everton 1907 (reprinted 1998)	£2.50
15	Prominent Footballers Leeds 1907 (reprinted 1992)	£2.50
15	Prominent Footballers Liverpool 1907 (reprinted 1992)	£2.50
15	Prominent Footballers Manchester Utd 1907 (reprinted 1992)	£2.50
15	Prominent Footballers Middlesbrough 1907 (reprinted 1998)	£2.50
15	Prominent Footballers Newcastle Utd 1907 (reprinted 1992)	£2.50
15	Prominent Footballers Queens Park Rangers 1907 (reprinted 1992)	—
15	Prominent Footballers Sunderland 1907 (reprinted 1998)	£2.50
15	Prominent Footballers Tottenham Hotspur 1907 (reprinted 1998)	£2.50
15	Prominent Footballers West Ham Utd 1907 (reprinted 1998)	£2.50
15	Prominent Footballers Woolwich Arsenal 1907 (reprinted 1992)	£2.50
20	Royalty, Actresses, Soldiers c1898 (reprinted 2001)	£5.00
25	Royalty Series 1908 (reprinted 1998)	£6.25
15	South African Cricket Team 1907 (reprinted 1992)	£7.50
25	Territorial Regiments 1908 (reprinted 1996)	£6.25
25	Thames Series 1903 (reprinted 1996)	£6.25
20	Victoria Cross Heroes (Nos 1-20) 1900 (reprinted 1996)	£6.25
20	Victoria Cross Heroes (Nos 21-40) 1900 (reprinted 1996)	£6.25
20	V.C. Heroes — Boer War (Nos 41-60) 1901 (reprinted 1997)	£6.25
20	V.C. Heroes — Boer War (Nos 61-80) 1901 (reprinted 1997)	£6.25
20	V.C. Heroes — Boer War (Nos 81-100) 1902 (reprinted 1997)	£6.25
25	Victoria Cross Heroes (Nos 101-125) 1905 (reprinted 1996)	£6.25

TEOFANI & CO. LTD

24	Past and Present The Army 1938 (reprinted 2001)	£6.25
24	Past and Present Weapons of War 1938 (reprinted 2001)	£6.25

D.C. THOMSON

24	Motor Bike Cards 1929 (reprinted 1993)	£6.00
20	Motor Cycles 1923 (Wizard Series) (reprinted 1993)...	£6.00

TOPPS CHEWING GUM INC. (USA)

LT56	Mars Attacks 1962 (reprinted 1987)	£12.50
LT51	Outer Limits 1964 (reprinted 1995)...	£12.50

UNION JACK

M8	Police of All Nations 1922 (reprinted 2005)	£4.00

UNITED TOBACCONISTS' ASSOCIATION LTD

10	Actresses 'MUTA' c1900 (reprinted 2001)	£3.00

HENRY WELFARE & CO.

22	Prominent Politicians c1911 (reprinted 2001)	£6.00

W.D. & H.O. WILLS

EL4	Advert Postcards of Packings 1902 (reprinted 1985)	£5.00
50	Allied Army Leaders 1917 (C.C.S reprinted 2000)	£10.00
50	Arms of Companies 1913 (C.C.S reprinted 1999)...	£10.00
50	Builders of The Empire 1898 (C.C.S. reprinted 1999)	£10.00
L7	Cathedrals (from set of 25) 1933 (reprinted 2000)	£2.50
50	Cricketers 1896 (reprinted 1982)	£8.50
50	Cricketers 1901 (reprinted 1983)	–
L25	Dogs 1914 (reprinted 1987)	£8.50
50	Double Meaning 1898 (C.C.S. reprinted 1999)	£10.00
50	Engineering Wonders 1927 (C.C.S. reprinted 1999)	£10.00
L25	Famous Golfers 1930 (reprinted 1987)	£8.50
50	Fish & Bait 1910 (reprinted 1990)	£8.50
50	Flower Culture In Pots 1925 (C.C.S. reprinted 2000)	£10.00
50	Household Hints 1st Series 1927 (C.C.S. reprinted 1999)	£10.00
L25	Lawn Tennis 1931 (reprinted 1988)	£8.50
50	Life in the Hedgerow 1950 (reprinted 1991, Swan Vestas)...	£12.50
50	Life In The Royal Navy 1939 (C.C.S. reprinted 1999)	£10.00
50	Military Aircraft (unissued c1967) (reprinted 1991)	£8.50
50	Military Motors 1916 (reprinted 1994)	£8.50
58	Musical Celebrities 2nd Series including 8 substituted cards 1914 (reprinted 1987)	£9.50
25	National Costumes c1895 (reprinted 1999)	£6.00
50	Naval Dress & Badges 1909 (reprinted 1997)	£8.50
25	Naval Dress & Badges 1909 (Nos. 1 to 25 Naval Dress only reprinted) inscribed 'Commissioned by Sydney Cigarette Card Company, Australia' (reprinted 1993)	£6.25
50	Old English Garden Flowers 2nd Series 1913 (reprinted 1994)	£8.50
L40	Puppies by Lucy Dawson (unissued) (reprinted 1990)	£12.50
50	Railway Engines 1924 (reprinted 1995)	£8.50
50	Railway Engines 1936 (reprinted 1992)	£8.50
50	Railway Equipment 1939 (reprinted 1993)	£8.50
50	Railway Locomotives 1930 (reprinted 1993)	£8.50
12	Recruiting Posters 1915 (reprinted 1987)	£3.00
L25	Rigs of Ships 1929 (reprinted 1987)	£8.50
50	Roses 1st Series 1912 (reprinted 1994)	£8.50
50	Rugby Internationals 1929 (reprinted 1996)...	£8.50
50	School Arms 1906 (C.C.S. reprinted 2000)	£10.00

W.D. & H.O. WILLS (continued)

Qty		Sets
50	Ships Badges 1925 (C.C.S. reprinted 2000)	£10.00
50	Waterloo 1915 (reprinted 1987)	£10.00
50	Wild Flowers 1923 (C.C.S. reprinted 1999)	£10.00
50	Wild Flowers 1st Series 1936 (reprinted 1993)...	—
50	Wonders of The Sea 1928 (C.C.S. reprinted 2000)	£10.00
25	World's Dreadnoughts 1910 (reprinted 1994)	£6.00

W.D. & H.O. WILLS (Australia)

50	Types of the British Army 1912 (reprinted 1995)	£8.50
50	War Incidents 2nd Series 1917 (reprinted 1995)	£8.50

W.H. & J. WOODS LTD

25	Types of Volunteers & Yeomanry 1902 (reprinted 1996)	£8.50

THEMATIC LISTINGS

If you are interested in a particular subject the
thematic listings on our website may be of help.
Alternatively, lists can be sent on request.

SUBJECTS COVERED

American Football, Baseball etc.
Animals and Wildlife
Aviation, Space Travel and Astronomy
Birds, Butterflies and Moths
Boxing
Brooke Bond Tea Cards
Cricket
Dinosaurs
Dogs and Pets
Fantasy Art
Film and Stage Stars (1920-40 issues)
Fish, Fishing and the Ocean
Flags, Arms and Maps
Flowers and the Garden
Football
Golf
Horses and the Turf
Liebig Card Issues
Military
Motoring

Native North American Indians and
  Cowboys
Pop Stars and Singers
Railways
Reprints
Royalty
Rugby League and Union
Ships, Shipping and Naval
Speedway
Sports (general)
Star Trek
Star Wars
Tennis
TV, Films and Sci-Fi
Wrestling
Miscellaneous Cigarette Card Issues
Miscellaneous Trade Card Issues
Selection of Cigarette Card Sets £20
  and under
Selection of Trade Card Sets under £5

Website
www.londoncigcard.co.uk

Other Catalogues Available

Cigarette Card Catalogue 2014 Edition

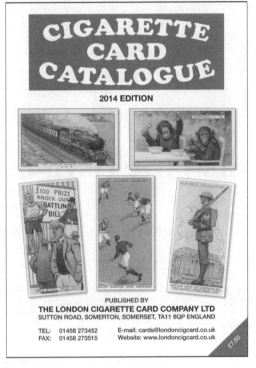

Price £7.50

This is the original price guide, now in its 85th year, updated for 2014 with every item dated and priced. To help even further, Section 1 has reference book numbers to help identify those tricky sets. This guide covers cigarette cards and silks issued by hundreds of manufacturers in Britain and around the world from the 19th Century to the present day, 224 pages giving selling prices for odd cards and sets in top condition. Over 7000 series with a colourful 8 page section with 84 illustrations.

Visit our website or order your catalogue via post or telephone — details on the front cover

Other Catalogues Available

Liebig Card Catalogue 2009 Edition

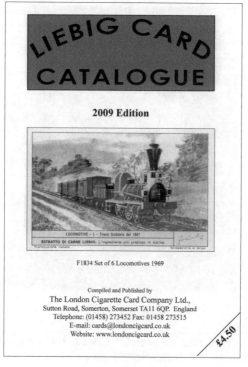

F1834 Set of 6 Locomotives 1969

Compiled and Published by
The London Cigarette Card Company Ltd.,
Sutton Road, Somerton, Somerset TA11 6QP. England
Telephone: (01458) 273452 Fax: 01458 273515
E-mail: cards@londoncigcard.co.uk
Website: www.londoncigcard.co.uk

£4.50

Price £4.50

This price guide lists over 1500 fascinating sets issued in the different European languages (all except the earliest) by this manufacturer. It includes a brief history of the company, an English translation of each set title, together with the 'Fada' reference number, the number in each set and date of issue from 1891 to 1973. The prices in the 2009 catalogue will remain until further notice.

Visit our website or order your catalogue via post or telephone — details on the front cover

Collecting Cigarette & Trade Cards

By Gordon Howsden

Price £17.50

Collecting Cigarette & Trade Cards by Gordon Howsden traces the history and development of cards from their beginning to the present day and includes the background of the issuing firms, thematic collecting, printing and production, grading, pricing and so on. Authoritatively written in an easy-to-read style and beautifully illustrated in colour, the book approaches the subject from a fresh angle which will appeal to seasoned collectors and newcomers alike. *Cigarette & Trade Cards* is not only an indispensable reference work but also a joy to read or just browse through.152 large-format pages with 220 colour illustrations featuring 750 cards and related ephemera.

Visit our website or order the book via post or telephone — details on the front cover.

NOTES

NOTES